What your teen is trying to tell you

Stella O'Malley is a psychotherapist, best-selling author, public speaker and a parent with many years' experience working in counselling and psychotherapy. Born in Dublin, Stella now calls Birr, Co. Offaly, home, where she lives with her husband and two children and runs her private practice. Stella is often invited to give talks to teens and parents.

What your teen is trying to tell you

Stella O'Malley

Gill Books

Gill Books
Hume Avenue
Park West
Dublin 12
www.gillbooks.ie

Gill Books is an imprint of M.H. Gill and Co.

© Stella O'Malley 2023

9780717196050

Design origination Graham Thew
Printed and bound by ScandBook AB, Sweden
This book is typeset in 10 on 16pt, Alda.

*The paper used in this book comes from the wood pulp of
sustainably managed forests.*

A CIP catalogue record for this book is available from the
British Library.

5 4 3 2 1

Information given in this book is not intended to be
taken as a replacement for medical advice. Any person
with a condition requiring medical attention should
consult a qualified medical practitioner or therapist.

To my friend Alasdair, with all my love, from one erstwhile crazy, mixed-up teen to another.

CONTENTS

Chapter 3

PART II GROWING UP IN THE 21ST CENTURY

Chapter 4

Chapter 5

Chapter 6

Chapter 7

PART III EXPLORING TENSION, FEAR AND RIGID THINKING

Chapter 8

Chapter 9

PART IV THE RECKONING: COMING TO TERMS WITH OURSELVES AND OUR BODIES

Chapter 10

Chapter 11

Chapter 12

PART V FACING COMPLEX CHALLENGES

Chapter 13

Chapter 14

Chapter 15

PART VI ESTABLISHING POSITIVE FAMILY DYNAMICS

A NOTE FROM THE AUTHOR

In the interests of confidentiality, names and identifying details have been changed throughout this book.

'The right way to wholeness is made up of fateful detours and wrong turnings.'

CARL JUNG

INTRODUCTION

I WAS A demonic teenager. When I look back, I can hardly believe that I acted in the way I did. I was filled with power and certainty and lived with almost animal-like instinct. Ironically enough, I had the reputation among my friends of being a 'deep thinker', as I charged around the place, filled with fury and intensity. Although I was certainly thinking hard, I was also manic, disconnected and totally out of touch with myself. I literally hadn't a clue what was going on.

In my work as a psychotherapist, I spend time in Planet Teen alongside unhappy adolescents and I have met hundreds of troubled teenagers who are just as mixed up as I was. I like them. We typically establish a warm relationship and I've seen first-hand the difference that some understanding and connection can make to these kids. Some of them are potential powerhouses, almost overwhelmed by the depth of their emotions. Others go the other way and seem to have shut down entirely: monosyllabic responses emerging from a hanging head communicate a slouching antipathy that can melt their parents' minds. Too much or too little emotion, it really doesn't matter – the reason you are reading this is because you are worried about your kid and desperately afraid that things are getting worse.

Parents can often feel at sea in the face of their teen's distress; they don't know what to do and they don't know what to say. These days, our instinct is often to 'get the professionals in', but the professionals don't always know how to help your teen – and anyway, nobody cares as much as you do. This book aims to help parents lean in to the challenges involved and help their teenagers as much as they are able. Through an analysis of the 'tasks' each teenager needs to tackle during adolescence in order to progress to adulthood, parents will know better when to intervene and when to allow the teen to work it out. Some kids have additional needs, and certain common conditions are examined in the context of helping teenagers to one day become better-functioning adults.

Witnessing a teenager in distress is so incredibly hard that the vast majority of people – be they siblings, fellow parents, teachers or other professionals – feel that somebody, somewhere needs to be blamed for the mess – and the parents are the easiest target. For many parents, it is heads you lose, tails you lose; you're either too strict or too easy, you either worked too much or not enough. Whatever you did, you did it wrong. Yet, although trashing the parents might be easy, it's not necessarily justifiable. Equally so for the teenager. I have written this book so that harried parents can refer to specific issues and hopefully find some self-compassion, a deeper understanding of what is going on for their teen as well as some suggestions that might improve the situation on some level. You may not read the book from start to finish; you might instead choose to cross each bridge as you come to it and approach the book section by section.

This book isn't too concerned with the easy-going teenager who is sailing blithely through adolescence – for those parents who have such an easy job, we wish you well (with perhaps a hint of dark envy); rather, this is for the parents of the teenager who is in distress. Although it is unsettling, most parents can endure common or garden bad behaviour from teenagers; what feels unendurable is when the teenager's behaviour seems incomprehensible.

I don't promise a miracle – false promises seldom help. Instead, I seek to help parents improve things, little by little. Although the situation might not be radically altered, it can be improved, and this is usually enough. If we can reduce the impact, the intensity, the length of time, the fallout and the frequency of distress, everybody's life will change for the better. Bringing some self-awareness, gentleness and compassion into everybody's life can make all the difference.

Some teens are sad, others are anxious; some teenagers appear to take on every difficult trait of adolescence and turn it up full volume. They may live at an intensity that is difficult to fathom. Many teens are a little on edge or just seem dejected. No matter what's going on, many teens need help with communicating and the parents of these teens need help to figure out what's being communicated. I will attempt to not only support these endeavours but also bring insight, awareness and compassion into the equation.

• • •

Using this book

This book is not exhaustive – I haven't tried to explain every possible distress that might manifest in teenagers. Rather, I have tried to give snapshots of common issues that arise in my counselling practice. I have used some recurring features throughout this book in order to provide practical support for parents and to highlight specific issues.

Case studies: A case study is an in-depth study of one person. As space is limited, I can't provide all the details of any given case study, and instead I point to what I perceive as the pivotal moments that happen during the therapeutic process. Certain details have been changed in the case studies to protect the identities of those involved and, in a bid to further protect confidentiality, I illustrate scenarios similar in kind but not in actuality to those I have heard from clients over the years.

Developmental milestones are a set of functional skills or age-specific tasks that most teenagers can do by the time they reach emerging adulthood. These milestones or 'tasks of adolescence' can be cognitive, emotional, social, physical or behavioural and it can be very helpful for parents to realise that their teen is struggling with a specific developmental milestone and might need some extra support in this area.

Coping mechanisms are conscious or unconscious adjustments or adaptations in our behaviour that decrease distress in a stressful experience or situation. Some coping mechanisms (also known as coping behaviour and coping strategies) are healthy and some are unhealthy. In the counselling context, therapists often seek to help the client become aware of and modify unhealthy coping mechanisms in favour of healthier options.

Parenting strategy features and the **takeaways** at the end of each chapter are offered as clear and concise suggestions that parents might try to see if they work in their household. I urge parents to only follow suggestions that sit well with them – you are the world expert on your child and, as with all suggestions in this book, the old saying, 'Take what you need and leave the rest' is very apt.

PART I
UNDERSTANDING THE TEENAGE MIND

CHAPTER 1

HALF CHILD/HALF ADULT

'We don't so much solve our problems as we
outgrow them. We add capacities and experiences
that eventually make us bigger than the problems.'

– CARL JUNG

When the clinical psychologist Lisa Damour was in graduate
school, the professor teaching the psychological testing course
presented her with a pile of Rorschach inkblot tests to score.
Before letting her loose on the tests, the professor warned
Damour, 'Double-check the age of the person whose test you
are scoring. If it's a teenager, but you think it's a grown-up,
you'll conclude that you have a psychotic adult. But that's just a
normal teenager.'[1]

For some, the storms and stresses of adolescence arrive with a bang; the teenager is suddenly unaccountably ill at ease, and many parents feel that It Has All Gone Wrong. One kid might swing madly from arrogance to devastating insecurity, from laughing wildly to screaming like a banshee, from giving affectionate hugs to trashing the kitchen. Another might completely disengage and live behind a thick wall of silence. None of us really knows what function the storms and stresses serve; perhaps teenagers need to experience this distress to prepare for adulthood? The psychologist Carl Pickhardt tells us that the task of adolescence is to break the spell of childhood.[2] Maybe the magic of childhood necessarily leads to crushing disappointment in adolescence as we come to a reckoning with life and realise that it isn't filled with magic and Hollywood endings and, in fact, is often really harsh. If an adolescent doesn't learn how hard life can be, will they truly be fit to become a functioning adult? As yet, psychologists remain unsure about this point, but most parents agree that the spell of childhood certainly seems to get smashed as the adolescent navigates the teen years.

'Why did I ever embark on this parenting lark?' the parents in my clinical practice rage. 'They hate me, I hate them; we never stop screaming at each other. What the hell has happened?' It can feel even more unsettling that some teenagers seem to behave in a manner that is designed to destroy their entire family. They might reject your views, your politics, your friends and your personal values. Even random inoffensive stuff, like your cooking, your soft furnishings and your taste in music, suddenly become the object of contempt. Some parents feel they can do nothing right during this tumultuous stage, and the insidious notion that parents are just hopeless fools can creep into the parents' mindset as they begin to believe the propaganda. 'Perhaps the kids are right,' they think. 'I can't follow all their jargon, and their way of life looks pretty insane to me. Maybe I'm just a hopelessly out-of-touch old fool?'

Yet, in many ways, we parents are *supposed* to be out of touch – we're not the new generation any more. And we are often hopelessly flawed; I'm flawed, you're flawed, we're all flawed – but that doesn't mean that we're fools. Most of the time, we parents still know more than teenagers. For teenagers to thrive, parents need to learn how to carry themselves with authority. It's important that parents don't give their power away and let the teenager think that they are vastly superior to their parents. The wisdom we have gained from experience might be dismissed in this era when youth is glorified, but our wisdom is hard-won, and teenagers feel more confident when they realise their parents have insight and experience that they don't have.

• • •

Why are some teenagers so irrational? (And why can't you be more like your sister?)

In my work as a psychotherapist, I have noticed that roughly a third of teenagers find adolescence relatively benign, about a third find it challenging, and for the last third, adolescence is a complete nightmare. This makes everything even more difficult for the family as the parent looks askance at the difficult teenager and wonders why the hell they can't be more like their siblings. But let's look at the bigger picture. It is readily acknowledged that some babies can be impossible to settle; they can cry all the way through those early years and then become perfectly happy children and healthily functioning adults. Some individuals are happy babies but then become whiny and moany in middle childhood, and then there is another turnaround: they are really quite manageable as teenagers and eventually become reasonable adults. Some teenagers can be impossible to please and can tantrum through their teen years but become contented adults. Sadly, some of us are difficult from the cradle to the grave. It's impossible to predict, and although many theories are floated, no one has quite figured out the reason for this.

Both brains and bodies develop at rapid, though differing, pace during the teenage years, and teens develop at different times. One adolescent might be going through a pubertal growth spurt at the same age as another is experiencing a period of cognitive growth. Not only that, but the huge influx of hormones and the many developmental peaks and troughs cause more tumult in the teenager's life. We don't quite know why some children walk at nine months while others learn to toddle at 18 months; neither do we know why one child can speak in full sentences at 20 months while another is still saying 'Mama' and 'Dada'. Intelligence is not always a factor, and neither is verbal competence or physical agility. Yet there is one similarity between all babies, children and teenagers – they all experience extraordinary surges in growth and development in a way that isn't replicated in adulthood. They are literally growing up, and one day it will all calm down. Their bodies and minds will become aligned, and they will be grown up.

If a person is a cranky baby, then becomes an unhappy child and eventually turns into a nightmare teenager, it is likely that there are certain unmet needs at play and this needs to be attended to. The parent might need to take a long, hard, honest look at this child's life so that they can accurately figure out what is lacking. Perhaps the teen is bored and needs more freedom? This might not suit you as parents, but if your teenager has the pent-up energy of an animal in the zoo, maybe they need to unleash some of it?

If the difficult teenager was reasonable as a child, it is more likely that either hormones and growth surges are impacting them in unimaginable ways, or else some unresolved trauma has caught up with them and they need extra help. Some people have harrowing experiences during early or middle childhood, and as a result they are thrown off course for some years. Early life experiences can really shape us, and if adverse experiences are the reason for your teenager's angst, it can be helpful to take some time to find the right support for them to process what has happened. When a teen fully understands what happened and has enough time to analyse the sequence of events with someone understanding and sympathetic, they can emerge from the experience with more wisdom. If they don't face this monster, if they continually look away and attempt to quickly move on from it, they can be unconsciously shaped by those early experiences.

No matter the reason for your teenager's difficulties, this life stage is such that they are likely to disregard their parents and instead turn to their peers for emotional support, fun and friendship (see Chapter 6). This works to varying degrees, and it is vitally important that parents don't give up at this crucial time. Although it is developmentally natural for the teenager to seek validation among their peer group, it is also natural for parents to ensure their child has a strong base to return to when life becomes overwhelming. As one parent said to me, 'I see myself as the lighthouse, and my child is out on the stormy seas.'

For a long time, much of the intensity, moods, attitude, conflict with parents, risky behaviours and other challenges associated with adolescence were assumed to result from the heavy influx of hormones that teenagers experience. However, developments in neuroscience over the last 20 years have brought a deeper understanding of the teenage brain, which has led to more insight into why teenagers are the way they are. These discoveries show us that brain development is another key reason why teenagers are so unpredictable, emotional and impulsive.

The human brain develops in two directions at once: bottom-up and top-down. The bottom part is the oldest part of the brain. It generates emotions and involuntary, unconscious reactions. The top part is the newest part of the brain. It generates rational thought, regulates impulses, weighs risk and reward, and modulates emotions. During adolescence, developmentally speaking, the bottom part outpaces the top part, so the instinctive, emotional brain is more powerful than the modulated, rational brain.

In her book *The Teenage Brain,* Frances Jensen, a neuroscientist and neurologist, looks to the latest developments in neuroscience to show us how the the brain continues to develop throughout adolescence. Although the brain is 90 per cent of its full size when we are six years old, studies in the last 20 years show that our brains aren't fully developed until we are 25 years old, so while the brain doesn't grow in size during adolescence, it gains complexity.

Inside the teenage brain

When we look at neuroscientific imaging of a teenage brain, we can see that it's like a half-baked cake; it may look fully formed, but we shouldn't be fooled! The inside is a mush of ingredients that have been mashed up together and aren't properly cooked. The teenage brain is characterised by low judgement, immature planning and underdeveloped analytical capabilities. This, combined with being easily bored, high emotionality, an excitable reward system and low impulse control, can be pretty dramatic. On top of that, the teenage brain is sensitive to social judgement, which is why teens will sometimes get led by the nose by their peers.

It doesn't matter how smart the teenager is or how good their grades are; they do not have the gift of judgement at their disposal. The rational and judicious part of their brain is not fully developed. So even if they have intelligence, they seldom have wisdom. Adults can think with the rational part of the brain, the prefrontal cortex. This prefrontal cortex understands the concept of long-term consequences, but this part of the brain *is not fully formed until early adulthood.* So teenagers are mostly driven by the emotional part of their brain, the amygdala. The amygdala is fast, filled with certainty and power, wildly illogical and given to seeing the world in black and white. The connection between the emotional part of the brain and the logical, decision-making centre is still developing. So while adults might be thinking, teenagers are busy feeling. Men may be from Mars and women from Venus, but teenagers are from Pluto.

Prefrontal cortex: Plays a central role in cognitive functioning, planning, reasoning and the processing of emotions

Adults: Fully developed at 25 years

Teens: Among the last regions of the brain to mature and so teens are significantly more prone to high-risk behaviour

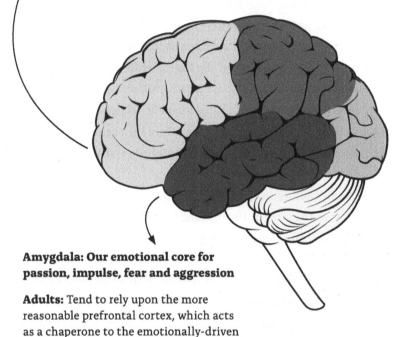

Amygdala: Our emotional core for passion, impulse, fear and aggression

Adults: Tend to rely upon the more reasonable prefrontal cortex, which acts as a chaperone to the emotionally-driven amygdala

Teens: During hormonal surges in puberty, the amygdala rapidly grows in size and becomes more active, which may lead to rash and emotional behaviour in the teen

. . .

Risk-taking and sensation-seeking behaviour

Just as most parents for thousands of years have suspected, recent evidence suggests that teenagers are chemically distinct from the rest of humankind. Teenagers' ability to assess risky behaviour and evaluate potential rewards is pretty much half-baked. Teenagers have uniquely loosely connected frontal lobes, which impact the decision centre of the brain, while the reward centre in the brain is on high alert. So when adults make a decision, they can correctly carry out a risk–benefit analysis. In contrast, when teenagers weigh up a decision, they see the pleasure in full technicolour but their ability to consider the risks is dulled.[3]

Worse than that, teenagers' ability to assess risk is even more muted when they are in the presence of other teenagers. The psychologist Laurence Steinberg ran a simulated driving study that showed that teenagers take twice as many chances when driving in the company of their friends than when driving alone – for example, running the lights when they are amber.[4] It is developmentally normal for teenagers to be more preoccupied than any other age group with social judgement and more sensitive to the potential for approval. This is why they feel compelled to engage in risky behaviour – they are sensitive to their peers' judgement, and their half-formed brains enjoy risk far more than mature adults' brains. Adolescents and adults understand potential rewards differently – teenagers see them as almost the full picture while adults' brains are better able to balance potential rewards with possible consequences, so the conclusions they reach can be vastly different.

The amygdala in the brain can drive emotional reasoning and teens are easily talked up – this is why they're so excitable. The adults in the room sometimes need to help teenagers to dampen their amygdala-driven behaviour rather than talking it up. Distraction is an under-appreciated but very valuable technique for adults to use if they want to help their teenager to calm their fevered mind. You can distract with a favourite dinner or activity or some interesting gossip you heard about somebody. If distraction works with your teen, appreciate this gold coin in your pocket, as it can be invaluable in helping to talk your child off the metaphorical ledge. If distraction doesn't work so easily, you can seek to slow down your teenager's brain by helping them fully understand the consequences of the issue. You might do this by initially listening with empathy to whatever is creating the high emotion, and then, with sensitivity, bring some other factors into play. You might say, 'I can see why you think you need to make this dramatic statement to the entire school year; but I wonder how Julie will respond to it?' From there, the teenager could easily move into a rant about Julie's nefarious actions. The parent can gently guide their teens to engage more about why Julie acts like this and what is driving Julie's motivations. From there, they could then begin to complexify the issue further by exploring how another person might respond. The end goal is to teach the teen the consequences of a proposed risky action by helping them to consider potential responses. When we become adults, we learn to better evaluate risks and rewards, and we – eventually – improve our ability to control our impulses and look to the long term.

Teenagers' risky behaviour might seem frightening to adults. Still, there are perceived evolutionary benefits to a propensity for risk-taking. Without this desire for adventure, teenagers would not be motivated to strike out on their own and would never leave their family of origin. The rise in 'failure to launch' among young adults (see Chapter 4) is a good example of how a risk-taking impulse is both needed and often impeded by other circumstances. Young adults who have failed to launch tend to stay in their childhood bedroom well into adulthood, safe and mollycoddled, some with no desire to move out and explore the big wide world, others feeling prevented from growing up by the current economic situation. Adult kids who are forced to remain living with their parents can cause much more distress to their parents in the long term than your average risk-taking teenager.[5] Believe it or not, we need young people to take risks – we also need them to seek to grow up and move on. (In addition, we need older people to provide a thoughtful counterbalance to excessively brave and risky behaviour.)

Another reason why parents need to endure rather than always seek to curb their adolescents' propensity to take risks is that, in evolutionary terms, risk-taking appears to have reproductive advantages. It is not only required for the adolescent to individuate from their parents but also necessary to impress potential mates. Even so, it's important to become more attentive and supportive when your child falls into risky behaviour. This might mean taking them away regularly for a night camping, mountain-climbing or go-karting – any activity that will engage their interest. If chosen correctly, the activity will be interesting and involve something exciting that satisfies their need for risk-taking behaviour without being thoughtlessly self-destructive. It's not easy and will require thought and commitment but, as the saying goes, 'You can lure them with a silver string, but you can't push them with an iron bar.'

Impulsivity and impaired inhibition

Of the many fears parents have about our kids – and most of us are terrified about several issues at any given moment – we are often most frightened by the fear that our beloved child will make a terrible mistake, an error perhaps born out of compulsive impulsivity and a low boredom threshold, and that this mistake will alter the course of their lives. We remember our own crazy behaviour and lack of inhibition. We might have seen our friends lose their way, maybe fall into drug addiction, or drop out of college, or harm themselves. Teenagers seek risk, sensation, mental stimulation and physical freedom. This is simply petrifying for parents – and, developmentally, that's perfectly appropriate; as fully formed adults we're right to be frightened! We often talk blithely about chicks needing to fly the coop, but it is not so well known that the most dangerous time in a bird's life is when they first leave the nest.

To complicate things further, though, not everything a teenager does is problematic. While moderate risk-taking and sensation-seeking are perfectly natural, parents tend to immediately conceive the worst-case scenario and catastrophise things. Parents need to steel themselves so that their teenager is free to learn from their own mistakes: sensation-seeking in early adolescence is both normal and necessary for teens.

It is arguably more important that parents watch out for impulsivity and impaired inhibition than for risk-taking or sensation-seeking behaviour, as a lack of cognitive control correlates with a higher risk for future issues. Appropriate risk-taking or sensation-seeking behaviour could be, for example, going to a carnival with a group of mates – there will be lots of excitement and there might be flirting, but it's not intrinsically dangerous. Impulsivity or impaired inhibition is deciding to jump from the top of the carnival ride or having sex without taking precautions because they get swept away by the moment. Therapists are taught to emphasise the patterns of behaviour more than any given situation. Similarly, it is most helpful if parents can evaluate the golden thread that represents the overall pattern of behaviour rather than tumbling from one problem to another without seeing the wider perspective and pattern of behaviour. In many ways, parents need to introduce the teenager to the teenager. We can do this by saying, 'I notice that this is a pattern of yours.' Rather than decrying the behaviour, it is far better to be neutral in the face of specific behaviour and instead point out the specific pattern of events that is repeating. This is what skilful therapists do, and it doesn't come easily. For example, if your child has been caught stealing, is this indicative of a pattern of impulsive, risky behaviour that has escalated to the point of criminality? Or is it a one-off impulsive act that could act as the much-needed wake-up call that your teen needs?

Parents often have a lot of valuable insights to impart to their children – the challenge is knowing how and when to make the point. Timing matters, and it is often much better to stay silent, bide your time and then, when you judge the timing to be right, land your point and walk away. If you have been careful in your communication and if you have chosen your time well, there will be no need to repeat what you say and no need to hang around to justify it. You might choose your moment and say something like, 'I've noticed a pattern of risk-taking behaviour that worries me. For example, you were caught vaping, and then you got into an unsafe situation with your friends after the party, and now you've been caught stealing. Your impulsivity and general lack of inhibition when it comes to risk seem to land you in serious trouble. Maybe it's time for you to learn how to take a deep breath, feel the soles of your feet, and step away for a minute before you make a decision?' It's like throwing pebbles in a barrel. You might feel like you can never fill the barrel – that nothing is going in – and then one day, you have a strange inkling that your child is learning something. Eventually, usually around the time when the teenager becomes a young adult, the synaptic balance in the brain becomes more inhibitory than excitatory (which basically means that the brain becomes more able to evaluate risk as it isn't so likely to become over-excited). So the ability to behave safely and logically has improved with time – and the barrel is finally full.

• • •

Behaviour management

Parents of toddlers will have learnt how a well-known psychological tool called operant conditioning – a method of learning that employs rewards and punishments for behaviour – can be very effective when it comes to raising kids. However, we often forget that this learning can reduce and even become extinct if we stop providing rewards for the behaviour. When the behavioural psychologist B.F. Skinner accidentally discovered how a conditioned or learnt response will decrease in strength or become extinct if not continuously attended to, he became very excited: 'It was a Friday afternoon and there was no one in the laboratory who I could tell. All that weekend, I crossed streets with particular care and avoided all unnecessary risks to protect my discovery from loss through my accidental death.' It is easy to laugh at Skinner's intensity, but the learning from his experiments turned out to be as significant as he thought it would be. Skinner's work shows that we can't take our teenager's learning for granted. Although you may have taught them – and taught them well – not to engage in sexting or inappropriate behaviour online, if you don't regularly reward them – even through mild verbal acknowledgement – for avoiding this, there is a danger that they will slowly drift towards it without even realising it. Simply put, children and teenagers will continue to demonstrate good behaviour *only* if we continually satisfy their reward centre and tell them they are great for avoiding bad behaviour.

At the same time – because nothing about parenting is simple – it is important that parents don't become the 'verbal wallpaper', with commentary becoming so repetitive that it is like the radio in the background, unnoticed, slightly annoying and always on. The delicate balance between the two is hard to achieve. We parents are always on a tightrope, trying to get it right, swinging to the right, veering wildly back to the left, failing, failing miserably, and then, sometimes, failing better. In the meantime, all we can do is give ourselves a break and bring some self-compassion into our lives, as parenting a difficult teenager is an extremely tough challenge to navigate.

EVIE, 14

On the first day of secondary school, Evie was as excited as any
12-year-old could be. She wore her new uniform with pride and
thought that, finally, now that she was in First Year, she was in the
big kids' world. That morning in school assembly, some older boys
from Third Year felt her bottom. Evie didn't know what to do. She
was shocked and embarrassed but flattered that older boys could
be interested in her. In primary school, Evie had found it difficult to
find a friend group, but suddenly, in secondary school, the boys were
giving her huge amounts of attention. Her status was automatically
elevated into the cool group. It didn't take long for Evie's behaviour to
become very sexualised.

Evie's parents had no idea that this early sexualisation was taking
place – they were happy that she seemed popular and content in
school and didn't think to ask anything more. Evie's mother had
already taught her all about safety online, so she knew all about the
risks of online inappropriate sexual behaviour. But these lessons
faded away as Evie became in thrall to the boys' compliments and
attention. Evie had a large bust and was intrigued to discover that
she was the recipient of plenty of male attention. She leapt at this
unlikely chance to shine and became proud of her sexual self and
proud that so many boys were sexually interested in her. She dressed
provocatively both at home and with her friends and regularly
posted sexually explicit pictures of herself online. One day Evie's
mother picked up her phone and saw a series of sexual messages
flash up on the screen. It became clear that Evie was engaged in a lot
of sexualised behaviour.

When Evie first came for counselling with me, she was happy that she
was the boys' favourite. She reckoned the other girls were jealous,

as was her mother. With the exuberance of youth, she felt that she was extraordinarily sexy and that all the boys loved her. It was heady stuff, and she found it difficult not to be sexual. She wore revealing clothes everywhere she went – even in the kitchen with only her mother and father to see her. Evie had become over-identified with her sexual identity. This identity had been foisted upon her when she was vulnerable. It had been the first time she felt like a social success and couldn't give it up easily.

Evie and I worked together for quite some time. This involved getting to know each other, learning to read the boys' behaviour, building real friendships and learning to notice hostile behaviour and learn from it. As Evie became more astute at reading social cues, her intense need for superficial approval from the boys diminished. Her parents introduced further restrictions on Evie's tech and imposed rules on her phone usage; she could only have a phone if her parents had the password. In the meantime, her relationship with her parents improved as they started to hang out with her more, watch films together, go shopping and generally re-establish a connection. Prior to counselling, Evie's parents had been distracted with their work and had not been spending so much pleasure-seeking time with her – indeed, most of their time together had consisted of hurried breakfasts, lifts to school and dinnertime.

All this effort took a lot out of Evie's parents. It was a difficult time for everyone. Her parents had felt very alienated from Evie's extreme sexuality. At the same time, Evie was almost addicted to the excitement of sexual approval. Sensation-seeking and risk-taking behaviour was the order of the day, and it took a lot of energy from her parents to help Evie enjoy more boring pursuits such as a day out shopping and a movie. But time and effort paid off, and eventually Evie began to integrate her sexualised identity into a larger identity. She still enjoyed receiving male attention, but she also found pleasure in building friendships with other girls, playing sports and having fun with her family.

• • •

Emotional regulation and information processing

We already know that teenagers are easily bored and more responsive to rewards than to consequences. To make matters even more challenging, changes in the limbic system in the brain also make teens less able to regulate their emotions. These changes also increase the pace and range of their emotions. When a person is more emotional, they're more likely to be more vulnerable as they are more likely to wear their heart on their sleeve.

It's not easy being a teen, but it's not all bad. The good news is that adolescents can process more information than adults, and their brains are developing all the time. During adolescence, their cognitive ability improves in five areas:

1 **Attention improvement:** Their ability to maintain their attention improves.
2 **Memory:** Their memory improves.
3 **Processing speed:** They develop the ability to process information quickly.
4 **Thought organisation:** Their thoughts become more organised.
5 **Metacognition:** Their ability to think about their thinking improves.

In short, they become aware of their own thinking patterns and gain more self-control and insight, and this leads to the development of more complex thinking processes. Thankfully for us all, their brains are fully formed by the time they are in their mid-twenties.

• • •

What parents can do

It feels torturous to watch your child make unnecessary mistakes. Whether they are dropping out of a valuable college course or alienating their good friends, we parents want to leap in and redirect them. Sadly, this seldom works. Their brains are half-formed, and we also know our children very well – better, sometimes, than they know themselves – yet it is not always our place to take charge of their problems. Sometimes, the failures we endure as adolescents are the very experiences that propel us to become healthily functioning adults. We can attempt to provide wisdom and insight when our kids seem at sea, and if we can help, all well and good; sadly, more often than not, our 'help' turns out to be more destructive than supportive (see Chapter 16, 'The difference between supporting and enabling').

Can we really sit idly by while our teenagers make mistakes? Although it is definitely the role of parents to keep our children safe, when it is more a matter of reckless irresponsibility it can be more valuable to allow our children to learn from their mistakes and provide love and wisdom when it is all over. We say we would take a bullet for our child; this bullet sometimes comes in an unrecognisable form. Sometimes it is imperative that we watch our child make a mistake; we say our piece so that they know what we think, but we allow them to make their mistakes and provide a safe and loving harbour for them when they are ready to seek help. This is incredibly difficult to do.

• • •

Takeaways

- Some teenagers are easy and some are very difficult – this is not necessarily a consequence of parenting.

- Ensure your teenager knows the reality of the unformed teenage brain so that you can point out that their ability to assess risk is impaired and you retain authority over decisions about their welfare.

- The amygdala can drive emotional reasoning and teens benefit more from dampening down their amygdala than from talking it up.

- Don't underestimate the value of distraction.

- Prop up information about brain biology with memorable stories you have gathered (through searching online) that demonstrate the impulsivity associated with the teenage brain; for example, reckless teenagers jumping off high rocks into the water and hurting themselves; driving too fast, etc.

- Parents need to be the lighthouse as the child is sailing in stormy seas.

- Teach your teens that they can be resilient and competent. The brain seeks drama, and the adolescent brain can swing wildly from one drama to the next. It is helpful if teens are regularly reminded that they will probably cope better than they think they will.

CHAPTER 2

CONNECTING AND COMMUNICATING WITH YOUR TEEN

'The single biggest problem in communication is the illusion that it has taken place.'

– GEORGE BERNARD SHAW

EACH FAMILY is like a tiny planet of its own, with its own particular climate. You might remember visiting your friend's house when you were a child and realising with a shock just how differently each family operates. The way family members behave, the way they laugh and how they communicate all combine to create the family dynamic that fosters each unique family atmosphere. Whether the family atmosphere is positive or negative is often unknown until problems arrive and the dynamics undergo pressure-testing. Most families tend to jog along in life, accepting their particular quirks, hoping for the best and navigating each problem as it arises, until, all of a sudden, a difficult teenager explodes like a bomb in the household, and the parents are forced to carry out a critical evaluation of the family dynamics.

Rather than waiting to confront issues when that pressure point is reached and the teenager has exploded, we should learn to improve connection as soon as the cracks start to show, so that conflict can be tackled in a healthy manner. Although this can be difficult, the entire family generally benefits from improving communication. Making some necessary adjustments to the family's communication style will lead to a significantly improved family dynamic – and life – in the long run.

The teenager will not be thinking about this on any level; there is perhaps nothing on earth more self-absorbed than a teenager who is in mental distress. This is why it is wholly up to the parents to lead the way in changing unhelpful dynamics and patterns of communication.

• • •

The different communication styles of the family

It is perhaps easiest to understand others by remembering that there are two main styles of communication: direct and indirect. Major problems can arise when direct and indirect communicators clash, as they are speaking two different languages.

Direct communicators give the headlines. They tend to disregard body language and tone of voice and instead focus on words. These people go by the motto 'I mean what I say and I say what I mean.' They value other direct communicators and can feel very frustrated by indirect communicators. They make their point with conviction, and it is easy to know where they stand on any given point. They tend to be forceful and often use words like 'should' and 'have to'.

Indirect communicators are very different. They may tell long, rambling stories with a tenuous link to the subject. They often use metaphors, body language and tone of voice to communicate their thoughts and emotions. They ask questions rather than argue the point and use qualifying words like 'maybe' and 'possibly'. For indirect communicators, 'It's not what I say, it's how I say it.'

Direct communicators think they are clear, assertive and efficient. The problem is that other people may think their clarity is rude, aggressive and insensitive. Indirect communicators often perceive themselves as gentle, sensitive, courteous and subtle, yet other people may see them as inefficient, wishy-washy, sly and even dishonest.

Julie, a teacher and a mother of two, came to see me for counselling as she felt overwhelmed by the huge fights that were erupting between her husband, Harry, and her son, Brian. Harry, a direct communicator, regularly gave orders to his son and could never understand why Brian seldom carried out the tasks. Brian was an indirect communicator and didn't like his father's rude manner. Rather than expressing in words why he believed that the stark orders were inappropriate, he chose to communicate his unhappiness with his behaviour – he went on strike. Both became irrationally angry with each other, but neither knew exactly why they felt so irked. Julie and I examined Julie's options, and she decided to intervene by first gently asking Brian what he thought was going on and then privately asking Harry for his version. Then, in front of the two of them, one evening after supper, at a rare moment when both were getting along well, she translated the words and the behaviours and pointed out that there was no argument here – there was only a different style of communication and that if the family were to jog along together, both Harry and Brian needed to appreciate the other's way of communicating.

There are many other aspects of communication: some people are goal-oriented, others are people-oriented; some people are thinkers and enjoy making plans, others are action-oriented and can be dismissive of plans. Figuring out communication styles within the family can make it easier to build bridges between warring factions.

It can also be important to note who is a verbal communicator and who communicates behaviourally. This is not necessarily linked to direct or indirect styles of communicating – in conflict, some direct communicators are verbal and say, 'I don't agree'; others are behavioural and will leave the room and slam the door to demonstrate disagreement. Indirect communicators in the same situation choose to tell a long story that contains the message that they don't agree with you, or, if they were more behavioural, they might gently remove themselves from the room with an elaborate excuse. The more parents can figure out how their teenager communicates, the sooner they can help their teen in the language that best suits them. Some people will never be talkative: they prefer slamming doors to shouting; they leave the room rather than explaining their problem. This is their preferred means of communication, and it can be pointless for parents to try to ensure that all their children are great verbal communicators. Some people prefer to communicate with their body language, with their music or art, with the food they make or with their facial expressions or their hugs. There are many ways to communicate, and it is not very helpful to hassle your teen into becoming a brilliant verbal communicator when they are more comfortable with behavioural communication.

Sally was an ex-client of mine who started back in counselling when she became concerned that her son, Paul, hated school. We worked together to try to make the experience nicer for Paul. Sally noticed that when Paul came home from school, he was often exhausted. Sally decided to make the kitchen feel really calm and pleasant and ready for Paul to eat a snack. She would then invite him to go to his room afterwards to decompress. Talking only stressed Paul further – what he needed was alone time to allow his body to de-stress. Some people benefit from a hot bath, others from a blanket on the couch, and some of us need to talk endlessly when we are distressed. It doesn't do to assume one way is better than the others. The most important aspect of communication is learning to honour both your communication and the other person's communication. This means actively listening with openness to the entire communication, including the words, body language, behaviour and tone of voice.

• • •

Five key steps to help you connect with your teen

Over the years I have worked with teenagers, I have found a pretty reliable approach to building a connection with one. Even though this approach can take some time and needs a certain level of skill to carry out, it is worth following. It doesn't even matter if you make a mess of it – as long as the hurt teenager knows you're trying, they will feel slightly consoled that you can see their distress and that you are making an effort.

Mistakes will be made. Indeed, many mistakes will be made, but that's all part of the process. Parenting is a long game. This is not about never making mistakes; this is about moving beyond the fake role of the infallible parent, connecting on a deeper level and being willing to repair ruptures in the relationship.

Step 1: Clarification

There is a French saying, 'Tout comprendre, c'est tout pardonner' – 'To understand all is to forgive all.' The parent needs to clarify exactly what is upsetting the teenager. If you can clarify what's really going on, you will reach a deeper level of understanding. This step requires the utmost patience. Although your daughter might profess to be unhappy because school is shit, her parents are shit and everything is shit, on closer examination you might find that her friends are treating her coldly and she doesn't understand why. Then, with further clarification, it can turn out that her erstwhile best friend is badmouthing her, and this is what is really causing the upset.

To figure out what's going on, you need to use open-ended questions that don't allow for a yes or no answer. You might need to allow the teenager to roll their eyes and become enraged when you don't immediately understand what's going on. Persist anyway. Questions such as 'I can see you're upset; could you help me better understand what's going on?' and 'Maybe I've got this all wrong, but what happened in your friend group recently?' or 'Please be patient with me while I try to understand what is most distressing for you about all of this. Is it the fact that your best friend has spread lies about you or is it that the others are siding with her?'

Step 2: Empathy

To be empathetic, parents have to roll up their sleeves and get down into the trenches with their children. It can be very painful to do this, so parents often shy away from it, preferring to instead believe that their child is just experiencing teenage angst or being histrionic. Brené Brown, a world-class thinker on empathy, tells us that 'empathy fuels connection. Sympathy drives disconnection [...] empathy is "I'm feeling with you. Sympathy, I'm feeling for you."'[6]

Empathy requires the parent to fully acknowledge their teen's wounds. This can be very painful and often needs courage. Acknowledging that your teen is hurting, without any judgement as to whether they 'should' feel this way, liberates them. They are freed from the fear of being a disappointment, and a sense of kindness and compassion fills the room. It's like tuning into the teen's radio frequency and experiencing the world in their shoes.

This doesn't mean that parents need to share the exact same experience that the teen is going through, but rather that you need to fully feel into your teen's pain. If you do this, your teen will know they are not alone. Empathy overpowers critical thoughts – you can't really be empathetic while you are criticising. Parents and teens who develop their empathy often automatically soften their critical attitude towards each other and increase their feelings of tenderness and compassion. Once the teen feels free to experience and express their feelings, it will be easier for them to feel more flexible and less rigid about any given situation. They will often soften and move to a place of self-compassion. Self-compassion helps us calm our nervous system and return it to a state of relative equilibrium.

Empathy comes quite naturally to some people and not so easily to others. But it seems to be teachable. You can help your teen to practise having empathy with any random person in their day-to-day life, such as the stressed-out shop assistant, the peremptory hotel manager and anyone else you meet along the way.

An important aspect of empathy is communicating your empathy. It is not enough to walk in your teen's shoes – you need to communicate that you are walking in their shoes. When you have communicated your empathy accurately, you will typically see a sigh of relief from your teen. Phrases like 'I can feel your pain' or 'I completely get it now, it's been so very difficult for you' are useful. Their shoulders might fall, they might take a deep breath, or perhaps they'll let out a sigh of agreement. Although this visual cue is not always present, it often is and is a real sign you're on the right track.

Step 3: Solidarity

Solidarity is an attitude that suggests to your teen that you will work shoulder to shoulder with them to improve the situation. This might entail you researching group dynamics so you can help your teenager better understand what's going on in their friend group, or it might mean liaising with the school to ensure your child is receiving sufficient support. It is vital that you communicate your solidarity. You could say something like, 'I can see how much this hurts, and even though it might take days or months or years, I'm willing to work with you to do whatever it takes to improve the situation.' You must show that you are ready to translate your words into actions.

Maura, an IT consultant, came to me for help when she found out that her teenage son was drinking alcohol alone in his bedroom every day instead of going to school. After some time deliberating about her options, Maura decided to take a six-month sabbatical from work and stayed home to be with him and help him out of this difficult patch. This was a difficult decision, but it communicated to her son that she was taking the issue deadly seriously, which had power in itself.

Step 4: Authenticity

Parents need to be authentic to properly connect with their teens. Although as a parent you might always be in the throes of cultivating your child's potential to live their best life, there comes a time, when they're upset and need a hand, when you need to down tools, forget about improving them and instead authentically connect on their level.

I had a difficult relationship with my father when I was a teen. One day, when we were sitting in the car together, he handed me a print-out of Philip Larkin's poem 'This Be The Verse'. The opening lines set the tone: 'They fuck you up, your mum and dad. They may not mean to but they do.' I read the poem, and then, in a spiteful gesture, I allowed the page to fall from my hand to the footwell of the car, as if I found it boring. I did this because I wanted to hurt my dad. Nobody could have guessed at the time that his attempt at authentic connection deeply moved me and I've never forgotten it.

Teenagers can spot fakery at a hundred paces, so you need to demonstrate that you are showing up authentically. Teenagers communicate their feelings through their behaviour and their words, sometimes in ways that are very unhelpful both to themselves and to you. Once the teen feels that you have authentically connected with the situation, they can stop showing you, maybe in a multitude of dysfunctional ways, how unhappy they feel.

When you are authentic with your teen, you show that you believe they deserve respect. If you don't agree with them, you need to find a way to gently and sincerely tell them which part you don't agree with. Don't forget that you probably only know half the story and that your teen might not want to explain the entire story, so they might be surprisingly accepting of your lack of agreement or understanding. Authentic connection shows your teen that you are meeting them where they are.

Step 5: Depth

Parents often miss the need for depth when their child becomes a teenager. During adolescence, teens must learn how to renegotiate their relationship with their parents. They also need to make sense of this world and find a set of values and beliefs they can identify with. For this, the teen often needs some depth. When the child is young, we parents know instinctively that it's not appropriate to allow our kids to see us upset, as it is too much for them. As they grow up, we continue with this approach. We cheerily pretend that life is going swimmingly, even when things are falling apart. However, this can lead to parents maintaining a fake persona in front of their teenager that can result in a superficial connection with someone we care about more than anybody else.

As teens grow up, parents need to ditch the 'parenting the child voice' – the childish voice that many parents put on when speaking with their children. Instead, parents should use their true voice so that they can begin engaging on a deeper level. By bringing some depth into their interactions with their teen, parents are helping them cultivate a deeper understanding of themselves. Rather than disconnecting from their behaviour, teens can learn to understand their thoughts and actions by confronting their inner depths. The teen can then begin to realise that there are endless complications in this world and that, although life is very difficult, it is also beautiful.

It is with good reason that teenagers have long been associated with creativity, music, art and poetry. It can be very consoling for the young person to realise that their emotions have a universality. This universality makes them feel less alone. Introducing them to a good film, such as *Juno* or *The Perks of Being a Wallflower*, or a poem, such as 'This Be The Verse' by Philip Larkin, or a song that has some substance, such as 'Hold Your Own' by Kae Tempest, can make a significant difference to a young person.

The ways family members approach conflict

You have probably heard of the fight-or-flight response as your body's natural reaction to danger. Further research has developed this, and now many experts describe this as the fight-flight-freeze-appease response (also known as flight-fight-freeze-fawn). This stress response has been with us since we were living in caves and it helps us react to perceived threats, like a growling bear or an oncoming car. Fight-flight-freeze-appease isn't a conscious decision; it's an automatic reaction we have little control over. But the more we know about how each person responds, the better equipped to handle conflict we are. For example, if the father tends to react by fighting, and so does the teenager, while the mother tends to freeze, huge fights can quickly break out between father and teenager while the mother is frozen to the spot. Suppose the father is forewarned that his fight response is causing huge conflict and inadvertently contributing to rendering his wife useless. In that case, he can perhaps learn to leave the room for five minutes as soon as the conflict breaks out so that the mother is provided with the opportunity to regroup and overcome her stress response.

The stress response instantly causes hormonal and physiological changes in the body and brain, and these changes enable us to react quickly to protect ourselves. When the stress response is activated, our body automatically prepares itself so that we can respond quickly and efficiently to the attack. It is worth taking a moment to appreciate how overwhelming our stress response can be:

- **Heart rate:** *Our heart beats faster to bring oxygen to our major muscles. During our stress response, our heart rate might increase or decrease.*

- **Lungs:** *Our breathing speeds up to deliver more oxygen to our blood. If we freeze, we might hold our breath or restrict breathing.*

- **Senses:** *Our senses become sharper.*

- **Blood:** *Our blood flow increases. An increase in blood sugar ensures that we are provided with immediate energy.*

- **Skin:** *Our skin might produce more sweat or feel cold or clammy. We may suddenly look pale or have goosebumps.*

- **Hands and feet:** *Our hands and feet might get tingly, cold or clammy.*

- **Pain perception:** *Our stress response may temporarily reduce our perception of pain.*

These responses can vary from person to person and an individual's physiological reactions depend on how they usually respond to stress. Some of us might also shift between fight, flight, freeze and appease. It is very difficult to control our response, and much more helpful to be aware of it and anticipate accordingly. The stress response is akin to a red mist, and it usually takes about 20 minutes for our body to return to its normal state. Afterwards, we can feel embarrassed, regretful and completely shocked that we behaved as we did.

The fight response
When our stress response is to 'fight', we go straight in for the argument, we keep arguing the point, tend to shoot our mouth off and sometimes say and do things we regret.

The flight response

When we respond with the 'flight' response, we avoid the problem by running away on some level, for example simply leaving the room.

The freeze response

When we 'freeze', our stress response is put on hold. In this case, we might disengage from the argument by closing down and becoming immobile. Those who tend to freeze experience the same physiological and hormonal changes as the fight and flight responses but don't fight or run away. They freeze like a rabbit in the headlights, staying completely still and waiting for others to make the next move.

The appease (aka 'fawn') response

People who tend to 'appease' their attacker experience the same changes in the body and brain, but their way of responding to an attack is to make friends with the attacker. For example, in the same way as a person who is being mugged can seek to be friendly with the mugger in the hope of escaping without being physically hurt, a parent who is triggered might instantly agree with their angry teenager or begin pleading and bargaining with them. In a way, this is a form of fleeing; it involves escaping through communication rather than escaping by running away.

• • •

Developing emotional intelligence

In his 1995 book *Emotional Intelligence: Why It Can Matter More Than IQ*, psychologist Daniel Goleman described 'amygdala hijack' as the way the amygdala in our brains disables our frontal lobes, triggers an emotional overreaction and hijacks our brain. Thankfully, as Goleman explains, although the body goes into automatic response, it is possible to deactivate your amygdala and activate your frontal lobes so that you behave wisely. Even though the amygdala can hijack our brains, our emotional intelligence can help us regain control. To do this, we must be sensitive to bodily changes when the threat lands. We need to take stock of our emotions and physical symptoms; we need to be aware that our amygdala has been activated and that we are likely to behave with animal instinct. We also need to be aware of our communication styles and know that they will likely come to the fore at this moment.

When we improve our emotional intelligence, we will begin to recognise our patterns of behaviour and the patterns of other people's behaviour, and this will help us to foresee and act on likely problems in any given situation. So the emotionally intelligent parent might spot that the teenager is looking particularly cranky on a given night and then notice the other parent, who is often equally flammable, is quite stressed from work. The emotionally intelligent parent might separate the two from each other that evening as it is obvious that a fight will break out if they spend much time together.

• • •

The Drama Triangle

The Drama Triangle is a model of human interaction that was proposed by Dr Stephen Karpman to demonstrate a type of destructive communication that can occur when conflict arises.[7]

The (often unconscious) goal of the instigator is to get what they want by dividing and conquering. This typically involves the use of indirect communication, often behind someone's back. Triangulation can occur between the teen, the mother and the father, or the teen, the therapist/teacher and the parents. In this dysfunctional communication system, one person is the victim, another is the persecutor and the third the rescuer. In a family triangulation system, one person can be used as the messenger or as a substitute for direct communication. A parent might send messages through the teen to the other parent, typically expressing dissatisfaction. In more extreme cases, the teen can be forced into the 'surrogate spouse' and 'rescuer' role, rather than maintaining the child's role.

Triangulation is often an issue for teenagers as they are learning to renegotiate relationships with the adults in their lives, and they can almost unconsciously begin to play one parent off the other. In other contexts, the teenager (the victim) actively seeks to distract and avoid issues by ascribing the role of the rescuer to the therapist or other involved adult and the role of the persecutor to the parents. Parents need to be vigilant against triangulation occurring as it causes harm to everyone and doesn't improve our mental health in the long run.

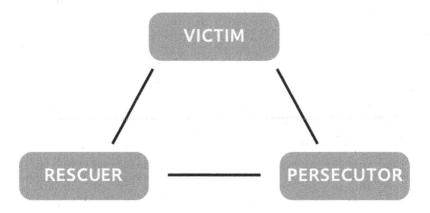

As parents, it is important to spot triangulation when it is happening and to take steps to mitigate it. Parents, even warring ones, need to create an equal partnership so that the teen can't widen the divide. You can do this by engaging with your partner or your ex as an equal rather than a superior or inferior. It will be difficult for the teen to triangulate if the adults engage in healthy and compassionate communication that clearly communicates thoughts and feelings. It is imperative that you resist the urge to vent to your teen in the case of relationship conflict. You can refuse to engage in triangulation when you spot it – this entails refusing to act the part of the victim, rescuer or persecutor and not retaliating when other individuals in the triangle play their parts. Instead, state your position clearly but gently. It can be difficult for some people to assert themselves; but instead of blaming, punishing, manipulating or using passive-aggression, it is healthier to take responsibility for your position. Say what you mean and mean what you say. Boundary-keeping is essential for any triangulated situation. This might mean that you support and empathise but don't take over. All of this requires skilled communication and can take some time to learn – be gentle with yourself during this process.

• • •

Blended families

Diverse family structures need their own attention, and yet, whatever your family's structure, teenagers are often facing similar challenges. When parents split up, there can be some time before a new world order emerges. Blended families can bring about a lot of complexity that some teenagers find difficult to handle. This doesn't necessarily mean the teen dislikes a new partner; it might mean that they simply find the complex emotions difficult to comprehend. Sometimes, though, the teenager doesn't like the new partner, which can cause significant issues within the household. It is important to give this situation the respect it deserves. It can be hard for a teen to realise that their parent is not only having sex but also having sex with someone who is not their parent. On top of that, it can be challenging for a teen to learn to live alongside a usurper of their parent's attention. None of this is easy, and further reading about this subject is recommended so that the parent can lead the communication and the teen can feel free to speak about their complicated emotions.

• • •

What parents can do

It can be very helpful for parents to become aware of their style of communication and of their stress response and start to learn how to respond more appropriately. Taking a breath or a glass of water before responding can be helpful. Leaving the room can be a game-changer – you can always come back in when your heart rate has slowed down. At first, this will feel impossible, but with commitment it can eventually become second nature. For example, perhaps your teenage daughter comes home drunk. Your amygdala immediately swings from zero to a hundred as you become furious that she would be so irresponsible. You start shouting your head off at her. She screams and cries and throws things. You behave equally badly. The entire episode is a train wreck. Afterwards, you analyse what happened. You realise that your rage stemmed from fear as you realised your daughter had walked home alone and drunk. The next time your child comes home drunk, you walk out of the room. You stand outside in the back garden. You make a conscious effort to control your breathing. You take a glass of water. You tell your teenager to go to bed and that you will deal with it in the morning. The next morning there is no 'both sides were wrong' argument. The teenager was drunk, and they need to face the consequences.

Parenting strategy: Mindful breathing

During the height of the stress response, mindful breathing can be a powerful tool to help you regain equilibrium. Think about the speed of your breath, and try to slow it down. Breathe in through your nose. Hold it. Breathe out more slowly through your mouth. Focus on how your body feels as you inhale and exhale. Try to find a calm, natural rhythm. Concentrate on how the air makes you feel and notice how your body is clenched. Unclench your muscles. Soften your jaw. Drop your shoulders and take one slow, deep breath. Take another. Consider your options before you respond.

• • •

Takeaways

- Learning how to handle conflict helps teens to manage complex relationships.

- Acknowledging our methods of communication builds self-awareness.

- If parents can develop their emotional intelligence, the entire family will benefit from wiser parental responses.

- Connecting with your teen can involve a lot of emotional effort.

- Open-ended questions that do not presume the answer can elicit a more accurate description of what is going on for your teen.

- Parents often shy away from depth, but teenagers need depth to properly understand how their world has changed since childhood.

- The amygdala's stress response was useful to early humankind as they regularly experienced real, immediate physical threats. Today, that's not the case, and it often leads us to overreact.

- Although we often respond to stress as if it were physical stress, we can gain control over our brain's irrational emotional reactions.

- Don't get into the boxing ring at the wrong time – it can sometimes be much more valuable to avoid the argument and instead wait until the time is right to bring in consequences.

CHAPTER 3

WHAT TEENAGERS NEED TO LEARN DURING ADOLESCENCE

'Make no mistake, adolescence is a war. No one gets out unscathed.'

– HARLAN COBEN

WE HUMANS have been turning 13 for hundreds of thousands of years, but only in the last hundred years or so did we consider that the bridge between childhood and adulthood deserved its own name. Indeed, before the twentieth century, there were just two main stages in life – childhood and adulthood. The concept of the 'teen-ager' first came into public consciousness when the psychologist G. Stanley Hall, the first president of the American

Psychological Association, advanced the idea of a psychology of adolescence with his 1904 tome *Adolescence: Its Psychology and its Relation to Physiology, Anthropology, Sociology, Sex, Crime, Religion and Education.*[8] Since then, business interests, among others, realised the major potential of the market, and the net result is that in the last hundred years the teenager has grown to occupy a significant cultural space. But we are still in the early years of learning about this development phase, so we need to proceed with caution.

• • •

Teenagers' milestones

Although teenagers are aged between 13 and 19, childhood these days has become shorter, so children are described as entering the 'tween' stage at about eight or nine years. The adolescent stage has recently come to be perceived as a much longer stage, and the new concept of the 'emerging adult' reaches well into adulthood. All the same, there are certain developmental tasks that adolescents need to overcome during the teen years if they are to achieve fully functioning maturity in their adult years. These developmental milestones have been formulated from various theories of human development during the twentieth century, such as Havighurst's developmental task theory, Erikson's theory of psychosocial development, Piaget's theory of cognitive development and Bandura's social learning theory.

Many of these theories suggest that adolescents are required to successfully complete certain tasks as they progress (not necessarily in a linear manner) through a series of stages of development. Although other theorists will undoubtedly have a different understanding of the teen years, my therapeutic work with teenagers over the years has led me to outline certain common challenges (or 'tasks') that adolescents in the twenty-first century benefit from tackling. It is typically recommended that these challenges are approached at any time between the ages of about 10 to 25 years. One individual might be way ahead on one challenge and massively behind on another, but by the time the person is 25 or so years old, they should have made some degree of progress towards maturity in almost all areas.

Teenagers who find adolescence manageable will confront these tasks reasonably well; however, the teenagers I meet in my work have typically got stuck on some or all of the tasks and need an extra hand. It is valuable for parents to be mindful of all the tasks of adolescence facing their teenager, as it doesn't do to focus on some and neglect others. Parents can help their teens to spread their wings and face their challenges head-on; through encouraging them to confront these challenges, you are literally helping them to grow up, just as once you taught them to tie their own shoelaces. The common challenges that adolescents need to overcome these days are outlined below.

1 **Develop coping skills:** Understand emotionally complex experiences; learn emotional regulation and behaviour management.
2 **Learn to maintain relationships:** Understand other people's perspectives, understand peer relations; renegotiate relationship with adults; manage complex relationships.
3 **Acquire healthy methods of communication,** both in real life and online.
4 **Learn to cope with independence:** Become more self-sufficient.

5 **Come to terms with the body and the sexual self:** Adjust to body development, sexual maturation and the need for health.

6 **Develop a sense of personal identity and purpose:** Develop a purpose with career or vocational goals; adopt an appropriate occupation or social role.

7 **Identify meaningful moral standards, values and belief systems:** Acquire a set of values to guide behaviour and become socially responsible; become aware of the need for societal values and social responsibilities.

8 **Begin to reach emotional maturity:** Move towards self-acceptance; accept limitations and flaws.

The challenges that often face teenagers if they fail to conquer these tasks can be as significant as toddlers who don't reach their milestones – for some, it merely means that maturity will come to them a bit later, but for others it can be an indication that they might be facing other serious challenges. Babies (and their parents) can become very distressed when they can't achieve a certain task; however, teenagers may develop disordered behavioural patterns or cognitive patterns when they feel unable to overcome certain challenges.

During these pivotal years between 10 and 25, adolescents grow in size, sexual maturity, emotional maturity and thinking capacity, and the developmental changes they experience rival those of infancy and early childhood. As with toddlers, milestones are achieved gradually; and, just like learning to ride a bike, there are often cuts and bruises along the way. Each task is linked with other tasks that need to be overcome, and they combine to propel the adolescent towards fully functioning maturity. Even so, reaching maturity doesn't mean that they will suddenly leave immature behaviour behind – they won't. Mature adults do, however, have many more qualities and more complex brain power to draw on than the half-formed adolescent. This is why we need to have forbearance and patience while they figure themselves out.

• • •

Develop coping skills

During adolescence, teenagers need to build their ability to understand emotionally complex experiences; initially, they might see everything in black and white, but with some experience, guidance and patience, they will eventually learn to see nuances. As their ability to understand things increases, teenagers learn to regulate their emotions and manage their behaviour accordingly.

It's important that parents don't minimise their adolescents' feelings if at all possible. Comments like, 'Oh sweetheart, I'm sure this won't happen,' or 'You're making a mountain out of a molehill' might calm you – the parent – but are likely to enrage your teenager, and they can add it to the evidence that you don't understand them. Teenagers can go the other way and 'turn up' their emotions to communicate to both themselves and their parents that they are very upset.

Some teenagers are processing when they are displaying their emotions in this way. It is more helpful to validate the strength of their emotions. This, in turn, can bring about more self-awareness so the teenagers can begin to figure out what's going on for them. And so you might say, 'I can see how horrible this is for you, you must be feeling a whole range of emotions from anger to sadness to disappointment.'

• • •

Learn to maintain relationships

It is valuable for parents to teach their teens the value of maintaining relationships rather than encouraging them to burn their bridges. Teenagers need to learn how to understand other people's perspectives and how to interact with other teens around them. This can take time and a lot of drama for some. It can be very challenging for some teenagers to learn how to expand their friendships beyond their one best friend or the family. Ultimately, adolescents need to learn how to get along with many other people.

Teenagers' friendships can often be fraught for two main reasons: the teens haven't yet learnt how to manage complex relationships; and it is developmentally appropriate for teens to become very focused on their social relationships. Some teens might need to learn that their 'best friend forever' has faults just like the rest of us, while others might need to learn how to make friends or how to keep them. Sometimes self-discipline is required as some teens might need to learn how to lead without dominating the proceedings — it can be immeasurably hard for some teenagers to take the lead and just as difficult for others to learn how to allow others to take the lead. Many adults fail to handle relationships and they are often the most complex aspect of our lives, so parents may take the long view on this.

Teens need to also renegotiate relationships with adults so that more complex relationships can develop. When we are children, life is relatively simple – the adults are in charge – but it is much more complicated for adolescents. Sometimes it's appropriate for the adults to be in charge, and other times it is better for teenagers to take the lead. This leads to continuous renegotiation between teenagers and adults as the nature of their relationship is constantly changing.

• • •

Acquire healthy methods of communication

Some people find this challenge reasonably easy and can competently communicate their thoughts and emotions, while others find it a much more arduous task. If your child has difficulty in figuring out their emotions, they will often have difficulties in communicating why they are distressed. We parents need to help these teenagers find a way to communicate effectively. Some teenagers get into a habit of constantly contradicting their parents, and it might be valuable for parents to explain to their teen some more constructive ways to put forward their opinion. For example, in the face of yet another contradiction, the parent might say, 'Clearly you hold another view on this. Could you perhaps explain your opinion without trashing mine? Because this feels like the vanity of small differences.'

Of course, among the digital generation, the reliance on devices to communicate is almost overwhelming for children these days. The day the child finally receives their first mobile phone can be as big a deal as when children of previous generations made their confirmation – indeed, it is often considered their first entry into adolescence. It's recommended that parents teach their children good online etiquette *before* they own their first phone. This can be done by repeating stories from the media about children losing the run of themselves online and showing them the lessons that need to be learnt from this (see Part II, 'Growing Up in the 21st Century').

I worked with Matilda, whose mother, Sarah, was very anxious about online influences. Matilda first got an iPhone when she was 12 years old, and Sarah was very strict with parental controls on the phone at all times. As Matilda became older, she felt hemmed in by these controls and she renegotiated the terms of use by suggesting that if the parental controls came off the phone, she would provide her mother with passwords to all her accounts so Sarah could monitor her behaviour. By doing this, Matilda, who was by then nearly 15, could access more content. Matilda's mother took the 'trust, but verify' approach and allowed this to be an experiment for a month. It worked out, and Sarah commented to me that knowing the passwords was better than using technology to maintain behaviour.

Learning how to communicate healthily includes learning the difference between venting and complaining. Complaining suggests that something needs to be fixed; venting indicates your child needs to be understood. Being able to complain in a healthy manner is a gift for life. It is often helpful to ask your child, 'Do you want my help right now, or are you just venting?' But you mustn't allow your teenagers to expect you to experience their hardships instead of them. Although most parents would gladly do this for their teens, it doesn't help; in fact it impedes the teen from achieving maturity.

• • •

Learn to cope with independence

In an era when technology acts as an emotional blanket for adolescents to remain tethered to the mothership for much longer than was previously considered healthy, coping with independence and learning self-sufficiency has become one of the key challenges facing adolescents today. Parents can help with this by giving their children more freedom to fail. They do this by encouraging their teens to leave the safety of their bedroom and allowing them to be unavailable for some time when they are outside. When the digital support machine is turned off, teenagers can learn to make decisions for themselves. Sadly, many parents will encounter resistance because many teenagers today are filled with fear. They often don't want more freedom and instead insist on remaining connected to their parents when they go out. Yet teenagers need to learn to become more self-sufficient. They will not achieve independence unless they have heaps of opportunities to be self-sufficient. Continuous gentle encouragement to move beyond their comfort zones can be extremely valuable for their developing maturity.

• • •

Come to terms with the maturing body and the sexual self

Children often grow up alongside the opposite sex without being overtly conscious of the differences between the sexes, but then puberty strikes, and they can barely breathe in the same room as someone of the opposite sex, or of the same sex if they are gay, lesbian or bisexual. Their hormones are raging and they don't quite know what has happened to them. Negotiating their sexual self can be very challenging for many teenagers, and they can be disoriented when they first realise they are looking on their peers as objects of attraction.

Developing a sense of our sexual orientation can take some time, and it can be particularly difficult for gay, lesbian or bisexual young people to come to terms with their sexuality. Parents might need to seek and find appropriate role models for their teenagers to learn how to negotiate their burgeoning sexuality. Films, art, music and literature can also be explored to help their teenager along the way.

Some adolescents respond by becoming combative with the opposite sex. I witnessed this recently when my 14-year-old went to the local disco. In what could only be described as a fit of hormonal madness, some of the boys decided to bring along eggs and throw them at the teenage girls dressed in all their finery. This sort of aggression can be difficult to manage, and the adults in the teenagers' lives must confront such aggression with straight talking and appropriate sanctions (for more on porn and sexually inappropriate behaviour, see Chapter 11).

The bridge between childhood and adulthood involves the body becoming sexually mature, a point at which teenagers need to explore their sexual development in a safe and hopefully loving manner. The teenager's family's attitudes to sex, love and family life can be very influential, but with easy access to high-speed Wi-Fi and hardcore porn, it is not the only influencing factor. Parents can help with this by monitoring their teenagers' devices. Some parents will not agree with this; but I have worked through so many horrible incidents involving technology and adolescence that I firmly believe that parents need to maintain strong boundaries with technology in the household – just as you would with junk food, alcohol or drugs.

Perhaps because body development arrives at the same time as a deeper level of self-consciousness, self-loathing and body hatred are huge issues for teenagers (see Chapter 10 for a more detailed analysis). Parents can help by modelling a forgiving approach to their own bodies. If you can raise a teen who is mildly aware of their body without focusing too much on it, you've won the lottery in today's world, as a combination of vanity and body-loathing is so common among teenagers.

Adjusting to one's developing body and understanding the need for a healthy body is often a natural part of sexual maturation. As teenagers gain more independence, they realise that they can eat whatever they want. I remember a pivotal moment in my own life when I realised that I could buy a box of biscuits for 53p, which was cheaper than buying two bars of chocolate at 30p each. This revelation led to a happy summer of gorging on biscuits in my bedroom: I thought I had figured out the art of living. However, it also led to a heap of weight gain and a new layer of challenges that added to my difficult relationship with my body.

···

Develop a sense of personal identity and purpose

Humans need a sense of purpose, and this can most often be found within a person's job. However, it's valuable for teens to widen their bandwidth so they can perceive their sense of self in terms of their personality, values and beliefs. A sense of purpose can help build the young person's identity. Indeed, the focus on identity among young people today could be a direct consequence of the lack of a solid future path that was previously offered to young people, which often provided a sense of meaning and purpose.

Up until fifty years ago, adolescents' vocational choices were limited, and they tended to know where they were going. They would probably follow the road either their parents or their relatives had set out on before them. The generation born towards the end of the twentieth century seems to be the first generation in which the majority had a vast choice of career paths. The results have been mixed and, without a clear trajectory to follow, this next generation appears to be floundering

These days, the burden of choice weighs heavily on teenagers' shoulders as the message of 'You can be anything you want to be' has been interpreted as 'You should be something special because you have untold opportunities.' Many teens are nervously focused on what they will 'be'. The future is wide open – too open – and many teens feel overwhelmed by this. Parents can help relieve this burden by allowing their child to cycle through different identities with a neutrally supportive approach. They can also take the pressure off by explaining how the concept of the 'job for life' is less likely these days and that it is more helpful to focus on what they want to do over the next five years than imagine what they think they'll be doing for life. Neutrally discussing the working life of any given career choice can help the teenager figure out what training and skills are most necessary for these options. You will find your teenager is much more interested in the conversation if you can show rather than tell. This could entail you noticing the work your teen seems interested in and finding examples in real life or online that demonstrate the working life. It can be more beneficial if you search and find a podcast or a YouTube video that shows a person describing their working day and/or the highs and lows of their career rather than telling your teen about it. The general idea is to help the teenager have a good understanding of the typical day of any career they might be interested in.

When adults place undue emphasis on the logistics or the challenges attached to any given career or future pathway, many teenagers become frightened and cut off mid-stream. Equally, if parents wax too lyrical about the fabulousness of another career or lifestyle, they can create a pressurised environment where the teenager believes that this is the only route to follow.

I vividly remember standing at my front door with my brother and telling him that I would quite like to be a psychologist. I was about 16 years old and quite mad at the time. My brother was immediately sceptical and implied that I wouldn't have sufficient sympathy for this job. I didn't say anything much in reply, but it made a difference to my outlook on my future. I didn't go to college after school, and it was about 15 years later before I finally began studying for a degree in psychotherapy.

My sister was just as easily thrown when my mother explained to her that she could never be a lawyer – only rich people became lawyers. We weren't of a social class that would allow her to become a lawyer, apparently. And so the world lost a brilliant and lawyerly mind. Loose lips sink ships.

• • •

Identify meaningful moral standards, values and belief systems

It is a fundamental task of adolescence to develop an outlook towards life that is based on what is important to the self. Teenagers often acquire values that guide behaviour as they become more socially aware. This is one reason why so many teenagers are heavily involved in social justice causes, and this is exactly what they should be doing at their age.

The teenage self is changing all the time, so what matters to a 15-year-old might not be so important to them at 25. The challenge for parents is to help keep their teen steady when their zeal might restrict their options. A teenager could easily burn their bridges in their new job waiting tables because their manager disregards their veganism and requires them to serve meat to customers, which they refuse to do. This reaction is in keeping with the passion and idealism of adolescence, so the parents' role might be to allow them to leave this job and also allow them to suffer the consequences of having no money.

Adolescents need to learn to behave in a socially responsible manner (for example, to learn not to throw eggs at girls who are dressed up for the disco!). They learn this by being taught the concept of *other people*. Of course, teenagers are very self-absorbed, so parents need to play the long game with this task. Social responsibility will come – but it might not come very soon. Parents can begin in the home by ensuring that teenagers consider the feelings of other members of the household when they behave in a certain manner. Over time, the teenager can bring this social responsibility out to the wider community.

Teenagers are often wildly idealistic and have little interest in logic or reason in the face of a vision of fairness. In our post-religious world a vacuum has arisen in terms of moral codes to live by, and at the same time we live in a heavily technological era, so our teenagers' moral standards can be wildly different from our own. Their online community might have nothing in common with the real-life community in which we have chosen to raise our family. This can create significant tension between parents and teenagers, and it can take a lot of time before a truce is called.

Parents can help with this task by ensuring their child is exposed to many different outlooks in life – this might mean holidaying in a range of places, where your child is exposed to societies with great wealth and societies in poverty, to technological cities and wild nature. If the budget doesn't stretch that far, you can use social media and film to ensure that your child is exposed to different sets of moral standards. Films such as *Once We Were Warriors*, *Cinema Paradiso* and *Goodfellas* can show your teenager that there are many ways to live. You can also search for social experiments or interesting history or other subjects that might interest your teen on TikTok or YouTube and share it with them.

Begin to reach emotional maturity

Emotional maturity is a well-recognised task of adolescence, but few adolescents attain it. We may move towards self-acceptance and learn to accept our limitations and flaws, but many people remain emotionally immature until quite far into their twenties and beyond. Emotional maturity is when someone can manage their emotions and their behaviour. Such people are reliable and honest; they take responsibility for themselves. They can own their mistakes and apologise when necessary, without blaming other people or having a meltdown. They have no need for secrets. Emotionally mature people can show empathy for other people but also set healthy boundaries – often a difficult challenge for the average teenager. Essentially, emotionally mature people have emotional intelligence and live their lives with integrity.

• • •

Takeaways

- Adolescents have a number of tasks to work through if they are to become healthy, functioning adults. These tasks are often difficult, yet there are no other options if the person is to achieve emotional maturity.

- Each task is linked with other tasks. A teenager might be great at one task but hopelessly behind on another, which skews development.

- If you wish to assess how your teenager is doing in the larger sense, you could ask yourself, 'In which tasks is my teenager progressing, struggling or stalling?'

- Teenagers benefit if parents can show rather than tell, but this needs creativity and a calm mind.

- Emotional maturity is achieved through learning to face reality.

PART II

GROWING UP IN THE
21ST CENTURY

CHAPTER 4
IMMATURITY: WHY DOESN'T MY TEEN WANT TO GROW UP?

'Maturity of mind is the capacity to endure uncertainty.'

– JOHN FINLEY

ACHIEVING EMOTIONAL MATURITY is a vital challenge for adolescents if they are to become fully functioning adults. The American Psychological Association defines emotional maturity as 'a high and appropriate level of emotional control and expression' – a quality of being that doesn't necessarily arrive when we reach our twenties. Emotional immaturity, in contrast, can be described as 'a tendency to express emotions without restraint or disproportionately to the situation'.[9]

Some teenagers have great difficulty with this developmental milestone; they don't want to grow up and they prefer to remain childlike and immature. The parents of immature kids can feel really torn. On the one hand, it is very comforting to have your child remain by your side, showing no desire to leave Mum and Dad; on the other, we parents know that we're supposed to give our kids roots and wings; we know that we should be encouraging our teenagers to look beyond the family home. This was not a major issue for previous generations as they looked forward to having the freedom to do as they pleased when they were grown up. Children today, though, have a pretty easy life at home. They typically have their own bedroom, with their own tech, they can have friends over for sleepovers, and, when they're older, their partners can stay over. The upshot of all this is that the desire to mature is missing.

Developmental milestone: Coping with independence and understanding complexity

Many young people resist maturity because they haven't yet tackled certain developmental tasks, such as learning to cope with independence and with complexity. It can be distressing for individuals to come to terms with these difficulties, but this is often a necessary and worthwhile pain that the adolescent needs to experience if they are to move towards emotional maturity.

The daunting nature of adulthood

Nothing is simple for this generation. Never before have most machines and systems been so complex that few among us understand them. Our parents' generation, born roughly in the middle of the twentieth century, understood most machines by the time they came of age. Radios, cars and electricity were the height of complexity, and it was possible to teach the average teen how they worked. Parents of this generation, born towards the end of the twentieth century, were faced with more complex machines such as televisions, computers and labour-saving appliances. These were less easily understandable but still within reach. Nowadays, children born in the twenty-first century are confronted with a vast array of highly complex devices that only people with PhDs in the field can understand. This means that the majority of us don't really know how anything works any more. How does Wi-Fi work? What about Bluetooth? What on earth is the ethernet? When we don't understand things, we feel uncertain – and research shows that uncertainty leads to anxiety.[10]

An example of the off-putting nature of this complexity is when a child opens their first bank account. This is a symbolic and practical rite of passage that many children benefit from as it puts them on the road to financial independence. When I was a kid, it was reasonably easy: my mother brought me down to the post office with my birth cert, and I was asked to sign on the dotted line. I remember feeling thrilled at the time because I felt powerful and grown up. When I helped my children to begin their own financial journey with a credit union account, we entered into a Kafkaesque nightmare that involved four tedious trips to the credit union with various documents and photos to prove that my children were my children and that they lived where they lived. This was despite the fact that we live directly across the road from the credit union and everyone in the credit union knew us personally.

Initially, when we went to the credit union, my kids were ebullient and waxing lyrical about how great it would be to have their own account. By the fourth visit, they were slack-jawed and uninterested – the whole thing had become a boring headache of passports, proof of residence and guardianship. They didn't feel like participants in the process as it quickly became a complicated adult situation. The reason for all this protocol is to prevent money-laundering and fraud. But there is a fallout, and the fallout impacts this generation of children. Yet another important rite of passage has become filled with tedious form-filling and stress, and this is off-putting for children.

What has all this got to do with immaturity, you may ask. Well, pretty much everything. Young people today are given no indication that the adult world is attractive – indeed, it feels impossibly complex and boring. Consequently, many of them do not wish to grow up – it feels too difficult and comes with the sense that you'll be penalised if you make mistakes.

• • •

The cultural shift

The resistance to maturity from children born from the 1990s onwards has not gone unnoticed. The US psychologist and expert on generational differences, Jean Twenge, author of *iGen: Why Today's Super-Connected Kids Are Growing Up Less Rebellious, More Tolerant, Less Happy and Completely Unprepared for Adulthood*, points out that 'the whole developmental trajectory has slowed' as there has been a cultural shift across demographics, with a trickle-down effect impacting 20-somethings. Twenge led research on data from 1976 to 2016 on more than eight million US adolescents between the ages of 13 and 19 to figure out the differences between the generations. This research revealed a decline in engagement in all activities that involved growing up. For example, in the US in the 2010s, 17–18-year-olds got together with friends less often than 13–14-year-olds in the 1990s. On average, adolescents today are significantly less likely to have sexual experiences, use alcohol or drive than adolescents in the 1990s, the 1980s or the 1970s.[11] Although, on the surface, this seems to be a good thing, when we drill deeper into these figures we see a generation who feel overwhelmed by the idea of adult life and instead prefer to pretend to themselves that they are doing their growing up online. But they're not. Just as online sex is a facsimile of real sex, growing up online is a facsimile of growing up in real life. Yes, it requires courage to engage in real life, but, as we experienced during the Covid-19 lockdown, online life is an unsatisfying substitute for real life.

Jeffrey Arnett, a research professor of psychology at Clark University in the USA, coined the term 'emerging adult' to refer to this new phenomenon in which young adults try to avoid taking on adult responsibilities for as long as possible. These young adults stay in education for longer, marry later and have their first child later. According to Arnett, 'Thirty is the new twenty.' They don't want to learn how to drive, they're not interested in alcohol and have much more limited dating experience. Reflecting on the lives of his 19-year-old twins, Arnett remarked, 'My own teen years were pretty wild in comparison.'[12] On the one hand, this seems like a lovely phenomenon: teenagers appear to be safer and much more connected with their parents. On the other, a whole generation of young people being pretty resistant to becoming adults is a fairly depressing indictment of adult life.

Why don't teenagers today want to grow up?

They don't want to learn how to drive – Uber is easier and carries no responsibility.

They don't want to date – it feels too scary, so they prefer to engage in online sex.

They don't want to drink alcohol – it feels like things might get out of control.

They don't want to get a part-time job – it's too nerve-racking and intimidating.

They don't want to move away to go to college – remaining closer to home is more comforting.

They don't want to explore the big wide world – they feel scared by it and prefer to taste freedom virtually from the safe confines of their childhood bedroom.

···

Limited opportunities to gain maturity

Another reason why so many teenagers are emotionally immature is that they have little opportunity to gain maturity through experience. Society has become so protective that we don't allow teens to grow up. For example, they have very little opportunity to earn their own money, while opportunities to socialise without parental input are limited as youth clubs, discos, amusement arcades and other teenage hangouts have closed in their droves in Ireland in recent years. The reasons are many: increased insurance costs, increased emphasis on health and safety and increased volunteer responsibilities mean fewer adults are willing to run teenage events. Equally, the radius of activity (the distance that children will venture outside the home on their own) of children and youths has been severely curtailed compared to previous generations. Then when they hit the magical age of 18, the teenagers are suddenly expected to be adults, having been infantilised until the day before their eighteenth birthday.

It is essential that parents help their teens by providing them with opportunities to grow. This is a concept that ideally continues throughout our lives. Echoing Rainer Maria Rilke, who believed that the purpose of life was to be defeated by ever greater things, the Jungian analyst James Hollis says that we shouldn't ask ourselves what makes us happy but instead, 'Does this path, this choice, make me larger or smaller?'[13] Adolescents need to be taught that reality can be both absolutely brilliant and challenging and that's OK. The biggest threat to our wellbeing is not challenges or problems but despair and stagnation. Practically speaking, this involves parents allowing their child to go to the disco (and helping to organise one if there are none). It includes encouraging teens to head into the city to go shopping with their mates. Basically, teenagers will enjoy growing up if adults can cheer along when they choose life-expanding activities rather than the safer, narrower option that involves staying at home.

Parenting strategy: Role-modelling

The importance of role-modelling cannot be overestimated. If you, the parent, aren't really enjoying the reality of your life, there is more chance that your teenager will feel a sense of dread about adult life. The good news is that you can start to address this by seeking out life's little pleasures. Maybe you need to start going to art classes or resurrect old friendships? Or maybe you need to start travelling as you always said you would? If you can begin to bring more pleasure into your life, you will automatically teach your child how to seek pleasure in a healthy manner.

• • •

Compulsive lying

Many parents describe how their teen has become habituated to lying. Teens typically tell lies either because they have something to gain – be it attention, a treat or some other gain

– or they are incapable of discerning the truth, perhaps because they have difficulty confronting the truth in general.

Pathological liars tell lies when they have no motive and nothing to gain from it, but there are often many reasons why teens lie to their parents. Perhaps they were engaging in forbidden behaviour; perhaps they believe their parents won't understand or will judge their friends; perhaps they don't want to betray a confidence. Sometimes the most important aspects of your teen's life will be kept from you – you might hear that Isabel is a pain in the ass these days, but you won't hear that Isabel embarrassed your teen by mocking her in front of her mates when she was drunk. Your teen might not want to admit their sense of shame to themselves or anybody else, and they might also not be able to explain the full context to you.

A common reason your teen lies to their friends is probably low self-esteem. They may want to impress and perhaps gain positive attention from their lies. If parents are to help, they need to ensure that teens learn about the consequences of lying. There needs to be a precious line brought in that cannot be crossed. The teen should learn that if they do something bad, you will issue sanctions but it'll be OK in general; but if they do something bad and then lie about it, you will go nuclear. The sooner the teen learns this serious lesson, the better. Going nuclear in one family might mean no devices, at all, for a month; in another family it might mean no devices for the rest of the year. You know your kid, and so 'going nuclear' depends on your parenting style.

Stealing and delinquent behaviour

'My 14-year-old was arrested for shoplifting make-up this week,'
said Angela, a mother of two. 'I don't know how to react – is this
just normal teenage behaviour? Or is it something more serious?'
Angela rang me determined to engage me as a therapist for her
teenager, but, as I explained to her, this behaviour very much
depends on the context. Was her daughter's behaviour reflective
of an overall pattern? (In which case Angela might need to
seriously address the underlying issues by leaning in to her
teen's life with love and boundaries.) Or was it just an impulsive
act brought on mostly by teenage impetuosity?

Some teens steal as an act of bravado or from a sense of
adventure. Parents might remember engaging in such behaviour
when they were young – and this memory should be recalled
as it will help you build empathy and connection with your
teenager. Teens who persistently steal may have difficulties with
their attachment bond (see Chapter 6) and find it hard to form
close relationships. Rather than feeling guilty, these teens may
blame their behaviour on others, arguing, 'Jane made me do it,'
or 'It's not fair that we've no money.' Such teens need to build a
more complex understanding of life – why some people are rich,
why some are poor; and what is the most appropriate response
to living in poverty. Other teens need to explore why they want
to live dangerously. Are they bored? Can they do something
productive that will make life less boring?

When teenagers steal within the family by robbing from their parents or their siblings, they often add to the sense of chaos by lying about it. The volume and frequency of the stealing needs to be evaluated. If your teen's problem is chronic, you would benefit from consulting mental health professionals. Forthright honesty is essential rather than colluding in secrecy; indeed intense secrecy is often an integral aspect of lying and stealing.

Stealing can also be an aspect of general delinquent behaviour that might be a manifestation of inner distress or could be the result of peer pressure. At times like this, parents need to take an in-depth examination of the pattern of behaviour so that they can be sure to respond appropriately.

• • •

The carrot and the stick

It is easy to track how the greater freedom and ease of relationships with parents has led this generation to seek to maintain the status quo when they become older – they typically want the parents to hold the worry and responsibility while they continue to live an easy life. Previous generations were very keen to grow up because growing up equalled greater freedom and more control over their lives. When they were grown up, they would be able to have their own car, a sex life, a social life and freedom to live without comment or scrutiny. Young people nowadays know that they can have all that and maintain the comfort of living in their parents' house – there is no upside to moving out, and there seems to be a considerable downside of pressure and responsibility.

Parents would be doing their children a favour if they could use both a carrot and stick to instil a sense of excitement and hope about growing up and living independently. Parents can impose certain restrictions on their teenager's life, such as ensuring that any lovers who stay the night do not feel like they own the house. Too many clients, both parents and teenagers, have described situations where the teenager's girlfriend or boyfriend has all but moved in. The boyfriend or girlfriend ends up camping out in the bedroom, entirely oblivious to the seething resentment of the parents. Some teenagers are in a situation in which they simply cannot afford to move out. For healthy relationships to be maintained, some boundaries need to be established – this might entail a clear message of what is expected from both sides.

Nature has made us so that we remain private about our sex lives – often especially to our parents and siblings – perhaps this triggers a natural disgust reflex to combat incest? The natural order of things suggests that when your teen is ready to have a regular sex life, they are also ready to strike out on their own and live independently. Although this is difficult to manage these days, if parents are to retain authority within their own healthy household, it is essential that either boundaries are maintained or the young adult moves out.

• • •

Failure to launch

As parents watch their adult children remain in their childhood bedrooms into their twenties and beyond, support groups about adult children's 'failure to launch' are mushrooming.

Even though this generation of teenagers is more educated, conscientious and socially engaged than any previous generation, I regularly meet 15-year-olds who feel unable to do their own laundry, 16-year-olds who can't get themselves up in the morning without parental input, and 17-year-olds who rely on their parents to speak with their teachers about difficulties in school. On a societal level, we seem to have collectively done a great job in creating magical childhoods for our children yet a conversely bad job selling adulthood to teenagers. For the first time ever, this generation of young people does not expect to be richer than their parents. Nothing about getting older feels secure or pleasant for many teens today. They often need help in seeing adulthood as something they might want to be a part of – we need to create *a desire* in these teenagers to grow up.

DANIEL, 20

Daniel was always an immature child; his mother and father didn't worry unduly when he seemed slow to catch up with his peers. They became more concerned, though, when Daniel showed little interest in applying for college or seeking a job after school. He seemed perfectly content to lie about the house, playing video games and eating snacks from the fridge. His hardworking single mother, Hilary, was appalled. Hilary and her ex-husband and co-parent, John, wondered how, with their keen work ethic and strong moral values, they could have raised such a lazy layabout.

Hilary booked very expensive career advice for Daniel. The conclusion was that he would enjoy a job in the arts. This was not altogether unsurprising, as Daniel was a movie buff, but it created the perfect excuse for Daniel to explain why he was loafing about doing very little with his life – you see, he wanted to be a film director, but it was almost impossible to get into this line of work, so everybody just needed to have patience. Stardom and success would take some time.

Daniel's mother enrolled him on a film studies course which did little to improve the situation, as it was there that Daniel met Rebecca, who quickly moved into the family home and spent her nights watching movies with Daniel in the den and her days sleeping and having sex with Daniel in his bedroom. This was a small house, so it was perfectly obvious to everyone, including Daniel's siblings, Elizabeth (16), Colm (13) and Jack (11), exactly what was going on.

The sex noises during homework time, dinner time and family TV time were one thing, but the nightly raids on the fridge became even more annoying as tomorrow's lunch would be plundered by the fun-loving couple. Hilary came to me out of sheer frustration with this impossible situation. She had no idea how to bring about some sort of maturity in her happy but hapless son.

Daniel and Rebecca liked to characterise their immaturity as being 'easy-going'. This insulated the couple from recognising that they weren't taking responsibility for themselves either financially or emotionally. Daniel and Rebecca expected greatness to come around the corner to meet them any day soon. They were entirely unconcerned about their future and had no plans to move out anytime soon. Instead, they were saving whatever small amount of spare money they had from their university grant and their parents' generosity for a dream holiday in Greece. They were perfectly happy to maintain life as it was and saw no reason to be concerned about things – indeed, they often told Hilary that she should really try to 'chillax'.

Hilary decided it was time to bring in the carrot and the stick. She imposed some household rules. Nobody was allowed into the kitchen between 9 p.m. and breakfast time. She said it was too disruptive for everyone else, and anyway, it was her house and her rules. Hilary was strict about this. Every time the couple tried to cook something in the middle of the night, she would come downstairs and order them out of the kitchen. She did not back down.

Hilary then decided that it was time that the entire household lived on the same schedule – again, it was too disruptive for everyone else to hear Daniel and Rebecca watching movies at night. So Hilary would come downstairs and insist that they couldn't watch TV in the living room at night – they could, of course, watch things on the laptop in the bedroom, but Hilary would be in every morning, opening the curtains, sitting on the bed and insisting they got up and got dressed like everyone else in the household. This was met with huge resistance from Daniel. He moved from being cheerful to becoming very angry with his mother for ruining his idyllic existence. Hilary, supported by regular counselling, stood her ground in the knowledge that this was not a healthy lifestyle and she was no longer willing to support it.

Hilary had correctly guessed that Daniel's next move would be to move in with his dad. Hilary let John know that there was a revolution unfolding in her household, so John was ready for the call when it came. He explained to Daniel that although he was perfectly welcome in his house, there would be costs and responsibilities involved as Daniel was by then 20 years old and needed to live the life of an emerging adult rather than a dysfunctional teenager. Daniel didn't fancy the ominous suggestion of money changing hands and stayed put. But he felt less comfortable and began to speak tentatively about moving out one day. Hilary encouraged this and started to bring in the carrot by prompting Daniel to imagine a life where he had no demands to bring the younger kids to their activities (Hilary had started to insist that either Daniel or Rebecca had to do this to contribute to the household), where he and Rebecca could do exactly as they wished, according to their own schedule.

Then one happy day, Daniel heard about a house share in his friend's house. Daniel and Rebecca realised that if they were willing to use their holiday money and had a bit of help from their parents, they would be able to move into this house. Hilary was delighted and decided to offer Daniel a specific amount each month for the next year. The catch was that the amount was reduced by €50 each month, so Daniel would need to make his own money by the end of the year. Daniel readily agreed to this with the blithe confidence of youth, assuring his mother he would be a famous film director by that time the following year.

'I don't think he'll be a famous film director this time next year,' Hilary told me, 'but I do think he'll be working, and that's enough for me.'

• • •

Where is the trade-off?

Psychologist and author of *Surviving Your Child's Adolescence: How to Understand, and Even Enjoy, the Rocky Road to Independence,* Dr Carl Pickhardt, has also tracked this current generation's reluctance to grow up and identifies the mixed messages that parents give children that don't help. Initially, we parents encourage our kids to act like a 'big girl' or a 'big boy' and then, once adolescence kicks in, we try to put the brakes on this and try to slow down the process of growing up, showering them with endearments such as 'You'll always be my baby.' At the same time, a conflicting message of hyper-sexualisation contributes to the complexity and uncertainty.

In many ways, the process of growing up is a trade-off, and if the child doesn't see a good trade they will be resistant to the notion. In late childhood, the child needs to be willing to trade the playful freedom of childhood with the promise of being the sophisticated teenager they catch glimpses of on their screens. Later, in adolescence, there needs to be a similarly glamorous path to adulthood. Parents need to ensure that there is a trade-off by imposing certain healthy restrictions so that their teenagers can properly look forward to adulthood.

• • •

Takeaways

- Some teens will take a lot longer than others to mature. This also happens with babies, toddlers and children, yet it may feel more significant in teens.

- The complexities of ordinary life feel alienating for children, which leads to a fear of growing up.

- Help your child to problem-solve by refraining from giving them the solution. Many teens today learnt to rely on the nearest adult to overcome challenges. Encourage them to seek a resolution to any given problem before you stick in your own tuppence worth.

- It can be worthwhile to allow your teen the opportunity to learn from mistakes by keeping your mouth shut and underreacting when they make mistakes. Mistakes are all part of the learning process. Let them find the valuable teaching moment by not intervening.

- Provide expansive experiences by asking them to make their own dentist's or doctor's appointment. You might go with them to the appointment, but they can ring to make the appointment. Ask them to buy the groceries and incentivise them with a few quid for doing it.

- Encourage them to participate in volunteering for people less fortunate than themselves – this will provide a wider lens for them to understand life.

CHAPTER 5

DRAMA AND CONFLICT

'The greatest advantage of not having children must be that you can go on believing that you are a nice person: once you have children, you realise how wars start.'

– FAY WELDON

SOME TEENS seem to be almost addicted to drama. They storm through the house, causing a disturbance in every room. They're like a hurricane, so when they go out for a few hours, it can feel like the actual walls are breathing a sigh of relief. Many parents are often astonished by this level of intensity and don't quite know how to respond.

At the root of adolescent intensity is often an enraging recognition that life is much harder, more incomprehensible and less fulfilling than the child had ever suspected it would be. During adolescence, the teen is expected to come to terms with some hard facts about life. They realise that they are essentially alone, that no one fully understands them, that they're flawed, that their friends and parents are flawed, that no one is in charge and that life is essentially unfair. The utter pointlessness of life can hit the young person hard, especially if they have no religious framework to rely upon. Previous generations of teens often went through a devout phase during adolescence, perhaps because religion was a way of making sense of the enormity of our existence. These days, many teenagers are so discombobulated by the sheer absurdity of this world that they feel completely derailed by it all.

Is it a coping mechanism?

Drama, fights and emotional dysregulation can be a coping mechanism for teenagers who have difficulties coping with complexity and developing emotional maturity. Often driven by a need for understanding and a response to feeling vulnerable, these individuals need to find healthier ways to function. Learning how to handle complexity is a gift for life that is well worth developing, though for some people this can be a lifelong challenge.

• • •

Drama queens and addiction to drama

The term 'drama queen' can be applied to boys or girls. For these individuals life is either wonderful or dreadful. The rollercoaster of emotions involved in living with a drama queen can lead to utter exhaustion and feelings of despair, so parents and siblings need to have boundaries of steel when there is a drama addict in the house.

Of course, few among us can totally avoid drama – extreme events happen to most of us at some stage. But some people lurch from drama to drama, often playing an active role in maintaining and exacerbating the drama and usually declaiming that they did 'nothing'. These dramas always happen to them. It is valuable if parents can figure out which needs are being met through an addiction to drama. It could be, for example:

- **Learnt behaviour:** Is there a parent or relative who also seems to have an unhealthy interest in the latest drama?

- **A need for fun and excitement:** Some people need more thrills than others; this is an emotional need, not a casual desire, so resolution comes about by finding healthier ways to meet this need.

- **Seeking control:** Creating drama can be a way to control and manipulate others. This is a form of passive-aggression that seeks to make other people feel guilty and feel sorry for the drama queen.

- **A lack of emotional independence:** This individual finds it difficult to be alone and uses drama to create bonding experiences.

- **Self-destruction:** A person who has experienced trauma can seek to recreate intense emotions as a way of processing what happened to them.

- **Personality or developmental disorder:** An undiagnosed condition such as bipolar disorder or borderline personality disorder can lead to out-of-control behaviour. In this case, parents should seek help from a qualified professional.

• • •

Attention-needing versus attention-seeking

It is said that all behaviour is communication and, as my old college lecturer used to ask, 'What's going on? ... Now, what's *really* going on?' This question is worth contemplating in the face of attention-needing behaviour. Some people seem to need more attention than others; indeed, some people seem to have an insatiable need for attention.

When a teenager needs attention, their means of getting it can be destructive. This is why it is valuable for parents to look beyond the behaviour to see what they think the teenager is trying to achieve. It is better for parents to identify the need that is driving the behaviour and meet the unsaid need than to focus on the specific behaviour such as a tantrum or some other episode of extreme emotion. Unexpressed needs, such as a search for connection, understanding or protection, often underpin drama addiction. Ask yourself if your teen is:

- seeking connection because they want to be heard, seen and met on a deeper level

- seeking understanding because they want their feelings or thoughts acknowledged and validated

- seeking protection because they want to feel safe.

Parents can find this difficult to comprehend when their teenager is throwing a strop because they can't find their favourite T-shirt, but if you can ascertain the need underpinning the teen's behaviour, you can cut out the middleman – the attention-seeking behaviour – and instead go straight to the heart of the problem.

• • •

Fights and emotional dysregulation

Teenagers often have the right feeling but at the wrong scale. They might be able to identify that they are distressed, but their response is inappropriately intense. They are filled with certainty and power but are caught in a hurricane of emotions. This emotional dysregulation (an emotional response that seems far beyond the typically accepted range of emotional reactions) of a teenager can be a shocking thing to behold.

For example, your child might feel stressed about an impending exam. They come home from school, and suddenly what seems like an actual nervous breakdown unfolds because you are cooking pasta instead of rice. They blow up at you, screaming you know they hate pasta (they don't); that they've always hated pasta (they haven't); and that you never listen to them (you do). It's very easy to react to this outburst, but if you can instead look past the behaviour and lean in with empathy, you will see beyond the shouting to the hidden place in their mind where they feel small and scared. If you can refrain from responding to the rice/pasta fight and instead ask your teen to talk to you about their stress, you might get a better response. Encourage them to have enough self-awareness to know that this is about something other than pasta.

My top tip: show, don't tell! Let them come to their own conclusions about what it is really about. This will help them to build their coping skills. It is important to note that this needs to be done either after or before the storm. There is no point in trying to get through to anybody when they are in the middle of a tantrum. After the storm, you can encourage honesty and insight. For example, you might come into their bedroom with a hot chocolate later on in the evening and sit on the bed, without cleaning all around you, or even noticing the mess, and engage in a dialogue that goes something like this:

Parent: How are you doing? You seemed so upset this afternoon.
Teen: I don't know. Everything is just so difficult.
Parent: It seems like there's a lot of stress raining down on you these days?
Teen: You have NO IDEA. It's all so difficult.
Parent: I'm so genuinely sorry that it's this difficult. I wonder is there anything I can do to help?
Teen: Well, don't cook me pasta when I hate it.
Parent: (silent, letting the sarcasm go, waiting for more)
Teen: It's just the exams ... and everything.
Parent: (resisting the temptation to speak about plans, schedules, homework) I remember how exams brought about such horrible feelings of foreboding.
Teen: You have NO IDEA how much HARDER it is than your day.
Parent: (resisting the urge to correct them) I really love you. Let me know if there is anything I can do to help.

Then you can leave the room. There is little point in ruining the warm chat with talk of grinds or anything substantial. It's enough to have sent a message of warmth and kindliness. You can come up with something more constructive a couple of days – or even weeks – later.

If you can help your teenager articulate what they are experiencing, you have some hope of bringing about some self-reflection. This might mean viewing certain emotional outbursts just as a sailor would view the last big waves after the storm – eruptions that could be dangerous but might be easily quelled. When you encourage your teen to sit with their feelings, without pushing them away, you teach them that although feelings are hard, they are necessary and not something to avoid. This is a process of maturity that approaches the necessary milestones that adolescents need to master.

Developmental milestone: Develop coping skills

It can take some teens quite a long time to develop their coping skills, but this is an essential task of adolescence that needs to be tackled. When they have no idea what came over them, they are unlikely to learn how to behave better, but when they begin to come to an understanding about what is driving their behaviour they will begin to learn better emotional regulation and behaviour management. Parents can help with this by introducing them to stress management techniques such as time alone, slow breathing or exercise.

· · ·

Teaching the teen how to manage conflict

If you have a conflict-oriented teenager in the house, it can be helpful to prepare for the long game and read up on conflict resolution as you wait for the teenage brain to mature. Conflict resolution can be a tool in your workbag. Still, it won't be the answer to all issues as some teenagers simply will not calm down and no sooner is one issue resolved than another erupts. Nonetheless, some skills and knowledge in this area, such as the following five options for resolving conflict, can be handy:

- **Accommodation:** This is a lose/win situation – the parent accommodates the teen or vice versa.

- **Compromise:** This is a more amenable resolution – both sides move a little towards the centre.

- **Avoidance:** This is a lose/lose option – neither side grows from the experience.

- **Competition:** Sparks can fly when both sides become determined to win. A long and horrible power struggle can ensue, and it can even end in violence.

- **Collaboration:** This is the healthiest option. Both sides work together to seek an achievable resolution. It requires buy-in from both sides and is often rooted in an acknowledgement that there is a problem to solve.

LISA, 15

When Lisa was a little girl, she was the apple of her daddy's eye. This was perhaps why Jason, Lisa's father, was inconsolable when Lisa, aged 12, began riding roughshod all over the family unit. Screaming fights with her mother, Maeve, were a nightly occurrence. Every single incident involved drama. Nothing was dealt with in a calm or rational manner.

Lisa's behaviour first changed when she was 11 and was being bullied in school. She felt isolated during those difficult months and became irritable at home. Jason and Maeve were preoccupied at this difficult time as Maeve was undergoing chemotherapy for breast cancer, so Lisa didn't get the attention that she needed.

Lisa built a brittle shell around herself, and when she turned 12, her behaviour became very self-destructive. She became friendly with a group of similarly disaffected kids, and they began drinking, smoking weed and being sexually promiscuous.

Bright and vivacious, Lisa found it easy to make friends, but these friendships never lasted long. There were always dramatic fights to contend with when Lisa was around.

Lisa's parents did their best to help their child. They attended the Child and Adolescent Mental Health Services (CAMHS) with her. They brought her to the GP when she felt depressed. They followed the professional advice, but it didn't do much good. Jason and Maeve had reached the end of their tether when one day, as a result of a recommendation, they made an appointment for me to see Lisa.

Lisa first came to our counselling sessions with a lot of attitude. It was evident that she was absolutely furious that she was yet again in therapy. Lisa made it clear to me that she believed that everyone in my industry was not only foolish but also dishonest. It took some time for me to establish a working relationship with Lisa, but as I presented my authentic self to her and told her about my own difficulties as a teenager, she gradually, ever so slowly, deconstructed her protective wall.

It turned out that Lisa felt unloved. Despite all the evidence to the contrary, she didn't believe that her parents cared about her. She was jealous of her older sister, who was, by all accounts, perfect in every way. She was a blank wall of resistance when I mentioned her mother's cancer diagnosis – it seemed that Lisa's brain was not yet ready to process this, so just refused the information.

Lisa thought that nobody was looking out for her – and maybe, for those crucial months when she was being bullied as an 11-year-old, nobody was. Life is sometimes extremely difficult, and perhaps it was impossible for Lisa's parents to attend to Lisa's problems because Maeve was sick with cancer and Jason was busy with a full-time job and a sick wife.

After this wretched time, Lisa found some friends who were also lonely and looking for something extra to fill their void. They started to look for thrills rather than satisfaction. Lisa became transactional in her relationships and didn't express any interest in longer-lasting intimacy, vulnerability or deep friendship. At a pivotal stage of development, Lisa hadn't learnt the value of supportive relationships and so began to view life as a dog-eat-dog situation. She began to live in a shallow and superficial manner, always ready to fly off the handle at any moment.

As part of the therapeutic process, it seemed necessary to show Lisa that I cared about her. A professionally manufactured false show of concern was not what Lisa needed, so I made sure to only show Lisa my authentic regard for her. She was a lost, crazy, mixed-up kid and, as I had been like her, I found it easy to have empathy and concern for her. Lisa seemed surprised and intrigued when she realised that I really did care for her. She tested me a few times – cancelled appointments, texted at inappropriate times, laughed at me.

Then one day she explained to me that she really, really needed to go to the local disco and, as she was mid-punishment, her parents weren't giving her permission. The old Lisa would have gone anyway but since working with me her parents were now imposing strict consequences for bad behaviour. Often sending a teenager to therapy propels parents into firmer and more boundaried responses, and Lisa knew her life wouldn't be worth living if she sneaked out to go to the disco.

Lisa and I worked together and came up with a reasonable strategy that her parents might go for, and then I invited Lisa's mother into the session. The deep love Lisa's mother had for her child was immediately evident and it was relatively easy to figure out a compromise. This was a risk as Lisa, Maeve and I were all aware that Lisa had messed up similar opportunities in the past.

We were all nervous when Lisa went to the disco. But she didn't get into trouble, and when she arrived back in my office the next week, she had a breakthrough. 'I didn't know my mother cared so much about me,' said Lisa. I heaved a sigh of relief and encouraged more of this. We discussed her mother and what her mother had gone through. Finally, some old wounds began to heal in this lost little girl who pretended to herself that she was a badass.

Over time, Lisa opened up sufficiently for me to show her that her parents loved her deeply. They had taken the eye off the ball at a vulnerable time for everyone and things had disintegrated ever since. There was a lot of unnecessary pain unfolding as a result but it was no one's fault.

At around this time, a nice, easy-going boy called Seán arrived into Lisa's life and Lisa's harsh exterior began to soften. She also learnt some self-awareness and realised that her passionate nature was leading her to make quick judgements that weren't necessarily true. Lisa became that little bit gentler and that little bit easier, and her parents were finally able to breathe again. Life wasn't rosy in the garden, but life became manageable for the household as Lisa, finally, began to accept her parents' love again.

• • •

Encouraging wellbeing

Drama-addicted teenagers can be stuck in the bad habit of jumping from one crisis to the next without taking a moment to pause and think. As parents, you can help with this, not by trying to prevent the drama – it's often too difficult to prevent – but rather by adding regular moments of wellbeing into your teen's life. If you can get buy-in from your teenager, they can learn some techniques to ensure that not only is the emotional stress response activated but so is a sense of wellbeing.

Some of us express our emotions with our behaviour or our physicality, while others express their emotions verbally or through overthinking. Teens who are more behavioural or physically orientated generally show distress in their body or their behaviour, for example with digestive problems, breathing difficulties and eating too much or too little. These teens might be more comfortable with behavioural techniques to help them reduce stress, such as:

- deep abdominal breathing
- focusing on a calming word or calming mantra
- visualising peaceful images
- meditation
- repetitive prayer
- yoga or t'ai chi
- regular exercise
- baths or showers.

Teens who tend to manifest their distress in a more cognitive/emotional manner – by worrying, anxiety episodes or overthinking, may prefer these cognitive/emotional methods to alleviate tension:

- counselling from a mentor
- meeting friends
- speaking about their fears to a kindly person
- writing in a journal
- finding consolation in literature, art or music.

It doesn't matter whether your teen is cognitive or behavioural – what matters is that you take the time to notice your kid's disposition and help them find what works for them.

What parents can do

Parents need to take the long view on this. It can be utterly exhausting living with a drama queen, so self-care for both teen and parent is imperative in this situation. If the parent can encourage the teen to reflect on their difficult feelings as useful pieces of information that signal what is causing them distress, the teen will be able to acquire coping skills to deal with the true issue. This will lead to a deeper understanding of themselves and an improved ability to cope with difficulty.

When to escalate, when to maintain, when to seek professional help

It can be very difficult to figure out if drama is just a bad habit that your teen has fallen into or a sign of something more serious. Individuals with a need for drama often display personality disorders, including borderline, bipolar, psychopathic, and/or narcissistic disorders. You can take a 'watchful waiting' approach while you figure out whether professional help could exacerbate the problems of the teen who is addicted to drama or if it would bring a steadying voice into the equation. As always, reading around the subject, watching good YouTube videos and listening to podcasts on the subject will help enormously.

· · ·

Takeaways

- Attention-seeking behaviour can be a sign that the teenager needs more attention.

- When your teen comes to you with a problem, ask them whether they are seeking solutions or if they just want you to listen.

- Parents are the most important role model that a teenager has. Although their friends are very influential, the parents are the scaffold on which everything rests.

- It can be valuable to remind your teenager of previous times when they thought they were in the middle of a disaster but it turned out OK. Collect evidence of these successes and hoard them like gold coins to be produced at the right moment.

- Try to remember when you were a teen. There were probably drama queens among your circle; many of them eventually calmed down.

- When your teen arrives with a huge problem, take the bullet and keep your cool. You can freak out later, but it is essential that you maintain a safe harbour for your child during the crucial moments.

CHAPTER 6

FRIENDSHIPS, RELATIONSHIPS AND SCHOOL LIFE: MANAGING THE SOCIAL CONTEXT

'Wishing to be friends is quick work, but friendship is a slow-ripening fruit.'

– ARISTOTLE

PARENTS ARE OFTEN distressed by the way some teenagers suddenly and unceremoniously dump their parents and dive headlong into their friendships instead; other parents become frantic because their teenager can't seem to make any friends; others still worry about why their teen makes and breaks friendships at a frightening pace. We parents console ourselves that this is all natural – we know that it is developmentally appropriate for teenagers to seek peer approval and we remember how confusing trying to socialise was when we were teenagers. Yet sometimes, teenagers' friendship patterns cause serious concern. We're probably right to give this some thought as the friendship patterns of the teen might raise the issue of certain weaknesses in their attachment bond and parents can sometimes make a difference to this by leaning in with love and boundaries.

Developmental milestone: Learn to maintain relationships

Adolescents need to learn to navigate more complex peer relations than they had in childhood. They need to learn how to handle more than one-to-one friendships and instead deal with the friendship group. They need to learn how to handle disagreement and disappointment. They also need to learn how to understand other people's perspectives. All the teenagers are learning this together at the same time, and as a result there can be many difficulties with friendships during this stage. You might remember the fraught nature of friendships when you were a teenager and then, in your twenties, you might have moved on to fret about your career and your potential partners. This is how we humans live; moving from stage to stage, worrying about different aspects of our lives. The trick is to try to knock some satisfaction out of life as we progress through the stages. Although it can be challenging, it is developmentally normal.

···

How attachment bonds form

The British psychologist and psychiatrist John Bowlby defined attachment as a 'lasting psychological connectedness between human beings'.[14] He believed that 'the infant and young child should experience a warm, intimate, and continuous relationship with his [or her] mother (or permanent mother substitute) in which both find satisfaction and enjoyment' and that the lack of this bond might have significant and irreversible consequences on an individual's ability to form relationships. Initially, a child will attach to their parents or caregivers. From this springboard, they then go on to form attachments with the friends and relations of existing attachments – for example siblings, a kindly neighbour, a loving uncle or whoever appears in their life.

One of the problems with this is that children's brains are wired to attach indiscriminately to whoever or whatever is offered. There is little selectivity involved, so a child born to violent, drug-addicted parents will attach to those parents. Similarly, if the mother duck is missing when the duckling hatches, the duckling will attach to any moving object, such as a piece of fishing line. Children are not quite so basic – they don't attach to random objects – but they will instantly attach to the first person who *appears* to offer relief from the attachment void – the blank space inside humans which we seem to seek to fill with human connection. Sadly, our attachment programming is blind to the need for quality traits such as dependability or kindness; we don't question our desire to attach; rather, for some reason, we humans feel a hunger to attach.

Many people feel irrationally attached not only to terrible parents but also to other awful people. The reasons why we are initially attracted to them are many and varied. The reason why we stick with them even after they have treated us badly is often because we have formed an attachment and are deeply uncomfortable with creating an attachment void. Some people, typically when they are a little older and after a series of difficult relationships, can decide to pull back from attachment as they fear the distressing emotions it can unleash inside them.

· · ·

Peer-orientation versus adult-orientation

Post-industrial society, with its emphasis on professional childcare and both parents working outside the home, does not encourage children to form strong attachments with their parents. Consequently, many children form a series of unstable attachments to peers and professional childcare workers. Of course, not all children from previous generations had stronger attachments to their parents, but they did have many more opportunities to form stronger attachments to extended family members, such as aunts, uncles, cousins and grandparents. These days, in our increasingly peripatetic and peer-oriented society, many parents inadvertently put more effort into encouraging children to form attachments with their peers rather than with family members. Sadly, this doesn't work out too well for many families; although strong family bonds can sometimes feel like chains, they also tend to remain reliably *there*, in a way that passing friendships seldom do.

Children have always been unkind to each other. Their consciences are not yet fully formed, so they can be self-absorbed and brutal, but it is only in recent years that peers have been held in such high regard in our children's lives. Friendship is indisputably important, but few among us have many quality friendships throughout our lives, and too much emphasis on friendship can lead teens to seek loyalty and depth that is not necessarily available.

Parents need to continue to strengthen their relationship with their teenager even while the teenager is pulling away from them. In the seminal parenting book *Hold on to Your Kids: Why Parents Need to Matter More than Peers*, Gordon Neufeld and Gabor Maté decry society's tendency to 'make children responsible for children'. They believe that not only is this too much responsibility for children, it also disregards the value that can be found in child–adult relationships. As they point out, 'Attachment voids, situations when the child's natural attachments are missing, are dangerous precisely because they are so indiscriminate.'15

• • •

Attachment styles in childhood

Our attachment style drives the gut feelings we tend to project onto our friendships and relationships. These styles are typically formed through our early relationships with our caregivers. As a parent myself, I understand all too keenly how much we parents wish to tell ourselves that our children are happy enough; they probably have a secure attachment style and all is well. It takes much more courage to look at the monster under the bed and honestly assess our children's attachment style. But if we can be courageous about the challenges our children face, we are much more likely to heal any lingering wounds they might have. As the old saying goes, the best time to plant a tree is 20 years ago; the second best time is today.

Although there are a range of different viewpoints and different terminology is often used, there are arguably four major attachment styles in childhood. Aspects of attachment styles can be seen in your teenager's approach to you, to their friendships and to their romantic relationships. Although parents might be quick to assign a disorganised attachment style to their teenagers, as many of them engage in the push-pull dance with their parents, it is much more informative to watch teenagers' peer friendships and evaluate their attachment style from this point of view.

It can be valuable to help your teen to understand when their friends are behaving badly and when they might have communicated ambiguous messages themselves. It is also helpful to take some time to consider your teen's attachment style (and your own attachment style), and when you have figured it out, it can be valuable to evaluate what is needed to strengthen the attachment bond between you. We all face many challenges, and it is more helpful to acknowledge the challenges in the attachment style than to pretend that everything's fine. Attachment styles don't condemn us to dreadful relationships throughout our lives – rather, they suggest where weaknesses might form. The following brief analyses provide a rough explanation of how these attachment styles might manifest.

Secure

A teenager with a secure attachment style feels confident in their relationship with their parents. They often feel connected, trusting and comfortable with having independence and freedom. They are ready to explore the wider world and assume that their home life is a secure base to which they can return when they need support. They may make friends easily but are not overly attached to these friendships and can allow a natural ebb and flow to take place during the teen years.

Anxious

Teenagers with an anxious attachment style tend to crave emotional intimacy, even when the situation is inappropriate. These kids often feel dependent on others for approval and place their self-worth in other people's hands. This can become a destructive cycle of negative reinforcement as their craving for approval, responsiveness and reassurance from their peers can feel oppressive and needy – and they can feel even more anxious when they don't receive the desired approval.

Avoidant

Teenagers with an avoidant attachment style tend to be emotionally independent – often overly so. They feel uncomfortable when others get too emotionally close to them, and they don't trust others easily. When these kids feel a little bit vulnerable or rejected, they are very quick to pull away. Avoiding closeness, they often pride themselves on not needing emotional intimacy. Just because this child acts as if they don't need emotional closeness doesn't mean that it's true. Research shows that even highly avoidant people feel happier and better about themselves when they feel accepted or when a good relationship with others is fostered.[16]

Disorganised

Teenagers with a disorganised attachment style can be confusing. Essentially, they want emotional closeness and at the same time they push it away. They are afraid to trust others and yet they often seek approval or validation. They can be fearful, they tend to be reluctant to express their feelings and often deny any feelings, yet at the same time they can be rabidly jealous and are quick to perceive other people as potential rivals. These kids are hard work and can lose friends as often as they make them.

SOPHIE, 16

Sophie was the youngest of three in her family. She presented as a bright and bubbly teenager with a lot going on. As a child she seemed happy-go-lucky and yet she also suffered from behavioural problems as a young child – always a fussy eater, there were long periods when she would only eat about four different foods. Sophie was sent to me because her parents believed they couldn't control her and the school had told them that she might not be allowed return after the summer holidays unless her behaviour improved.

When we first began to work together, Sophie concentrated on regaling me with her exploits. She was funny and charming, and I laughed at these stories, and yet most of them didn't quite add up – as if she forgot or didn't notice vital elements to the story. Sophie's parents had told me that she was a compulsive liar, so I couldn't help but wonder whether the full truth was being told.

When I decided that we had formed a sufficient therapeutic alliance, I began to gently challenge Sophie on her stories. As she launched into yet another tale, I would stop her and ask her how she felt. Sophie would just look at me blankly and wave away this question with a quip.

Sophie hadn't yet learnt to go inward. Everything in her life was for 'shits and kicks'. She wanted to be entertained NOW and she would do anything to keep her mind busy. If this meant throwing a trolley in the river or chucking a bottle at a passing car, so be it. Sophie seemed to be compelled to move forward at all times. She made friends and she lost friends but none of her friendships lasted.

She found it hard to sit still, so it was little wonder that school didn't suit her. She was funny and constantly played up in the classroom. My job, as her therapist, was to bring a pause, some self-reflection, into her life. It wasn't easy.

Before Sophie would arrive at my clinic, I would light candles and put some effort into my own mood so that I wasn't driven by Sophie's energy. It was more helpful if I could slow the pace of conversation and instead turn it to a more reflective discussion. I would often ask her, 'But why did he/she/you do that?' She would try to respond flippantly, and I would continue to ponder, throwing out different ideas, 'I wonder was it because she felt nervous?' or 'Would it have been because he was annoyed at the time?' Usually Sophie would snap, 'Yes, I think so,' and return to the story.

It was only when I began to ask Sophie about her early childhood that she showed any ability to self-reflect. It turned out that Sophie was quite annoyed about certain aspects of her early childhood. She reckoned her parents were working all the time and her neighbours had brought her up. She believed that in hindsight her fussy eating had been some sort of strike, as it was the only way she had any control in her life.

Sophie's parents were hardworking Polish immigrants who had sacrificed a great deal to give their children everything they themselves had missed out on as children. Yet children seldom appreciate their parents' self-sacrifice and instead tend to believe, rightly or wrongly, that less sacrifice might have been a better choice.

Sophie began to zero in on her mother, Katja, in our counselling sessions. She had always had a tricky relationship with Katja and then, when puberty struck, and Sophie became quite self-destructive, it had become intensely emotional.

Katja had been studious and hardworking when she was a little girl. She had been routinely ignored by her busy parents and her tremendous efforts in her schoolwork were dismissed as irrelevant to real work. Katja was determined that Sophie would get all the attention that she had missed, but Sophie was a more rambunctious girl than Katja had been and had little interest in sitting quietly and studying. Sophie had no interest in schoolwork. Katja thought she was showing her love by taking an extreme interest in Sophie's work, but Sophie was more physically motivated and hated the elaborate arts and crafts projects of her early childhood.

When I pointed out that her mother must have been there at least some of the time, if they had extended periods of doing art together, Sophie waved her hand and said, 'That was for my mother. I hated it.'

It seemed a perfectly horrible situation. Piotr – Sophie's dad – and Katja had done nothing wrong; they had worked hard and done their level best to provide Sophie with a lovely life, and yet Sophie dismissed it all. What could be done?

It was possible that Katja and Sophie were diametrically opposed. Could it be that they just didn't suit each other? Katja was serious, hardworking, quiet and intense, while Sophie was loud, lively, cheerful and playful. They weren't each other's types and if they had met as peers, they probably wouldn't have gravitated towards each other. Piotr was more similar to Sophie in that he was physically motivated. He didn't like to sit still, and when he wasn't at work he was usually to be found in his workshop in the back garden. Sophie's siblings, Elena and Max, were studious and got on very well with their mother. It became obvious that Sophie was the cuckoo in the nest. She was lonely and disconnected from her mother and siblings, and her fidgety father was never at home. Rather than suffering the psychic wound of feeling rejected and not good enough as she was, Sophie projected everything outwards.

Sophie insisted that she didn't care that her behaviour didn't suit her mother's values – she thought her mother was a dreadful bore. I often wondered aloud how difficult it might have been to be loud in such a quiet and studious household. 'It was hell,' Sophie replied. I took this statement seriously. Sophie giggled then rolled her eyes and said, 'Ah, it wasn't that bad. It could have been worse.'

Therapeutic progress sometimes takes some time, and it was a testament to Katja and Piotr's deep love for their child that they continued for over a year with sessions that appeared to be going nowhere. I pointed this out to Sophie. She was by now used to my slow and ponderous pace and admitted that she was surprised they hadn't stopped the sessions. Her behaviour continued to be self-destructive but she had lost her edge. Sophie knew that no matter what happened, she would be engaging in some self-reflection about it in therapy. She began to anticipate my responses. She began to build self-awareness. Most of all, Sophie began to heal the wound of rejection that she had felt from her parents. She realised that they did love her; that she was different but that they still loved her.

Sophie also began to realise that her jealousy of Elena and Max was more intense than she had ever realised and started to reflect on this. We realised that she was often jealous of her friends too and that typically this ended up with a row and a break in the friendship. Cuckoos can have a difficult time. Sophie needed to love herself so that she didn't have to keep running all the time.

When I came across the line by Carl Jung, 'Everything that irritates us about others can lead us to an understanding of ourselves,' Katja sprung to mind. There often seemed to be a deep well of irritation within Katja towards Sophie, along the lines of 'Why can't you be thrilled with all I do for you?' It was true, Katja certainly did do a lot for Sophie, but sadly none of what Katja was doing was helping. Katja needed to start parenting the child she had and not the child she wanted to have, before it was too late.

With this in mind, I proposed a series of activity-based challenges for Katja and Sophie to carry out together. These activities, which included rock-climbing, abseiling and diving, took Katja well out of her comfort zone and gave Sophie the chance to excel. And excel she did – Sophie was absolutely superb at any activities that required grit, physical effort, courage and strength; Katja was pretty abysmal. As the weeks progressed and both Katja and Sophie returned every two weeks to tell me about their latest exploits, Katja developed a new-found respect for Sophie – she realised that Sophie's talents were plentiful but that they would never be found within the pages of a book. Katja realised that history was repeating itself – her parents had dismissed her talents in academia because they rated physical work more than book-learning and now Katja was dismissing

Sophie's talents because she rated book-learning over anything that Sophie could do. Katja was humbled by Sophie's courage in taking on any physical challenge with courage and cheerfulness. She set about finding work for Sophie in a children's adventure centre, and even though it was a long drive away, she set aside every Saturday to drive Sophie to her Saturday job at the centre. Sophie, in turn, began to appreciate Katja's generosity and determination to help her. She started to appreciate her friends too. Finally, some healing had begun.

• • •

School difficulties and school refusal

There can be many reasons why some kids don't like school. Some kids like primary school and end up hating secondary school. Some kids find the relentlessly social aspect of school draining. I know I did, so I have a lot of sympathy for kids who just don't want to go in. Some teens find the intense focus on popularity depressing and simply want to opt out of it. Others dislike the pointless rules – I remember one client telling me that she was way past being yelled at for walking the wrong direction in a corridor. Many of us will leave school and never again operate in such a large organisation – our experience with school will be enough for us to know that our wellbeing wouldn't be able for it. This doesn't mean that parents should allow their teens to drop out – but it can be helpful if parents can have sympathy for the kids who dislike school. Perhaps give them the odd day off or try to work with them so that you can help them to the finish line.

A few years ago, I counselled a teenager called Kyle. His parents' main objective was for me to simply help him make sense of why he should go to school when he hated it so much. Finally, after much ranting and raving, Kyle did his exams and he never looked back. I often meet his mother and he has thrived ever since the day he left school behind.

Parenting strategy: Adopt a broader perspective about your teen's education

Although your teen's grades might provide insight into how difficult life has become for them, I would urge you not to become fixated on the grades. School could very well be the most difficult time of your teenager's life. There are many, many ways to succeed in life – indeed, school grades are not even considered a major predictor of career success. As Sir Ken Robinson pointed out in his well-known TED Talk, the current school system is out of date.[7] It was designed at a time when convergent thinking and following directions were crucial to workplace success, but skills that are valued in the twenty-first century are based on innovation, problem-solving, communication and versatility. It is often more important for some teens to get through secondary school with their mental health and their self-esteem intact, as these can be enough to equip them for adult life.

The stepladder approach to school refusal

The stepladder approach is a way to learn how to achieve any desired outcome. In this case, the desired outcome is to attend school. Initially, though, the teen needs to accept that attending school is a goal worth achieving – maybe they have stayed home without access to electronics for long enough to realise this, or perhaps they know that school is a necessary evil if they are to one day attend college. If this process of re-attending school is to work, you need to get buy-in from your teen: they need to admit that their lives have become unmanageable, that they need to face reality and that they need to learn how to attend school. It is essential that this precedes the beginning of the action plan.

When the teen has admitted that they need to bring in some changes, the parent can begin by inviting the teen to imagine a simple stepladder with several rungs. The teen decides on the final goal, and this becomes the top rung of the ladder. For example, the top rung might be to attend school on a regular basis.

Next, the teenager needs to work out what tasks might serve as the first step and then the intermediate steps, with each step being a little bit more challenging than the last as they move towards the top of the ladder. It is important that your teen decides what tasks they add to their ladder. If they need your help, you should make a few suggestions so that they can choose for themselves what the next step should be. Perhaps they will attend the first two classes each day and leave at little break, or maybe they will go in for a full day three days a week. Maybe they will anticipate the remarks the 'cool kids' might make, such as 'Why are you never in school?' or 'You always get special treatment.' Perhaps you can think of appropriate responses together, such as nodding along and smiling blandly or having a good sentence that covers everything, something like, 'I'm finding it really hard to go to school at the moment because I hate it, but I'm trying to build up to it because I'm bored out of my mind at home.' This can alleviate the intense curiosity of the schoolmates and can work as a shield for your teen. As much as possible, the teen needs to be an active, motivated participant in the process, as this makes it more likely that they'll have ownership of the resolution and will be much more likely to stick with it.

Before you start, you could teach your teen some strategies for coping with their anxiety, such as slow, relaxed breathing or repeating a simple affirmation such as, 'This is just a thought and thoughts will pass' or 'I'm okay and I'll feel better soon.' It's a good idea to plan and practise these strategies with your teen so that they know what to do as soon as they begin to feel worried. It's also important that the teen stays in the situation until they feel even the slightest reduction in their anxiety, as they need to learn that anxious feelings don't last forever. (However, if the teen becomes hysterical, they will need to leave.) The task for them then is to enter the situation without tipping into a meltdown; in this case, not having a meltdown is a win.

Patience is required as the young person needs to wait until they have mastered one step on their ladder before moving on to the next. This might take one attempt or it might take a hundred, and it's always best to work at your teenager's pace.

Success must be rewarded, otherwise a relapse is very likely to occur. This doesn't need to be something expensive – it might be as simple as genuine, heartfelt praise or a shared celebration. As always, parents should try to be a good role model and show that they are willing to confront their own fears. If your teen has seen you panic and avoid, they will learn to do the same – perhaps you have panicked in the face of your child's panic and consequently they became even more scared? Reflect on the messages you give your children – sometimes we need to show our teenagers that we are also learning how to be brave.

• • •

Shutdown, withdrawal, disengagement

It is considerably more concerning if a teen's school refusal is because of a general disengagement and withdrawal from society. If your teen is showing the beginning of serious mental health challenges, such as depression or anxiety, it's important to speak to a mental health professional. *Hikikomori* is an extreme example of the severe social withdrawal that seems to be the result of mental illness, which can be cloaked, for example, in an obsession with gaming. Originating in Japan, this syndrome has spread to other countries and is characterised by young people who become recluses, often in their parents' households. These loners spend the vast majority of their lives in their bedrooms, just eating, sleeping and, typically, spending time online. They don't contribute to society and have no interest in life beyond the computer.

Parenting strategy: Lean in towards your teen

When you see your teen withdrawing from life, it is important to lean in towards them. This means entering the lair. Go into your teen's room regularly. You don't need to spend a long time there, but you do need to go in often. Try not to tidy when you're there, or to complain about the mess. This is important – once you pick up an item of clothing or a random cup, the atmosphere will change. Instead, make it a pleasant visit. You don't need to stay long and you can chat about light subjects, just for a few minutes. Tell them you'll be making a point of coming into their room because you're distressed by their isolation. Make sure you retain your authority – it's important that you don't allow your teen's room to become a fortress of isolation. Sometimes Muhammad must go to the mountain.

Many parents are surprised to learn that teens who have shut down emotionally or behaviourally are often a mass of emotions beneath their blank exterior. In fact, they are feeling so emotional that their bodies and minds have felt the need to shut down as a coping mechanism so that they don't mentally self-combust.

When parents tell me, 'He's so laid back, he's horizontal,' and 'Absolutely nothing will motivate him, he's just too relaxed,' my ears tend to prick up in concern. The natural state for a teenager is to be pretty excited and engaged by the many things that are happening to them. If a teen has withdrawn and is instead listless and disengaged it can be useful to figure out *when* they disengaged – was it during puberty? Or perhaps during a difficult school year or complicated friendship episode? The phrase 'paralysis by analysis' is brought about by overthinking. When we overanalyse, we can feel utterly overwhelmed and withdraw into a depressive cave in order to avoid all thought and emotion – many teenagers withdraw because they have fallen into a pit of over-analysis and need some help to find a way out.

Teens often feel overwhelmed by the magnitude of events and it scares them. Rather than tackling these complex emotions, many teens – especially boys – tend to opt out. They assume a blank expression; they say they don't care, that it doesn't matter. This can often be a cover-up as they don't want to admit to their parents or themselves that they do care and that they are frightened out of their wits.

● ● ●

When the bond becomes cold and transactional

Teenagers with an insecure attachment style with their parents can form intense attachments to their friends and become overly attached to a peer. From this, a coldness might arise from the teen towards the parent, perhaps because they feel they no longer need or want the parent – this can be as a consequence of immaturity or because they have come to believe they are not loved for who they are because maybe they felt over-criticised or dismissed in some way. Whatever the reason, when the teen doesn't respond to the parents, the parents, in turn, often don't know how to respond to the fact that their teen's heart is no longer warmed by their parents' presence. Everyone is left in a colder, more distant and transactional arrangement.

These teenagers begin to see and treat their parent as a bank or convenient provider of certain objects. The parent feels resentful that they are being used but helpless to know how to connect in any other way with their child. The parent and the teenager both feel the loss of the bond, but neither quite knows how to re-establish warmth. The teenager looks outward for resolution and disregards their relationship with their parent, while the parent feels like they've failed and relies on their sense of parental responsibility to get through this difficult period. There can often be bitter hurt on both sides: the parent feels the teenager represents their failed parenting – and even their failed life – and the teen feels unloved and lonely. The way to get around this is to approach the issue with sincerity. Talk about how much love you have for your child and remind them of your sense of kindness. You can still provide the 'stuff' they want, but you can bring love, affection and warmth into the transaction. You can let them know that you know you're being played and, because you love them, you're allowing them to play you.

• • •

Lonely and desperate for friendships

Friendships and romantic relationships hold huge significance for teenagers, and it often feels like our precious child's happiness is in the hands of random callow youths who couldn't care less about them. Our role as parents during these tumultuous years is to try to keep up with the many ups and downs of these relationships and get to know the cast of thousands, yet not involve ourselves too much. As a challenge, this feels almost impossible. You may feel out of your depth as your teen rolls their eyes dismissively when you innocently suggest they contact their old friend Izzy, whom they had always liked right up until two seconds before this conversation.

During the research for my book *Bully-Proof Kids*, it became evident that the most common reason why children didn't tell anyone about the bullying was that they didn't want to admit that they were being ostracised. They preferred to tell themselves that everything was just fine, that everyone liked them and that each episode was just a blip. Public disapproval triggers a sense of shame in all of us – even when we know we are right and they are wrong – and for teenagers, who in developmental terms tend to feel like their entire existence seems to rest on social approval, this sense of shame is so overwhelming that they often simply cannot admit to themselves or others that they are being ostracised.

Loneliness is a debilitating state. If your teen seems lonely it can be helpful to try a multi-pronged approach – try to figure out who in their social circle might be open to fostering a friendship; try to expand their social circle by joining clubs and following interests; and try to help them find sustenance in music, art and literature, as this can deepen your teen's understanding of their place in the world.

The intensity with which some teenagers grab onto their friends can be challenging for everyone concerned. Insecurely attached teenagers are susceptible to move from craving people to craving drink or drugs as they frantically seek to attach to a perceived solution to their feelings of loneliness. This loneliness is part of the human condition – we die alone – but the insecurely attached teenager can feel like the loneliest person in the world.

TARA, 15

Louise was a mother of four and always worried about her third child, Tara, a quiet, shy and lonely girl. When Tara entered secondary school at 13, their weak relationship became weaker as Tara became even quieter and sadder. Louise decided to take the situation in hand and booked a few nights away with Tara. This caused a lot of dissent in the household as her other children were outraged by the special treatment, but Louise stood her ground. Tara was unreceptive for the first night away, but when she realised this was not a short-lived project but a regular monthly event, she began to look forward to their nights away. It was costly and caused a lot of hassle, but it was worth it in the end. After about two years – 24 nights away together – Louise felt that their bond was sufficiently strong not to need these nights away. They had a chat and decided to continue with them as they were enjoyable. They both agreed that it was scary when they disconnected. Louise said, 'I could have easily spent that money on therapy for Tara rather than leaning into our relationship. I shiver when I think what I would have lost if I had done that.'

• • •

Teaching social skills

Just as some kids need help with their reading or writing, perhaps because of dyslexia or some other reason, other kids need help with their social skills. This should not be left unattended – how can these kids learn unless we, the adults, point out which social skills are effective and which are ineffective? The kids for whom social interaction doesn't come easily might benefit from you speaking a lot about different interactions you have in your day-to-day life. You could talk about how you manage to deal with a colleague who often criticises you or about an annoying interaction with a delivery person you had that day – it doesn't really matter whether you come out of the interaction well, what matters is that you are teaching your teen about the give and take that happens in different social scenarios. You can also explain to your teen how you noticed that a person was annoyed with you because you saw them grimace or reveal some other behavioural or verbal giveaway. This all might seem perfectly obvious to you, but then knowing how to spell 'obvious' is perfectly obvious to many people, and yet there are whole swathes of people who are never quite sure how to spell it. Break down social skills for the teen who needs it; highlight verbal cues, behavioural giveaways and some optional responses.

• • •

The attachment void

Swiss psychoanalyst Alice Miller tells us that 'the truth about our childhood is stored up in our body' and that those with insecure or weak attachment bonds can feel a void within them that they feel compelled to fill.[18] Addicts' description of the 'hole in the soul' is a good analogy to demonstrate the deep yearning a person can feel when insecurely attached.

Peer attachments are safest when they are formed as a result of existing attachments that have already been formed – for example, with the wider family or friends of the family. This is how communities have existed for millions of years. Our recent promotion of children finding friends who have no connection with the family is a relatively new phenomenon. Previous generations were less peer-oriented than we are, but it looks like future generations will be a good deal more peer-oriented. Our increased mobility favours peer-orientation as we no longer live near our extended families. The secularisation of society, our heavy emphasis on full-time work schedules, early childcare, an increased number of divorces and greater numbers of blended families also favour peer-orientation.

The unnaturally heavy burden of parental responsibility is weighing many parents down. Now that we often don't have an extended family to rely on, many parents are instead seeking a combination of professional support and peer interaction. Parents can help relieve this burden by maintaining friendships with other families – through invitations to anything from birthday parties to annual meetups, teens benefit from seeing themselves in the eyes of other adults and children who have known them since they were babies. This takes effort on the parents' part, as often the teen won't reciprocate. Still, it is often worth it, especially in the early teen years.

Both parents and children need attachment behaviours, such as a warm hug, a kind smile and a soft gaze. Everything becomes colder and more perfunctory if we don't feel attached to a person. It's important to note that we can be physically present but emotionally absent. For example, the anxious, depressed parent might be physically present but filled with internal fear and unable to be emotionally available to their children. This can cause confusion between the child and the parent as both can consciously or unconsciously feel the impact of the chasm between them. The parent knows that they have been physically present; they have turned up to all the important events and have done their level best, so they can't understand the lack of emotional warmth between themselves and their child. The parent might feel guilty and, as a result, never have the courage to confront this issue and, tragically, never dare to make a concerted effort to strengthen the attachment bond.

• • •

What parents can do

If your child seems to have an insecure attachment style, give yourself some time to address this. Parenting is a long game, and you probably have plenty of time. Just as it can take a couple of years to lose a couple of stone, it can take some years to improve the health of the attachment bond. The teenager will not be overjoyed with your attempts – it is, after all, developmentally appropriate for teenagers to look beyond their family relationships during adolescence – and yet it is valuable to insist on putting in the time to the relationship. This makes the parent–child bond healthier, which can improve the teenager's ability to form friendships. This is not to say that a parent should become like a puppy dog following their teenager around – far from it. Rather, parents need to acknowledge that parents and teens are developing a new way of being, with new parameters and ways to have fun and connect on a deeper level.

Just as the children in a nursery school learn to take turns and co-operate with each other as a direct consequence of the children's attachment to their nursery teacher and the teacher's intuitive support for them when they lose their way, the parent of the adolescent needs to continue to nurture a sense of attachment with subtle, carefully considered groundwork and boundaries.

Some parents are over-involved and others are under-involved – few among us have the Goldilocks level of just right. Parents need to be honest and evaluate whether they need to back off from their child and provide them with more space to develop their social skills or if they should lean in and strengthen the attachment bond. No matter what, we are responsible for our children. They are not responsible for us. They might reject us, deny us, betray us, it doesn't matter. Our job is to be the steady rock that offers safety, comfort and understanding when life is hard. This can be very difficult, so it's essential for parents to practise self-compassion and obtain the support they need to help them through the difficult years.

Parents need an attachment bond to give them the strength to endure the difficulties of raising children. Children need the attachment bond to provide them with the desire to seek their parents' approval and to form relationships throughout their lives. Without it, we are all adrift. We parents need to make sure that we continue to strengthen the attachment bond with our teenagers so that they don't become vulnerable to having an attachment void that drives them to make a series of inappropriate attachments. Teenagers need their parents, but they often don't know it.

• • •

Takeaways

- It is developmentally natural for children to move towards their peers during adolescence, but that doesn't mean our job is over.

- Society currently favours peer-orientation over adult-orientation, emphasising a weak attachment over the opportunities for stronger, deeper attachments.

- A structured plan consisting of baby steps in exposure that is worked on together can be a valuable way to confront avoidance of social situations, such as school.

- An insecure attachment style can create an emotional gap between parent and child.

- The insecure attachment style can happen inadvertently and does not necessarily suggest a lack of love – indeed, it can be the consequence of too much love.

- A weak attachment can create an emotional void within an individual, but this can be strengthened with commitment and focus from the parent.

CHAPTER 7

THE CHALLENGES ASSOCIATED WITH THE OVERUSE OF TECHNOLOGY

'We now expect more from technology and less from each other.'

– SHERRY TURKLE

AT A LAUNCH EVENT at MacWorld in 2007, Steve Jobs slipped an iPhone out of his pocket and changed the world. Back then, few of us had heard of Facebook or Twitter. Instagram, Snapchat, TikTok and other social media platforms had not even been thought of. But even then, we had already started to worry that we were addicted to our phones. Today, we have entered into an entirely different realm of dependency.

By 2012, more people had a smartphone than a 'dumb phone'; and the impact of new technology on teenagers' mental health since then has been startling. The kids of the digital generation, born anytime from 2000 onwards, are the first generation to grow into adulthood with high-speed Wi-Fi in their back pockets, and this ongoing experiment is not going well. Don't get me wrong – I'm writing this on a laptop, and I really enjoy social media – I love good technology. However, we would be foolish to disregard the heavy impact that screens have on children today.

We in Ireland and the UK can get a pretty good idea of how the overuse of technology will play out by looking at the USA, which is often a few years ahead of us and where technological developments have completely taken over childhood and youth life. The research already tells us that overuse of technology can permanently alter and impair the brain's anatomy, chemistry and neural pathways. Teens who overuse technology report persistent body sensations of overall 'shaking', increased breathing and heart rate, and a general state of unease (also known as a 'persistent hypervigilant sensory state') as the child remains on alert for the oncoming assault in the mode of constant notifications from their phone or virtual attacks from the latest video game or even unpleasant comments on social media. This state of chronic stress weakens the young person's immune system and can lead to a variety of serious diseases and disorders. Of course, this is just the physical impact. The psychological and emotional impact is outlined below in more detail.

• • •

The illusion of companionship

When a teenager in my practice told me that 'life is better online; my online friendships are better; there is more fun; the sex is better; everything is better online,' I had no answer. It didn't seem likely, but I wasn't a digital native. Perhaps this generation was moving into a different dimension? As a therapist, it is my job to hold neutral space for the client – we don't judge clients, rather we hold a space for them to unpack their feelings. For this reason, I was open to the idea that this could be a healthy lifestyle choice – even if my intuition shrieked a loud 'No'. Then along came the pandemic and we all became acquainted with living online. I soon saw for myself the significant issues related to the shallow nature of online intimacy. Indeed, I was thankful for this aspect of the pandemic; before 2020, I had met so many digital natives who argued that I didn't understand the satisfaction of a life spent online that I was almost convinced. Then I sat through the interminable Zoom calls during the pandemic and realised that there is a world of difference between having a coffee with a pal in real life and 'having a coffee with them' online. The warmth of real life is impossible to replicate.

Sherry Turtle, social psychologist and author of *Alone Together: Why We Expect More from Technology and Less from Each Other*, explains that technology 'can provide the illusion of companionship without the demands of friendship, without the demands of intimacy'. Although we can pretend to ourselves that online socialising is just as good, we know that it's not. Worse than that, meeting a person online is deceptive. While it is sometimes wonderful and can offer some powerfully intimate moments, more often than not technology offers an illusion of intimacy that doesn't really stand scrutiny.

Although technology is brilliant for keeping long-distance relationships and friendships alive, it should not be a replacement for meeting people in real life. Too many teenagers I know don't bother meeting their friends in person – they meet some mates in school and think that's enough. They spend the rest of their time and all their holidays meeting friends online. Late into the night, they message each other back and forth – some of them speak online on video chat but most prefer messaging. A fake persona often develops, sometimes inadvertently. In my clinical practice, I have heard hundreds of stories about teens messaging late at night about their dark secrets involving issues such as self-harm and self-loathing. The faux intimacy is exciting, yet it's not heart-warming. It feels slightly illicit.

Then the next morning they often feel disconnected from the previous night's revelations; these messages don't bring the soul-closeness that a real-life confession would bring. It's deceptive – it offers intimacy without vulnerability. But there can be no intimacy without vulnerability; in many ways, it's all fakery. The day comes when the young person is feeling lost or lonely. Suddenly, in their hour of need, the emptiness of online friendships can feel bitterly isolating.

• • •

The pursuit of pleasure and the avoidance of pain

In Freudian psychoanalysis, the pleasure principle is the instinct in us that satisfies biological and psychological needs by seeking pleasure and avoiding pain. Specifically, according to this theory, the pleasure principle is the driving force for all our bodily needs and wants and our emotional impulses and desires. Dopamine is a type of neurotransmitter that, in lay terms, drives the pleasure principle as it motivates us towards pleasure and away from pain.

Social media, and the internet in general, is driven by the pleasure principle. For every 'like', 'share', page-load or email, we basically receive a small 'squirt' of dopamine as we anticipate pleasure from pressing these buttons. The brain interprets each squirt of dopamine as an act of seeking pleasure and avoiding pain (even though, in reality, we may not achieve this pleasure).

Studies have shown that mice will continue to press buttons that stimulate the reward system until they die of starvation

– this expectation of pleasure supersedes everything else. Without dopamine, we have no motivation to do anything. When dopamine is blocked by scientists, a mouse has little motivation to sleep, mate or eat. If food is placed in the mouse's mouth, it will eat it. But without dopamine, the mouse will not exert enough energy to walk over to a tray of food to satisfy its hunger, and it will starve to death. When a willing female is presented to the male mouse, the dopamine-starved mouse will fail to mate with her.

Nowadays, many of us who feel psychologically dependent on social media are just like the mouse pressing the button, seeking dopamine (pleasure) to the detriment of all else in life. With the overdeveloped rewards system in their brains (as seen in Chapter 1), teenagers are arguably particularly susceptible to the pleasure principle. So it is the parent's job to ensure that other pleasures are brought into play. Otherwise, the teenager's world will narrow into ever-decreasing circles, just like the mouse in the cage, eternally driven online to seek pleasure and avoid pain.

Every time we put our phone down, a multi-billion dollar industry is working to convince us to pick it up again. The Netflix documentary *The Social Dilemma* revealed how social networks are designed to exploit human weakness with a psychological ploy known as positive intermittent reinforcement. In an article written for *Psychology Today*, Dr Mike Brooks explains that we have difficulty resisting our screens because of the 'Vegas effect'. According to Brooks, we keep checking and checking the notifications on our phone because we occasionally hit the jackpot: 'Like a box of chocolates, we never know what we are going to get. Who posted to Facebook? Who commented on my post? Let me check my news feed just one more time [...] the moment our smartphones buzz or chime, this dopamine reward system is activated.'

Facebook's first president, Sean Parker, claims that Facebook's founders knew they were creating something addictive and knowingly exploited a 'vulnerability in human psychology' from the outset. In 2004, Parker said that the main question he and others involved in getting Facebook off the ground had was, 'How do we consume as much of your time and conscious attention as possible?' According to Parker, 'And that means that we need to sort of give you a little dopamine hit every once in a while, because someone liked or commented on a photo or a post or whatever. And that's going to get you to contribute more content, and that's going to get you [...] more likes and comments.'[19] Parker now sees himself as 'something of a conscientious objector' to social media.

• • •

The echo chamber

An unexpected development of teenagers' dependency on technology is that their political beliefs and causes are being shaped in unknown ways by algorithms that create their very own echo chambers. *The Social Dilemma* captured how a distorted view of current affairs can emerge from the online echo chamber. Although we are told that social networks are simply a tool for communication, this so-called tool doesn't just sit there, inert, waiting to be used. Instead, it nags us incessantly, seducing and manipulating us with notifications and suggestions about what to watch and who to contact. As Tristan Harris, a former Google design ethicist and one of the experts interviewed for *The Social Dilemma*, says, 'It has its own goals and it has its own way of pursuing them by using your psychology against you.'

Teens tend to be more idealistic as their stage of development propels them to seek a moral framework and beliefs that can make sense of the world (see Chapter 12). Consequently, they are more likely to be attracted to new concepts and causes in the hope that they can fix the world. Users can end up with a skewed sense of reality and might need this balanced by parents who ask them about their online content and are willing to question these issues.

Is it a coping mechanism?

Heavy tech users often have difficulty handling complexity and need help in tackling their emotions. They may not like the uncertainty or vulnerability they feel when trying to develop real-life friendships, so they revert to more easily understood screens. Parents can help with this by setting boundaries on tech use and insisting on some real-world engagement in the form of joining a club or shopping for the family.

The anxiety-inducing feeling of social media

Ironically, the dopamine hit we receive from pressing 'like' or 'share' is more likely to induce feelings of anxiety than the pleasure we anticipate. Most of us know well the anticipated pleasure of choosing the picture, writing the post and waiting for the response. We recognise the thrill of a heavily shared post. We are familiar with the ping of dopamine that can come from the number of likes. We also know the distress that can happen when the post is disliked, when people take issue with your content, or you feel utterly ignored. This distress is mostly low-key, so it doesn't feel like a big deal. Yet, over time, the whole thing can creep up on you. What started as a benign pleasure can become a tense, stressful aspect of life that you keep returning to – because you hope that it will provide you with pleasure, despite the fact that it more often produces anxiety. Very similar to the highs and lows of betting in the bookies, social media can feel like great fun and yield great returns, but it can also bring about feelings of dread and anxiety. We often have no idea whether it is producing more pleasure or pain – but we tend to *believe* it will produce pleasure.

Teenagers today don't feel like they have any choice – life has been set up so that they are fed into the media machine from babyhood. They live on and through their devices. As soon as they get their first phone, they start building their numbers on the platforms and learn to view their pals through their numbers of followers and online presences. The issue of 'tech rage' has started to impact us as we can become irrationally murderous when our technology doesn't work and we can't figure out why. The sheer powerlessness can feel overwhelming. The number of passwords, usernames, and other details that we need to keep track of can also add to our stress.

In my book *Fragile*, I explored how the number of people experiencing anxiety and depression is skyrocketing. Since 2012, studies have shown a consistent spike in mood disorders among teenagers, which correlates with the popularity of social media and smartphone ownership. A review of 84 related studies found that 'excessive smartphone [usage] is associated with difficulties in cognitive-emotion regulation, impulsivity, impaired cognitive function, addiction to social networking, shyness and low self-esteem. Medical problems include sleep problems, reduced physical fitness, unhealthy eating habits, pain and migraines, reduced cognitive control and changes in the brain's grey matter volume.'[20]

Although teenagers tell us they urgently need their mobile phones to live, studies show this harms their mental wellbeing. Teenagers urgently want lots of things – a boyfriend, a girlfriend, certain trainers, etc. – and it is the role of the adults not to be swayed by the intense sense of urgency and instead keep a cool head as they assess the need. A big emotion does not have to be met with a big emotion. Indeed, just as we deal with toddlers, it can be more helpful if a big emotion is met with calmness; we don't need to meet the devil halfway.

KATIE, 16

Katie's parents experienced a difficult path to having a baby, filled with false hope and devastating lows through a series of fertility procedures. Finally, after eight rounds of IVF, Marilyn became pregnant with Katie, who was perhaps adored even more than most babies. Katie was Marilyn and Joe's only child, but they would have loved three or even four children, so Katie received an overwhelming level of focus from her parents. When she said she liked the horsey in the field, she was whisked off to private horse-riding lessons. When she danced around the kitchen with her mother, she was immediately enrolled in ballet lessons. Every utterance that came out of her mouth was taken very seriously, but rather than giving Katie a sense of confidence, it had the opposite effect. Katie felt the burden of expectation over her every move, she felt like she was being constantly monitored and learnt to approach the world almost like a world-famous celebrity as she knew that every single offhand comment would be taken very seriously, noted, memorised and repeated back to her for ever and ever.

Katie's childhood was lovely. There were many trips to magical places, and Katie was encouraged to have magnificent dreams about how she would be a success in everything she chose to do. At first, Katie believed her parents when they told her she was especially brilliant. But, as it often does, reality kicked in when she was around 11 and started to look outward rather than rely on her parents' worldview. Katie's schoolmates made it clear to her that they didn't think she was all that great. This made Katie feel dreadfully insecure as she realised that two narratives were taking place: in her home, she was a beautiful, charming and delightful genius; and in school, she was a quiet, anxious, often-overlooked bore. This led Katie to distrust everybody, and she fell into a more secure world of books and art.

Puberty hit Katie like a sledgehammer. She found it difficult to navigate her periods and felt embarrassed about her lack of breast development. Over time, Katie became very anxious about being in school. She was intimidated by her peers, who seemed incredibly sophisticated, and she was afraid of the boys, who made it abundantly clear that they weren't impressed by her. Katie began to develop stomach pains every morning and would beg and plead with her mother not to make her go to school. Whenever her mother relented, Katie would reward her mother by working really hard on her schoolwork. Slowly but surely, Katie became more and more determined to avoid school. She would ring her mother in a panic during the little break and tell her she had to collect her. Her mother worked from home, so she could always collect her.

Katie retreated into a world of fantasy in her bedroom. She had always been a great reader and became immersed in Tumblr, Discord and other online platforms that offered socially awkward girls like Katie a different reality. This online world was always available. By the time she turned 14, Katie had spent thousands of hours hanging out online in her bedroom with her new virtual community. Her bedroom was so dirty that her parents viewed it as a health risk.

Katie became very involved in online communities that were focused on victimhood, oppression and mental health concerns. Katie diagnosed herself with a range of conditions, such as attention deficit hyperactivity disorder (ADHD), autism spectrum disorder (ASD), gender dysphoria, bipolar and complex post-traumatic stress disorder (PTSD). When Marilyn heard about Katie's self-diagnosis, she made appointments with psychologists and psychiatrists – she believed that Katie's room was so dirty and her intensity around school was so intense that there had to be *something* wrong with her. Her father, Joe, didn't think she qualified for any of these diagnoses and privately believed that she was just a sad, lonely and disappointed little girl trying to avoid school and make sense of her world. Nonetheless, Katie underwent a plethora of assessments and evaluations. She ended up at CAMHS. Professional input can sometimes create more problems than it solves, and Katie began to use her mental health problems as reasons to avoid school.

Katie's initial avoidance of school grew to become an unwieldy beast, and by the time she ended up in my office, she had attended fewer than four of the previous 50 school days. The pattern was that Katie tended to experience stomach pains or anxiety attacks every morning before school, and her mother excused her from school. If her mother made her go in, she would inevitably receive a call before the little break explaining that she had to be collected. Once Katie was off school for the day, she would go online, doing her schoolwork and hanging out with her virtual friends – usually discussing her mental health, writing fandoms, and drawing idealised versions of herself on DeviantArt or similar platforms. But nature abhors a vacuum, and her body and mind required more input than online communities. Katie needed to confront the developmental tasks of adolescence, and her avoidance impeded her progress. This disconnect between doing and thinking caused an excess of energy. This, combined with the self-loathing that was further cultivated by her online life, led Katie to begin self-harming regularly. Katie needed adventure, risk, complexity and depth. None were easily available online, but manufactured versions were available in her self-harming ceremonies.

It took some time for Katie and me to build a therapeutic alliance, as she was somewhat distrustful of other people. But as we met each week, we eventually became more connected. Katie explained her utter disappointment with school. She had believed the scenes on social media and TV – she thought she would be a cool teenager who went on dates with good-looking boys. Instead, she felt ugly, completely ignored, isolated and excluded from the teenage experience.

Katie and I engaged in long, complex conversations that remained completely abstract without any practical application. Katie had retreated from real life because she found it too hard and instead immersed herself in social justice causes. It sometimes felt strange to hear this 16-year-old Irish girl speaking with an American accent about Black Lives Matter and Joe Biden but who barely knew the name of her own president and had never heard of issues such as Travellers' rights. Katie was an online Walter Mitty: brave, powerful and sassy behind the screen but a shy wallflower in real life.

It took a lot of time to help Katie re-enter society. She had left behind all her childhood activities and had little interest in anything except her online community. She stayed at home all the time. When I realised she hadn't been in a café or a restaurant in over two years, I realised that some direct action was needed. One day, during yet another cerebral and highly abstract conversation about why she should really go outside more often, I gently suggested that she and I could meet in the café across the road from my clinic as part of the recovery process. This was shocking to Katie, and it gave birth to six weeks of conversation about whether we should have a conversation in a café.

In the end, we went to the café. I ordered a coffee for myself and invited Katie to order for herself – despite her request that I order on her behalf. Katie rose to the challenge and ordered a hot chocolate. That was the first of a series of meetings in public places as the reintegration process began in earnest.

The school refusal continued, and Marilyn decided to enrol tutors to ensure that Katie would maintain her very high grades. This decision encouraged me to focus on what would happen after she left school. Our therapeutic sessions began to move beyond the local café. We started to meet in the cafés belonging to the university near where Katie lived and which she planned to one day attend.

I set Katie and Marilyn the task of visiting the university library regularly. They visited everywhere in the university environment and eventually found clubs that Katie could join. With this very soft lead-in, Katie eventually finished school and started to attend university. We ended the therapy with an invitation that she could come back in the future if she ever needed to. It was an unsatisfactory ending, but thankfully the self-harming had ended, Katie was attending university and she acquired some friends – and even a short-lived boyfriend. We had made some progress.

• • •

Sexting and inappropriate online content

The Secondary School Digital Trend Report surveyed over 3,200 secondary school students from 30 Irish schools and found that:[21]

- 32 per cent of First Years have spoken to strangers online.

- 70 per cent of Sixth Years have spoken to strangers online.

- 8 per cent of First Years have met strangers in real life after initial online interaction.

- 38 per cent of Sixth Years have met strangers in real life after initial online interaction.

- 13 per cent of students (17 per cent boys, 9 per cent girls) in secondary school have sent a nude or semi-nude photo or video of themselves to someone.

- 34 per cent of Sixth Year students have sexted (sent online sexual content).

Teens these days are more likely to be sexting – sending sexual content to another device – than actually having sex. This calms parents as they often perceive online sex as less dangerous than real-life sex. But there are many issues with online sexual behaviour: the lack of intimacy associated with sexting has a more insidious influence than many realise. Sexting can quickly lead to a view of sex as a transactional event, and romance, intimacy and love are left behind in favour of a colder, business-like arrangement. Sexting is also risky. Although there is currently no law governing sexting, the Child Trafficking and Pornography Act 1998 forbids sharing or possessing explicit images of a minor. A teenager who shares or stores a sexual image of a minor on their device can be convicted of child pornography. Sexting gives teens a quick thrill, but the fallout can be devastating to young teens who are innocent enough to believe that it won't be passed around. It is notable that the major online catastrophes I hear about tend to happen among younger teens – by the time they hit 15 or so, they have generally learnt some sense.

A distorted view of sex and sexuality can emerge from online sex. Teenagers who engage in sexting may have little experience of the physicality of kissing or even holding hands with their crush and instead view sex as being centred on looks. The self-absorption, vanity and even narcissism that seem to emerge among young people who are very focused on their selfies, profile pics, likes and shares can be all-consuming. These teens might not have been madly vain to begin with, but spending a vast number of hours perfecting photos to send to someone else in the hope that it gives them sexual pleasure can encourage vanity.

· · ·

Digital self-harm

Self-harm can be a form of self-aggression ranging from physical to psychological abuse (see Chapter 14). Digital self-harm is a form of self-harm that involves anonymously posting hurtful and/or verbally abusive remarks about yourself online. It is more common than many people think and it is mainly seen in adolescents. Digital self-harm is focused on emotional harm rather than physical harm, although countless teens also post videos of themselves self-harming and the results of their self-harming.

Many teens explore their identity and figure out different facets of their psyche by creating entirely separate personas online. Still, when teenagers post hate-filled comments targeted at themselves, they are creating a dark web of pain and self-loathing. Teenagers have described this cyber self-bullying to me as a way to beat others to the punch. They think that everyone hates them as much as they hate themselves. Sadly, bullying often brings about self-loathing in the individual. Their online self-trolling is a way to communicate all the dark thoughts in their head. Although parents might find it hard to understand, digital self-harm is like other forms of self-harm and requires the same patience, compassion and understanding from parents.

· · ·

Chronic sleep deprivation

When I look back on my teenage years, I shudder at how little sleep I was getting. I now know myself well enough to know that I get emotional and depressive when I'm tired, and I wonder how tiredness impacted my teenage depression. Sadly, I will never know. My tiredness wasn't due to tech overuse (I was socialising), but the net result was the same, and I used to be wrecked every morning. There was war every day as I would not be able to get up out of bed. I never ate breakfast – I was almost vomiting with tiredness and couldn't even contemplate it. I was infamous for falling asleep in class – indeed, I used to regularly hide away in quiet places in the school building to take a nap. And I was pretty much depressed the entire time. Now, all these years later, I know that if I don't get sufficient sleep, I will become distressed, emotional and over-sensitive, and existential angst will creep inexorably into my mind. In hindsight, lack of sleep certainly contributed to the angst of those terrible years when I slogged through life feeling miserable, tense, desperate and suicidal.

I often think of my tired and depressed teenage self when I meet the chronic gamers who are sent to me. They are often a mix of wired and tired – being overtired can literally make us restless, and technology also provokes a nervy restlessness. If your child is overtired from gaming or other online activities, you must lean into the situation and face the fact that your child's online life is out of control. Serious commitment on your part is required to retrieve the situation.

• • •

Online gaming

Research shows that the number of Irish boys who use
gaming consoles is double that of girls. This is arguably
driven by biological factors – for example, victorious gamers
enjoy a surge of testosterone when they vanquish strangers
online. Multiplayer video games are said to tap into the same
mechanisms as warfare, and the effect of testosterone on
aggression is advantageous to the players.[22] Perhaps in some sort
of atavistic driven instinct, males feel stimulated when they
protect their world against strangers? A result of all this virtual
warfare is an unbalanced nervous system. It makes teenage
boys feel nervous and aggressive, as the sensory imbalance leads
them to respond too quickly, and their distorted views of the
incoming attack makes their response out of proportion. Some
gamers seem to also develop a sense of numbness to brutality
and a casual attitude to cruelty as they become inured to the
bloodthirsty violence they see online.

An under-acknowledged psychological issue associated with
online gaming is that heavy gamers often feel disaffected and
alienated. The constant adrenalin and intensity of gaming
means that ordinary pleasures, such as a nice meal, a laugh
with mates or a good conversation, feel boring. This sense of
boredom can also mask a serious discomfort with feeling out of
control. The teenager who says they felt bored when out with
their friends might have felt anxious and hidden this under a
mask of boredom.

• • •

Online gambling

A report shows that people as young as 15 are betting online from mobile devices. Barry Grant, director of the Extern Problem Gambling Project, said, 'We regularly receive calls from parents whose teenage child has maxed out the parent's credit card, gambling online, where there has been no effort by the gambling operator to verify the age or identity of the person creating the account.'[23] This is an underexplored phenomenon that is particularly prevalent among teenage males who play sports such as GAA, soccer or rugby. Teenage brains are simply not equipped to handle gambling – the overdeveloped rewards centre in their brains and their propensity to take risks mean that this offer of instant gratification is particularly dangerous. If your teen is participating in online gambling, it's recommended you talk to them about it as soon as possible, and keep talking to them, as well as operating some restrictions on their tech use so that they cannot access online gambling platforms.

• • •

Parental controls

Microsoft founder Bill Gates and his wife Melinda had strict guidelines on technology for their children. Apple CEO Tim Cook warned about overuse of technology and believes there should be limits to the use of technology in schools. He declared, 'I don't want my nephew on a social network.' When Steve Jobs was asked by a journalist what his kids thought of the new iPad, he famously replied that they hadn't used it: 'We limit how much technology our kids use at home.' Indeed, many leading technology innovators and CEOs of tech companies limit their children's screen time. These experts have seen the impact of too much technology, so they distinguish between 'consuming' technology and 'creating' technology and also limit screen time for their beloved children.

Our teens' digital habits should be viewed as we view their other habits: are they healthy? What are the issues that need to be addressed? Few argue any more about whether parents should limit their child's online content – the questions these days are by how much and how to go about it. In a 2018 survey of more than 2,000 Irish tweens, 30 per cent of 12-year-olds said they could go online whenever they wanted. Almost one in three of these kids, aged between eight and 12, said they had friends or followers online who were strangers in real life.[24] Parental controls are often recommended because they give a semblance of control over tech use – not because they resolve the problem. Many parents prefer to tell themselves that their kids can easily swerve the parental controls. I have told myself this, so I empathise. But it's a lie we tell ourselves, usually because we simply can't face setting up the parental controls. (This is why it might be worth your while to offer some tech-savvy young person a few quid to set the controls for you!) I recommend that parents seriously consider paying for a service such as iKydz, Circle Home Plus or Net Nanny, as this will reduce the number of fights about tech usage.

A service that offers controls for specific devices and platforms is valuable. For example, your teen will know they have 10 hours per week on a particular device or platform. Some parents allow the teen to use their hours in whatever way they choose, while others believe that it is more important to designate a certain number of minutes per day on each device or platform. Some teens, if they had the choice, would happily spend 10 hours on the platform or the device in one day as they enjoy the trance-like state they can go into when spending long hours uninterrupted on the platform or device. These extended periods can be damaging, and it is recommended that parental controls are used like stabilisers on a bike – to begin with, the parents might control every aspect of their child's online life and then, as the teen grows older, they learn some self-control and how to manage their time on their own.

It is not only the amount of time online that matters. There is also the issue of harmful content. In recent years, I have come across too many young people who have grown-up feral online. With no guidance from their parents, the content they consumed gradually became extremely harmful. Their behaviour changed and their parents had only a vague idea that 'the internet' was causing it. The world-leading cyber-psychologist Dr Mary Aiken believes that minors are put at risk by being exposed to technology with 'little or no guidelines'. We are seeing 'feral behaviour online because [...] the reality is there is no one in charge.'[25] Dr Aiken is concerned about how society is facilitating these unhealthy habits in children: 'It does not take a rocket scientist to figure out that something is wrong, and that we need to act now.'[26]

MARK, 15

Mark was a fun-loving, sporty kid who fell deep into online gaming when he became a teenager. By the time he was 13 years old, he was still very small and was self-conscious about his height. This self-consciousness led Mark to stay at home in his bedroom, playing games rather than developing friendships with his peers. Mark became in thrall to Clash of Clans and obsessed about his scores. Any attempts his mother made to reduce his playing led to screaming tantrums and, often, smashed furniture.

Mark's parents were gentle, peace-loving souls who decided it was better to leave Mark be and let him play his games. This didn't work out, though, as Mark started playing all night and couldn't get up for school in the morning. Interventions led to further tantrums. The last straw came when Mark threatened his mother with violence, and he was brought to me for counselling.

We worked together for some time. He got to know me, and I got to know his world of gaming. Not much else was going on for Mark, so all he could really talk about was gaming. He didn't like meeting mates or going to school – he said it was boring. We explored the feelings related to 'boring', and it turned out that being in social situations made him nervous and uncomfortable. Mark didn't like feeling vulnerable, so he stayed at home, online.

Eventually, hormones kicked in and Mark realised that he wanted a girlfriend. He became conscious that he had not spent time developing his friendships. This was my 'in', and I worked with it. We spoke about the emptiness of online life – how it had a veneer of excitement but flirting with a girl he liked in real life offered much more excitement. Mark started to accept that his world was unacceptably narrow and agreed to return to soccer and rugby, which he had previously enjoyed. This led to further social engagements, and he even attended the local disco. Slowly but surely, Mark realised that Clash of Clans was more boring than the outside world.

• • •

The power of micro habits

If you have identified what is driving your teen to be so dependent on screens, you might begin to bring some micro habits into the situation. Micro habits should be related to a stress point, but they need to be specific, small changes: for example, no tech in the kitchen. Parents can create this one micro habit centred on one stress point, then make one rule about this. They should wait until the new situation is an accepted habit in the household before they bring in another rule.

Micro habits need to be supported by a system. That's what makes them doable. For example, you might suggest that your partner goes outside to take their call because there is no tech allowed in the kitchen. These habits also need to be too small to fail; it is up to the parent to create habits that are so small that you'd be embarrassed if you couldn't check the box each day to say you managed this. If no tech in the kitchen is too big for your household, perhaps no devices in the bedrooms at night might work better? Or no tech until 9 a.m. every morning? It doesn't really matter what the rule is – the point is for it to slightly improve your family's tech habits.

Micro habits seek the 'power of tiny gains' rather than big wins, which can apply to all parenting matters and life in general. The power of tiny gains is a mathematical representation of our lives improving by just 1 per cent each day. If we can do this, then, according to James Clear, a leading expert on habit formation, we will be 38 times better at the end of the year.[27] When we are overwhelmed, humans often seek the big event as it feels psychologically satisfying, so we decide that we're going to lock up all the technology and not allow anyone in the family to access anything. Then, because this is unsustainable, we inevitably fail – perhaps it turns out that the kids need their devices for school – and the big event turns into a non-event. Although these large gestures might give us a sense of power at that moment, they seldom have as much long-term power as a series of tiny gains.

The power of tiny gains

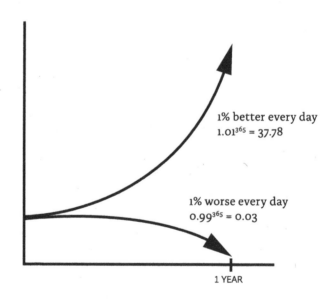

1% better every day
$1.01^{365} = 37.78$

1% worse every day
$0.99^{365} = 0.03$

1 YEAR

Source: Atomic Habits *by James Clear*

• • •

What parents can do

To begin with, the parents need to assess the family's habits. Where are the problem areas? What is causing fights? What works? What are the impediments to progress? Do you, the parents, need to engage in this process too? (Yes, you do.)

Then the parents might choose to sit the kids down and explain that they will make sure the household's tech habits are healthier. This might require some serious rules. There might be significant fights – so be it. We don't allow our children to eat sweets all day, every day; we don't allow adult kids to drink vodka at the breakfast table; equally, we need to bring in some rules around our technology into the household. The phrase 'digital hygiene' is usually used in the context of cleaning our laptops or in reference to scrubbing our personal details from the internet or regularly changing our passwords for security, but I believe 'digital health' is a term that needs to be used in the context of a healthy approach to our technology.

The following guidelines are often useful.

Make some rooms tech-free
For example, the kitchen, the bathroom(s) and the bedrooms. Just as many of us gave up smoking when we were forced to smoke outside, we will learn some boundaries around our tech usage if we have to leave the room to take a call or send a message.

Take all technology out of the bedrooms

Parents are often very resistant to this as they want to keep their own devices in their bedrooms and they also don't want their kids downstairs gaming in the sitting room. And yet, for as long as your children have the space to game all day and all night, they will – it is our job as parents to make sure that this is difficult to do.

Make some times of the day tech-free

Most parents agree that devices should be shut down at a certain time at night. But it is also recommended that we don't start our day by doom-scrolling through social media platforms. It could be helpful, for instance, to turn off the Wi-Fi at 10.30 p.m. and keep it off till 9 a.m. The children won't like that – indeed, none of you may like it; but the shocking impact technology overuse has on our health should perhaps guide you.

Use the 'trust and verify' approach

You trust your child to bring their technology downstairs at night – and you check that they do. You may also trust your child doesn't send sexualised content – and you check that they don't.

Maintain access to your teen's passwords

Considering how damaged children can be by certain technology, I recommend that parents have access to their teen's passwords. This doesn't mean that you break their boundaries – respecting boundaries is an essential aspect of emotional maturity – but it does mean that you can check in on their content every so often; perhaps once a week or once a fortnight you might randomly check in on their content. And you tell them you will check so that they know this will happen.

Discuss the nuances of privacy

Many teenagers believe they can have extended privacy on their phones. This isn't true, and parents can ensure teenagers realise this. If teenagers want privacy, they can have real-life discussions with their friends and call them on the phone. Online messages are not private as they can be screenshot, so parents should consider having access to all messaging apps and social media. This is in keeping with our working lives, where email, text messages and other communications sent during the working day are not considered personal by companies, and so it is a good habit to instil in young people. A teenager who wants to write out their private thoughts can keep a diary. The phone is too immediate a device and too easily shared among friends to be considered a tool for privacy.

Create micro habits within the household

Micro habits are tiny, everyday habits that steer a person in the right direction. These habits need to be small, easy and not time-consuming so that they are easy to incorporate into family life.

• • •

Takeaways

- Technology offers a false sense of intimacy.

- Humans can become over-reliant on the dopamine fix that technology offers, and we don't yet know how this is impacting teenage brains.

- Bring in rules as early as possible and promote the idea that your household is taking a healthy approach to technology.

- Tackle technology as you tackle junk food. Families often slip into unhealthy habits around food, sleep or screens. Although it takes energy to rectify, it is eminently possible.

- Many parents don't bother using parental controls as they believe the kids will find a way around them. They should use them, though, as they can be very helpful.

- Interrupt your child from spending long hours in a row online. Some individuals enjoy the altered state of mind induced by long hours spent on a screen. Equally, some people enjoy the stupor that binge-eating can bring. This is not healthy, and it is recommended that teens get intermittent access to their tech rather than extended binges.

- Involve yourself in your teen's online life, ask them what they like about their music, their favourite TikTok videos and their preferred video games – you don't have to like them, but you can be interested in why your teenager loves them.

- Certain rules, although hard to establish, will make life easier and reduce fights.

- Tiny gains and micro habits can be longer-lasting than huge showdowns.

- Privacy is a fallacy when messages can be screenshot.

- Parents need to have some control over their teen's online behaviour.

- Parents might need to trust and verify, but it's also important not to over-control.

PART III

EXPLORING TENSION,
FEAR AND RIGID
THINKING

CHAPTER 8

ANXIETY AND DEPRESSION

'We are more often frightened than hurt; and we suffer more from imagination than reality.'

– SENECA

THESE DAYS, whenever mental health practitioners meet at a conference or a more informal gathering, it never takes long for the subject to turn to what can be described as the pandemic levels of anxiety, distress and fear that dominate the teenage experience. If it weren't so tragically debilitating for these kids, it would be almost funny that previous generations had so much more to be anxious about, yet this generation, who have never been wealthier or better resourced, seem to be significantly unhappier and increasingly unable to cope with typical adolescent challenges. But why is it, psychologists across the world ask, that teenagers today are so filled with fear and anxiety? We are collecting data like never before but have no data from previous generations to compare with data from today. It could be the impact of technology and social media. That might be some of the story, but it is unlikely to be the whole story. There also seems to be a perfect storm of pressure to perform that has built up among young people, and this seems to be resulting in unbearable tension. The sheer pervasiveness of this phenomenon shows us that it is society, not teenagers, that is causing the problem with anxiety among young people: there is something about our way of living that is making teenagers very stressed. Yet, as these wise words, attributed to Jiddu Krishnamurti, tell us, 'It is no measure of health to be well adjusted to a profoundly sick society.'[28]

• • •

The impact of the Disneyfied childhood

Many children today have what I often call a Disneyfied childhood. Their lives have been filled with magic and fairy tales from the moment they were born. Special days out, themed parties and fantasy films combine to create children who believe that the good guys always win; and that if they wish hard enough, their wishes will come true. And until they reach puberty, their wishes often do come true!

The commercialisation of childhood gathered a lot of pace in the 1990s, when commercial interests around the world cottoned on to the massive profits that could be made from fulfilling childish dreams. Prior to this, children weren't so heavily encouraged to believe in a fairytale life. Parents of previous generations allowed children to have their innocence – but they didn't create vast palaces such as Legoland, Harry Potter World and Lapland to concretise these fantasies (and make vast amounts of money from them). In my book *Cotton Wool Kids*, I explored the reasons for and the impact of the cosseted childhood. The problem is that this dream childhood sells a lie to children as it lays a false yellow brick road before them (with adults standing like sentries ready to provide entertainment, protection or information whenever required). Then, when adolescence strikes, adults often begin to become uncomfortable about (or maybe exhausted by) upholding this fantasy existence. Parents then tend to suddenly and haplessly decide that the teenager needs a dose of reality.

A good example of how the young person experiences a short, sharp shock of reality is how the vast array of extra-curricular activities that children attend these days typically take on a very competitive edge around puberty. Suddenly, winning and performance take precedence, while the fun often goes out of the window. Lots of things become competitive when puberty strikes, and kids move from wishing on a star to being slapped into a hard brick wall of reality. This world is much harsher than the average child has been led to believe, and they often feel a deep sense of disappointment and even panic when they come to realise this.

Disappointment and shock are often evident when I meet young teens in my clinic. These youngsters honestly thought that they would have an adolescence like the scenes on TV. Why wouldn't they? Their childhood was filled with the promise that being a teenager would be cool and exciting. But puberty is not at all easy; indeed, it is very difficult for many. Their bodies feel out of control. Periods often feel impossibly depressing for girls – and very far from the image of the cool teen girl they've seen on social media. Boys also often feel out of their depth and intimidated by the idea of ever becoming a man. Childhood has been shortened considerably, so tweens are introduced to complexities such as puberty, sexuality, and the importance of online etiquette when they are as young as eight and nine. Just like they can't understand Shakespeare's *Hamlet* at that age, they cannot understand these complex concepts. Yet we have them living in a weird world in which they believe in the innocent fantasy of Santa Claus while simultaneously learning about complexities such as sexual consent.

Mae, a 22-year-old beauty therapist I know, told me that she was drunk when she first realised there was no such thing as Santa. 'I was thirteen, it was Christmas time, and I went to a party with my mates. We stole from the parents' drinks cabinet, and I got plastered really quickly. I kept asking everyone what they were getting from Santa, and then the girls started laughing at me and told me there was no such thing as Santa. I burst into tears and ran home crying.' A sad way to lose the innocence of childhood.

It won't help if parents suddenly start muttering darkly about the horrors of real life when they realise that their child is shielded from reality after reading this. Children need to look forward to the future, not dread it. It can be helpful, though, to bring some reality into childhood so that children learn as they go along that although the good guys don't always win, life can be great fun, and it is their own job to make sure they lead a satisfying life.

· · ·

An uncertain and complex world

Families today tend to be more individualistic and less likely to have an extended family nearby. Not only that, but our lifestyles often involve moving house more often, and, for some, a good deal less involvement in community affairs. The result is that teens today are less likely to know their wider community. Today, communication is more likely to be based on access to Wi-Fi, and teenagers generally feel their 'community' is their online community. This online world is often a bunch of unknown people who cultivate their online personas in a way that is seldom representative of their real-life selves; other times, they are real-life friends who spend more time online than communicating in person. But the online world is sophisticated. There is a maze of content to get through and a complicated new language and behaviour to learn – all this is anxiety-inducing for most teens.

Psychologists tell us that we can handle bad news much better than we think but we find it significantly more difficult to handle uncertainty.[29] Teenagers live in an unformulated world driven by a technological beast that knows no rules and very little protocol. This is quite confusing, as the real world seems to be laden with a multitude of policies and protocols, while the online world is like the Wild West, where there is no rulebook and anything could happen.

Social friendships in the teen years are much more complex than childhood friendships. Anyone who isn't socially adept or emotionally sophisticated can be side-lined as the cool group emerges at school and in other social contexts. Parents can help with this by having exploratory conversations about why x said y in school and helping their child to work through the finer points of social interactions in order to help them to better understand the interaction. Added to this is the complex new language that has evolved in recent times, where teenagers are told, 'You can't say that' on a regular basis. This thought-stopping ban on free speech has led to more anxiety as young people begin to believe their thoughts are wrong in some way and should be censored. The impact of all this complexity is that teenagers feel utterly weighed down by anxiety, their brains are turbo-charged, they're afraid to relax and are never quite sure about what is going on and whether they might be judged to be 'wrong' on some level.

• • •

Symptoms of anxiety

Often the teenager isn't actually aware that they are feeling anxious – they know that they are feeling distressed, but their brains feel like a mass of mixed-up emotions. They haven't cottoned on to the fact that all these dizzying thoughts or all these uncomfortable physical ailments can be traced back to one word: anxiety. It can be helpful if parents can become aware of certain symptoms of anxiety.

Emotional and cognitive symptoms of anxiety can include:

- feeling on edge, restless or wound-up
- feeling tired all the time, being easily fatigued
- having difficulty concentrating

- being irritable

- feeling consumed with rage

- difficulty controlling feelings of worry

- paralysis by analysis.

Physical and behavioural symptoms of anxiety include:

- headaches, muscle aches, stomach aches or unexplained pains

- breathing problems

- digestive ailments

- rapid heart rate, chest tightness

- trembling

- dizziness, light-headedness

- sweating, clammy hands, shivering

- sleep problems, such as difficulty falling or staying asleep

- exhaustion, shutdown.

• • •

How anxiety happens

The most reliable explanation of anxiety that I know of is that anxiety results from an overestimation of the danger combined with an underestimation of our ability to cope.

ANXIETY

=

OVERESTIMATION OF THE DANGER

+

UNDERESTIMATION OF OUR ABILITY TO COPE

Many people engage in a maladaptive vicious circle, where they initially overthink and overestimate the threat when they perceive the danger. They exacerbate their distress by underestimating their ability to handle this threat. Many of us then make matters worse by avoiding the anxiety-making situation. The short-term relief that is achieved is based on a false promise, and the anxiety comes back a little bit worse the next time.

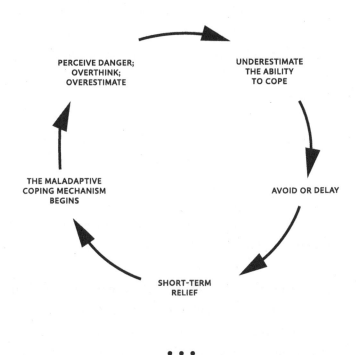

PERCEIVE DANGER; OVERTHINK; OVERESTIMATE

UNDERESTIMATE THE ABILITY TO COPE

THE MALADAPTIVE COPING MECHANISM BEGINS

AVOID OR DELAY

SHORT-TERM RELIEF

• • •

Negative thinking

In a similar way, depression is a tightening grip of negativity. The individual may perceive a problem as being bigger than it is, feels unable to cope, and then spirals into negativity and despair as an unhealthy coping mechanism. Others simply develop a very bad habit of negativity, where every thought, every plan, every suggestion is drowned out by the word 'No'. This can feel relentlessly difficult for the parent who is, after all, trying to create a happy home. It's not easy on the teen either though, as their negative thinking can create a self-made prison that can be difficult to escape from. If your teen is always negative, it can be valuable to try to catch them when they are in good form and point out gently that their negativity is ruining any chance they have of enjoying their life. Try to engage authentically with them on this matter – it is not helpful if you try to motivate them rather than taking the time to understand what's going on for them.

Parents might need to become aware of their own emotional reactions to their teen's pain. For example, if a parent has suffered a traumatic experience at a specific age, it is more likely that they will overidentify with their child's pain when the child is the same age, or they could completely dismiss their child's distress as it feels insignificant compared to what the parent experienced. Both are emotional reactions and neither are helpful.

Parents are often horrified by the depth of their teen's despair. Yet it is infinitely more helpful if parents can dare to confront the existential crisis that is so often at the root of depression rather than trying to jolly them out of their dark episodes. This might mean that the parent must confront their own nihilistic despair, which can be difficult. The great thinkers and philosophers can help us to process these big emotions; in my work, I have found that discussing the ideas of the Stoic philosophers Marcus Aurelius, Epictetus and Seneca can be helpful to teenagers. Kierkegaard or Nietzsche can be equally intriguing. Although it is fashionable these days to reach for bland positivity, teenagers in distress are often hungry for profound ideas that will help them make sense of life.

• • •

Symptoms of depression

Depression can often be masked in adolescence, and teenagers can present as cheerful when in reality they are very down. If you can manage to have an authentic conversation with your teen and they report the following issues, or you notice these symptoms, a visit to the doctor is recommended:

- sleep problems

- loss of appetite or other eating issues

- lack of energy

- loss of concentration

- problems with self-image or self-confidence

- ongoing thoughts of death or suicide (see Chapter 14).

• • •

When your teen won't get out of bed

If the teenager becomes unmotivated and the parents are too insistent or controlling, they may shut down. Some teenagers feel utterly alienated by school, college and the path before them. If this happens, it can be more valuable for parents to figure out why the teen feels disaffected and unmotivated than to try to motivate them. This listless teen may be impossible to rouse in the morning, preferring to stay up late on their devices. Maybe they don't care what happens to them because they believe that they have no agency and are merely puppets on a string and that either their parents or society will tell them what to do. The road to self-discovery can be blocked when the teen feels there are few options in life.

When teenagers believe that all effort is futile as they have no control over their life, no purpose or no meaning, they can begin to stagnate. They aren't quite sure what has happened to them, but they often seem to feel like caged birds and cannot respond as free and motivated individuals. If this feeling of oppression is all-encompassing or if it goes on too long, the teenager will not be able to think for themselves. Because the stakes are so high, it is recommended that the parents make sure to get professional help for the depressed teen. It is also very important to lean into the sadness rather than always trying to jolly your kid out of it. Although sometimes simple cheering up can work, at other times it can lead to an even deeper sense of alienation.

Parenting strategy: Consider your options

Parents who yell and beg their teens to get out of bed would often be better off allowing natural consequences to unfold. This can mean buying the teenager an alarm clock and letting them get into trouble for being late to school in the morning. If at all possible, try not to be involved in bringing your teen to school – it's developmentally more helpful if they can make their own way, by bus, bike or walking.

It can also be valuable to entice certain teens out of bed during the weekend with specific time-oriented events like the cinema at 12 noon. Although it might feel like you're spoiling them, you are also helping them form healthier habits at a difficult time in their life.

• • •

Nurturing resilience

'As safe as necessary' has recently replaced the phrase 'as safe as possible' for children and teenagers, as child experts have come to realise that 'as safe as possible' could entail locking young people up in a padded room – and this wouldn't work as their mental health would suffer. Teens need adventure, risk, challenge and fun to remain engaged in life. For these reasons, it is more valuable for parents to promote a healthy cycle of learning to tackle problems rather than encouraging avoidance of the problem.

This cycle of learning could begin with the teen perceiving danger and, instead of over-emphasising the risk, realistically analysing the threat. If they can realistically estimate their ability to cope, they can act appropriately in the face of imminent threats. For example, if the teen is faced with walking home alone, it is better if they can realistically evaluate the threat rather than immediately assuming that it is dangerous. If the teen is encouraged to celebrate any small wins they have over their anxiety and/or depression, they will feel stronger and more confident in the face of danger, and from this, a healthy cycle of behaviour and thought patterns can begin.

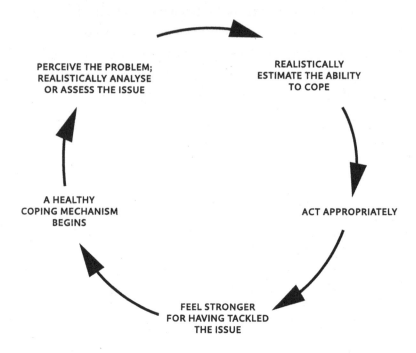

PERCEIVE THE PROBLEM;
REALISTICALLY ANALYSE
OR ASSESS THE ISSUE

REALISTICALLY
ESTIMATE THE ABILITY
TO COPE

A HEALTHY
COPING MECHANISM
BEGINS

ACT APPROPRIATELY

FEEL STRONGER
FOR HAVING TACKLED
THE ISSUE

The more your teen is encouraged to expect change to happen, rather than dreading it; to take charge of their emotions, rather than letting their emotions lead them; and to bring in flexible and realistic thinking, the more they will feel able to resolve difficult situations. Resilience, the ability to withstand difficult conditions, builds as a consequence of self-awareness, self-caring behaviour and self-caring thoughts. Resilience is also nurtured through positive relationships with loved ones who are willing to provide solidarity and a sense of purpose that helps the teen see a way forward. This can take time to achieve, but that's OK. Adolescence is long, and parenting is longer.

Avoidance, drowning and blocking

In my book *Fragile* I wrote extensively about how anxiety and avoidance can poison our future. Although avoidance may sometimes be used as a temporary coping mechanism, if we continue to avoid our problems, we are merely kicking the can down the road. The problem will inevitably boomerang back, a little bit harder each time. Teenagers today have in many ways assimilated the pop-psychology slogans of our time. They honestly believe that if something doesn't feel good, they shouldn't do it – not understanding that sometimes distress is a necessary feature of long-term contentment. Nor do they realise that the challenges of adolescence are often difficult, but these are exactly the challenges that need to be tackled if the teen is to become a fully functioning adult.

Avoidance reduces distress in the moment but often comes with long-term psychological costs. Things can go wrong when the unspoken message to the young person is that their negative feelings are something to be feared – in truth, negative feelings provide the individual with important feedback about their psyche. Ideally, we should take note of our negative feelings and then consider our options.

It can be useful to know that some of us are 'drowners'; drowning in difficult situations, drowning in fears and judgements and allowing our minds to become like a hurricane of powerful, emotional and often untrue statements. In contrast, others are 'blockers' who push through difficult situations by force of will, often with the help of food, distraction or avoidance tactics. Blockers avoid difficulties as much as possible but believe that they are relying on their mental strength. Blockers generally swerve wildly into 'drowning' every so often and then swing back into blocking again.

DROWNER	BLOCKER
• You drown in the difficult situation	• You 'push through' the difficult situation by force of will, often with the help of food, distraction, avoidance, etc.
• You drown in your fears and judgements	
• Your mind becomes like a hurricane of powerful, emotional and often untrue statements	• You avoid as much as possible, but you think you are relying on your mental strength
	• Until one day you swerve wildly into 'drowning'

Parents can help their 'drowner' teens by modelling realistic thinking and by helping them to adopt more realistic views. Challenge them when they say they know they'll fail the test; is this actually true? Is it more likely that they will not achieve the high grades they usually get, which is what is really stressing them out? Equally, blockers can be challenged by being gently prodded into reality with a few well-chosen questions. Might they be avoiding the reality of the test by being distracted by the latest drama on Snapchat? When the storm is happening, it can be helpful if parents follow these steps to help their kids calm their distressed minds.

• • •

Six steps to calm the anxious or depressed mind

When your teen experiences anxious episodes, it can be valuable for the parent to watch for the patterns and start to lean into the issue with the following steps. Sometimes you might skip some of the steps – this is not a linear process – and it is important that you don't underestimate your own intuition about what your teen needs in the moment. These steps may take practice, and you might get them wrong and receive a tongue-lashing from your teen, but that's OK, practice makes perfect.

1 **Approach the situation like a scientist:** Take a bird's eye view of what is happening. Imagine that you are watching what is going on as if you are watching TV, and consider what advice you would give the characters on screen. You might wonder aloud, if it's appropriate, what advice your teen would give.

2 **Distraction may work – learn to redirect attention:** This might mean encouraging your teen to play a game on their phone or chat with somebody about something else.

3 **Bring in mindful breathing:** Teach your teen how to slow their brain down. Take a slow breath in through your nose, hold it for a few seconds; release the breath very slowly through your mouth.

4 Use your intellectual curiosity: Help your teen
to figure out what's actually driving this; acquire
some understanding of what's going on. Parents can
begin this process by asking questions with genuine
openness and endless patience.

**5 Bring in self-compassion and compassion for
others:** Again, parents can help with this by showing
compassion towards the young person who is feeling
intensely distressed.

6 Find solidarity: If appropriate, help the teen to
engage in problem-solving with you, a (hopefully)
trusted confidante. This is where you can show
your children that you stand shoulder to shoulder
with them and are ready to engage in the long and
arduous process of problem-solving.

• • •

Overcoming fears

The term 'antifragility' describes something that gains from
being stressed; for example, when we work out, we stress our
muscles, and our strength grows.[30] Humans, and especially
teenagers, who are often moving from easy childhood to more
difficult adulthood, arguably need to experience pain and
complexity so that they can learn from it, grow from it and
ultimately become stronger and gain a deeper understanding of
life.

Although a little anxiety can be endurable, when individuals
become engulfed by anxiety, certain stress management

techniques can be required. For some people, it can be most helpful to focus on grounding techniques such as exercise, deep breathing or progressive muscle relaxation. Many find it more satisfying to work through the mind by journaling, meditating or visualising. Others feel better simply by chatting in a reflective manner about what is going on for them. There is no one-size-fits-all approach, but as long as the parent is aware of the dangers of short-term coping mechanisms, they can gently guide their teenager to become wary of avoidance in favour of confronting the roots of their anxiety. Ultimately, seeking a longer-term resolution for what works best for them will bring about more self-awareness and better outcomes.

Developmental milestone: Develop coping skills and begin to reach emotional maturity

Seeking to avoid something because of anxiety is often an unhealthy coping mechanism for a teenager who needs to tackle developmental milestones such as improving their coping skills and deepening their understanding of complex emotional experiences. Parents can help with this by chatting with them some time after the event so they can better process what happened and think of healthier responses for the future. If parent and teen talk before the event, the teen might become more anxious and shut down even more firmly, but sometimes there are opportunities for self-reflection after the event. Parents might ask, with a sense of open curiosity, 'I wonder, were there any other options that we didn't explore that would have resulted in a happier outcome?'

. . .

What parents can do

When a child is filled with fear and distress, it can feel as if the kindest thing to do is to allow them to use various methods of avoidance to cope. These coping mechanisms can be very convincing as solutions to the problem, but the solutions are short-lived. The role of the parent is to look to the long term and ensure their child learns to tackle the problem or they will never learn to move from the childish mindset. The teen needs to stop avoiding difficult challenges, such as exams, school, socialising and friendship difficulties, and to start developing healthy coping skills and learn how to process complex emotional experiences. If the parents allow the teen to continuously avoid difficult challenges, they will become stuck and won't achieve the necessary developmental tasks of adolescence.

There are many reasons why a teen might feel anxious or depressed, and it is valuable for parents to help their child figure out what is driving their distress. Parents need to gently guide their teen towards emotional maturity with baby steps that help them to confront these issues. It is worthwhile to begin with some psychoeducation that explains to the teen how existential angst, fear and anxiety are the challenges that they need to face; that avoidance is an unhealthy response and an unhealthy coping mechanism; and that tackling the elephant in bite-size chunks, as small as required, is the only way to deal with these issues. Then parents need to collaborate with their child to develop a plan together that confronts the avoidance slowly but surely. Perhaps the teen avoids real-life interactions? Maybe they can start by ordering a meal in a café? Perhaps you can help them role-play potential conversations in school? It can be helpful to anticipate blocks to progress and to plan in advance options for when things go wrong; and the stepladder approach in Chapter 6 can also work in this context.

• • •

Takeaways

- Past generations faced terrible difficulties, but they often had more secure formative years centred within a solid family and community.

- Today's younger generation feel uncertain as the world around them is much more complex.

- Uncertainty is more difficult to handle than bad news.

- Childhood today has become ever more magical and enjoyable, but an unforeseen consequence of such magical childhoods is that pubescent children face a bitter and sharp shock of reality.

- Disappointment in the reality of life often hits during adolescence and the crushing feelings associated with this should not be underestimated.

- Teens need to experience some hardship so that they can learn to deal with reality.

- There are ways to calm an anxious and/or depressed mind but it may take practice.

- It is valuable if parents can teach their children that reality, although sometimes difficult, can also be really brilliant.

CHAPTER 9

INTENSITY, RIGID THINKING, COMPULSIONS AND OBSESSIVENESS

'Prepare the child for the road, not the road for
the child.'

– PROVERB

IT IS PROBABLY not as well-known as it should be that flexible
thinking is a hallmark of healthy functioning and that the
opposite, rigid thinking, often creates significant challenges
for our mental health. Mental rigidity refers to an obstinate
inability in the individual to appreciate another viewpoint or
way of behaving and a tendency to perseverate (which refers to
an inability to change habits and/or attitudes). This tendency to

hyper-focus can lead to great achievement, and when we look at the obsessive work of Sir Isaac Newton, Michelangelo, Charles Darwin and countless others, we see the value in the individual who who will not deviate from their chosen subject. Sadly, not all obsessive thinking leads to pioneering work, and this type of thought processing can often negatively impact an individual's wellbeing.

The symptom of mental rigidity is a criterion for the diagnosis of certain conditions, including autism spectrum disorder, attention deficit hyperactivity disorder and obsessive-compulsive disorder. If this chapter seems to describe many of the challenges your teen is facing, it could be very worthwhile to seek an evaluation to see if this provides further insight into your teenager's challenges. Psychologists work within the diagnostic field, while psychotherapists like myself are less concerned about the diagnosis a person has and are more focused on the 'problems of living'. Therapists readily acknowledge that some of us have a certain type of brain that leads us to behave in a certain manner, but nonetheless, we focus on how individuals can function more healthily within any given framework while taking into account the way our individual brains perceive things. Individuals who are inclined towards mental rigidity often end up with certain mental health conditions such as eating disorders, OCD, body dysmorphia and gender dysphoria, so a good therapist who can provide continuous guidance in the long term could be necessary for your teen. This chapter leaves aside the specifics of each diagnosis and instead focuses on how parents can help when faced with rigid thinking, compulsions and obsession.

> **Developmental milestone: Begin to reach emotional maturity**
>
> Although we are often told to keep things simple, this is not enough for many of us to achieve mental wellbeing; some people need to be willing to complexify the narrative. For teens to begin to reach emotional maturity, they need to move towards self-acceptance and realise that confronting complexity, understanding shades of grey and learning how to handle our limitations and disappointment is an integral part of healthy functioning.

Manifestations of mental rigidity are:

- repetitive behaviour
- difficulty with unmet expectations and things going wrong
- obsessions
- compulsions
- polarised thinking characterised by the 'all or nothing' principle
- perseveration
- perfectionism.

• • •

Rigidly repetitive behaviour

When we feel anxious, our brain can feel like somebody has taken a snow globe and shaken it violently, and some of us use repetitious behaviour or speech as a way of calming down the chaotic noise in our minds.[31] Repeating the same behaviour or the same phrase over and over again perhaps gives our minds a chance to feel more grounded and allows us to catch up and process the new event.

Repetitive behaviour or repetitive speech can sometimes be very reminiscent of the prayers and rituals that have been used for thousands of years in organised religion. Catholicism, for example, with the various physical acts of blessing ourselves, kneeling, rosary beads and the repetition of prayers and magical thinking, was a perfect way for anxious people to feel calmer. Now that religion has unceremoniously fallen asunder all over the western world, many people feel adrift, without any life raft to cling to when they feel stressed, and they can find themselves turning to other coping mechanisms that make them feel more grounded.

Repetitive behaviour becomes problematic when it has a negative impact on the person's life or another person's life. This is often because the behaviour begins to occupy a significant portion of the individual's waking hours and interferes with their ability to tackle the challenges that life brings. The term 'repetitive behaviour' refers to behaviour that is characterised by repetition, rigidity, inappropriateness and lack of adaptability.[32] This includes any or all of the following behaviour:

- **Motor-stereotyped behaviour:** Repetitive, rhythmic, purposeful but purposeless movements such as thumb-sucking, nail- or lip-biting, hair twirling, teeth clenching or grinding.

- **Self-stimulatory behaviour** (also known as stimming): Often involves unusual body movements such as tapping, spinning, jumping, bouncing, counting, twirling, flapping hands, flicking or snapping fingers, rocking back and forth or side to side while sitting or standing, pacing or walking on tiptoes and/or repetitive blinking.

- **Self-injurious behaviour:** Picking, scratching or rubbing the skin, hair pulling, head banging, self-biting or other self-harming behaviour.

- **Verbally repetitive behaviour:** For example, echolalia (repeating words or phrases), whistling, humming.

- **Compulsive or sameness behaviour:** Rigidly following a complex pattern of routinised and ritualistic behaviour that forms a class of restrictive and repetitive behaviour.

An example of compulsive and/or sameness behaviour was evocatively described in the book *Our House is on Fire: Scenes of a Family and a Planet in Crisis,* in which Greta Thunberg describes how a 10-minute walk to dance class used to take almost an hour because her sister Beata felt compelled to walk with her left foot in front, refused to step on certain parts of the pavement, and insisted that her mother walk the same way. Beata also demanded that her mother wait outside during class – the girls' mother wasn't allowed to move, even to go to the bathroom.

• • •

Difficulty with unmet expectations and things going wrong

In psychiatry, 'magical thinking' refers to a form of thought disorder; however, it can also be a benign way of helping us to feel better. In childhood, magical thinking is perfectly appropriate, and, according to the developmental psychologist Jean Piaget, we outgrow this by around seven to ten years of age, depending on the child. Magical thinking can lead people to believe that their thoughts can directly cause things to happen – for example, thinking angry thoughts about a person can cause them to fall down the stairs. Although we are supposed to grow out of it, there is a distinct element of magical thinking involved in superstition and religion. Further, there is arguably a whole pop-psychology industry that is based on magical thinking. For example, the book *The Secret* by Rhonda Byrne is based upon the pseudoscientific 'law of attraction', which tells us that our thoughts attract events into our lives. Some people never outgrow this type of thinking, while others find the path beyond magical thinking incredibly disappointing.

Although our modern era offers many opportunities for happiness, and we have tried so hard to avoid disappointing children, this generation of teenagers often have little ability to cope when their expectations are frustrated. If your teenager hasn't had much experience in learning how to handle disappointment, then they need to learn – and parents need to buckle in for a rough ride, as the meltdowns might be very scary.

Some teenagers find it very difficult to let go of the idea that *expecting* something to happen will *make* it happen. It is our role as parents to introduce small disappointments in our kids' lives so that they can one day learn to cope with larger disappointments. Many people, including some professionals who work with neurodiverse adolescents, will argue that the solution is to avoid disappointment in the young person's life. This is arguably a self-defeating and exhausting endeavour that might work, to a point, during the school day but will inevitably fail for the family who is living with a teen who can't handle being disappointed. It is arguably better to teach coping mechanisms around disappointment than to seek to avoid disappointment; this might entail slow breathing, spending time in nature, and learning perspective by asking themselves, 'Will this matter in five hours? In five days? In five weeks? Or in five months?' Small strategies like this, which can be very helpful to teenagers, are sometimes underused by parents.

• • •

Obsessiveness

An obsession is a recurring thought of something or someone, over the short term or the long term, and can be uncomfortable and even disturbing. Obsessions can manifest in thoughts, dreams, urges and fantasies. The difference between an obsession and a worry is that a worry tends to be something that might possibly happen, while an obsession involves irrational and relentless thinking.

When parents hear the term 'obsession' many automatically think of OCD, and although many of the symptoms described in this chapter might suggest the potential for an OCD diagnosis, some people's tendency to obsess is a negative trait but not a clinical or diagnosable condition. These symptoms are effectively graded by their severity, and not every obsession needs to be thought of as a dangerous symptom of a mental health condition. I know that when I was a teenager, I often fell into almost dangerous levels of obsession with various boys in my life. I simply thought of nothing else. I lived for them. Looking back, I was filling a huge void in my life, an emptiness within, and my obsessions gave me a north star to follow when my mind was completely at sea. Nowadays, although I am certainly intense, I am seldom, if ever, obsessed – experience taught me to be wary of my intensity, and I eventually learnt how to bring things down a notch or two for the benefit of my (and everyone else's) wellbeing.

We don't know why some people's minds are prone to getting 'stuck' in a way that others simply don't, but studies suggest that there is a genetic predisposition. Perhaps we inherit our obsessive thinking process through our DNA. Others believe that obsessive thinking is down to a chemical difference in the brain, but this chemical difference is impossible to trace. It is also impossible to discern whether the obsessive thought patterns cause the potential chemical difference or the apparent chemical difference causes the obsessive thought pattern. Certainly, environmental factors also play a role in causing obsessions: when one of the parents is obsessive, there is a good chance that this will rub off on some of the kids, especially if stress is involved. A 'biopsychosocial' understanding of any condition – the understanding that a person becomes afflicted because of a combination of biological, psychological and sociological reasons – is often the most accurate.

ABIGAIL, 17

When Abigail first came into my office, she was determined to show me that she was a good girl and would be the 'perfect patient'. She engaged very well – perhaps too well – and always presented as cheerful and competent. But this didn't make sense to me. Her mother, Deirdre, had booked our sessions and told me Abigail was prone to fits of anxious rage, that she had developed some behavioural tics and symptoms of OCD and that she was desperately unhappy. So who was this cheerful head-girl type who was turning up every Saturday morning?

It took a lot of work before Abigail let down any of her defences. She had always been a high achiever, and as long as her results were brilliant, Abigail could cope. Sadly, life got in the way of this plan, and her difficulties with maths and science subjects created an identity crisis for Abigail. Who even was she if she wasn't 'All A's Abigail'? When Abigail received a series of less-than-perfect results, she spiralled out of control. She started to have panic attacks before school and convinced her mother she needed extra tuition, even though her grades were generally fantastic. Soon after, Abigail began to strictly curtail her food and over-exercise. She was determined to be brilliant at something, and losing weight became her thing.

Abigail was very articulate, and when she became angry with her mother, she became very spiteful. She used her mother as a whipping boy. Deirdre was willing to accept this as long as it helped Abigail. The problem was that it wasn't helping. The more Abigail raged at her mother, the more subservient the mother became, and the more infuriated Abigail grew. Abigail's perfect exterior was kept in check by an overpowering need to control. The perfect hair, the polished appearance – her entire persona was devoted to being perfect. But being perfect is exhausting. And it doesn't work because humans are fallible.

As we got to know each other, I often wondered where Abigail's father was. Where was Derek? It was Deirdre who made all the appointments and Deirdre who drove Abigail to counselling. Abigail informed me that her father was a very successful businessman who couldn't possibly involve himself in her minor problems. Deirdre agreed. But I persisted in trying to get to know this godlike figure – albeit on a second-hand basis.

It turned out that Derek was a strict, authoritarian parent. He laid down the rules and woe betide anyone who didn't follow them. Indeed, Abigail and her mother often lied to Derek about fairly basic details of their lives in order to avoid his wrath. Derek had Very High Expectations of his only child, Abigail. When Abigail was very young, he had encouraged her to become a doctor. As little girls often seek their daddy's approval, Abigail soon decided that she wanted to become a doctor. Then Derek explained to Abigail that she would need to work very hard to get sufficient points for such a demanding career. Abigail set about becoming the best little girl in the world.

All went swimmingly until Abigail found out that she didn't really have a mathematical brain and that English and art came much more naturally to her. This wouldn't do at all, so Abigail redoubled her efforts and started to get up at 5 a.m. every day to squeeze in more study. But all this effort came at the expense of her wellbeing. Abigail couldn't understand why she wasn't getting the results she wanted. She knew she was trying very hard, so she decided that something was wrong with her. Abigail's inner voice became a poisonous shrieking harridan that abused Abigail every chance she got.

As all this emerged, Abigail began to understand that she had internalised her father's high expectations and that they were driving her mad. We embarked on a course of psychoeducation in which Abigail learnt about her teenage brain. She began to realise that her simplistic, black-and-white thinking wasn't doing her any favours. Her impressive ability to gnaw at every problem without ever giving up came at the expense of her wellbeing. Abigail's immature brain led her to an intense fixation on success, and she needed to gain a more complex understanding of life. She needed to learn to let go of her tense grip on life. She found body-grounding exercises, such as becoming conscious of her physical body through deep breathing, Pilates, yoga or guided visualisation, were helpful in bringing about perspective. Abigail developed her self-awareness and, over a period of working together, Abigail slowly but surely found a softer, more compassionate inner voice.

• • •

Intrusive thoughts

Sometimes intrusive thoughts can figure in a person's obsession. These are unwelcome thoughts that pop into one's head repetitiously and without warning. Most of us have intrusive or unwanted thoughts from time to time, and not all intrusive or unwanted thoughts are obsessive. As with all mental health problems, it is when the intrusive thoughts have a detrimental impact on a person's life that there is cause for concern. Intrusive thoughts can be utterly debilitating, and they are often a sign that professional help is required. People can have intrusive thoughts about almost anything, for example:

- worrying about something you did or didn't do

- constant anxiety about offending other people

- fear of germs or sickness

- unwanted thoughts about hurting yourself or others

- fantasies about death

- worrying about doing something drastically wrong within a religion or belief system

- fear of losing control

- sex.

Is this a coping mechanism?

Obsessive thoughts and behaviours can be an unhealthy coping mechanism for a teenager who feels frightened by the chaos in the world. This teen needs to move towards self-acceptance by learning to accept the limitations and flaws in themselves and others. This can come about with psychoeducation – the teen is taught to better understand how they might cope with distressing thoughts and behaviours – and a willingness to experience uncomfortable feelings until they become more accustomed to this. Flexible thinking is the long-term goal.

• • •

Compulsive behaviour

Compulsive behaviour usually happens as the young person is trying to deal with obsessive or intrusive thoughts and they believe that if they do *x*, then *y* won't happen; it is effectively superstition writ large. Again this is echoed in religiosity, and when I see my mother doing a novena by going to mass nine days in a row for a specific purpose or fasting during Lent or not eating meat on a Friday, it is easy to see how this is a form of magical thinking. The difference is that compulsions take on obsessive or extreme intensity. For example, an individual might believe they might have to tap the door three times before they leave the house if they are to be safe. It's irrational and can be irritating, but it feels incredibly important to the individual.

Common compulsions include:

- making sure appliances are turned off, again and again

- checking multiple times that doors and windows are locked

- checking their body for flaws, weighing themselves, measuring themselves

- reviewing or going over events or conversations

- making sure they can't hurt anyone, for example by removing all knives from the kitchen.

Many conditions, such as OCD, body dysmorphic disorder, gender dysphoria and eating disorders, involve compulsive behaviours, and parents can feel at a loss in the face of the sheer intensity of the young person. While professional support is certainly recommended, it can also be helpful for the parents to encourage more flexibility in their teenager.

Teenagers often develop compulsions because they feel their (magic) behaviour can keep negative things from happening. It doesn't work – this is magical thinking at play – but it makes the young person feel calmer, so it is a dysfunctional (also called maladaptive) coping mechanism. The reason why it is dysfunctional is that it is based upon a false premise and the real reason for the distress continues to be ignored; this behaviour can also interfere with a person's ability to live their life. Ideally, the young person should be helped to find a more functional way to feel calmer. This can be done by pointing out to the individual that they have a coping mechanism which is helping them to avoid an important developmental task that they need to confront, such as reaching emotional maturity, moving towards self-acceptance and acceptance of others, and learning to live in a world that is filled with limitations and flaws.

• • •

Obsessive-compulsive disorder (OCD)

OCD involves excessive worrying or thinking about something despite efforts to stop thinking about it (the obsessive element) as well as having rituals, or things that one has to do in order to prevent something bad happening (the compulsive aspect). OCD should be diagnosed by an appropriate mental health professional; however, these days many people are described as having 'OCD traits' rather than a full-blown diagnosis. This is perhaps a more progressive way to approach things as it arguably provides more room for some individuals to move beyond it. Although rumination is typically perceived as a choice, people with OCD traits may feel compulsively compelled to ruminate. Meanwhile, individuals with Tourette's syndrome might demonstrate behavioural tics such as jerking movements or vocal tics such as humming or grunting, and they might also present with other OCD symptoms.

OCD is similar to a false alarm, as it causes a person to worry about something that is not harmful or dangerous or not likely to happen. It often runs in the family, so if you think about your extended family members, you might remember that you had a heavily religious aunt or uncle or cousin who was filled with compulsions or something similarly intense. Sadly, in previous times dysfunctional behaviour was unlikely to be treated and many people suffered in isolation.

People with OCD are more likely to obsess about issues such as:

- fear of dirt or germs

- fear of contamination

- a need for symmetry, order and precision

- religious obsessions

- body waste

- lucky and unlucky numbers

- sexual or aggressive thoughts

- fear of illness or harm coming to oneself or relatives

- household items

- intrusive sounds or words.

They are also likely to have compulsive behaviour that may involve:

- grooming rituals, including handwashing, teeth brushing and showers

- repeating rituals, including going in and out of doorways

- rereading, erasing and rewriting

- repeatedly checking homework

- checking rituals to make sure that an appliance is off or a door is locked

- rituals to undo contact with a contaminant

- touching rituals

- rituals to prevent harm occurring

- ordering or arranging objects

- counting rituals

- hoarding and collecting things of no apparent value

- cleaning rituals.

Teenagers with symptoms of OCD can feel scared and out of control and often keep the extent of their obsessions secret for fear of being labelled mad. This makes them feel lonely and isolated. The role of the parents is to make sure their child is attending therapy or has the right support so that the child can gain perspective and learn about how OCD manifests. This will help them both have a better understanding of what is going on for them and also learn to manage this condition – just as millions of people before them have. Parents can read about other people who have OCD traits and explain that OCD can take over many people's minds. A tangible story that you have found on the internet that your child might relate to can have a much longer-lasting effect than a bland sentence that tells them that one in 200 children experience OCD. Although parents will naturally reach for the positive stories, this is not the point of the exercise – indeed, many people who are in distress can feel panicked by Hollywood-type stories of fabulous recoveries. It is better to instead focus on the existence of a range of different stories with different outcomes so that the teen begins to realise the complexity involved.

Parenting strategy: Practise gratitude

Individuals with OCD traits can benefit from using gratitude to calm their minds. The word gratitude comes from the Latin word *gratia*, which means grace, graciousness or gratefulness. In many ways, practising gratitude encompasses all of these meanings. For thousands of years, religious practices involved ceremonial thanksgiving, and research shows us that gratitude is strongly and consistently associated with greater happiness.[33]

Parents can bring a sense of gratitude into the household by leading the way on this. Perhaps you could start a gratitude journal? Or regularly list three things you're thankful for during dinner time? Gratitude meditations can also become calming strategies for the over-anxious mind. This strategy involves the parents sprinkling a sense of gratitude within the household. It could be months before the children begin to be influenced by this approach. Pebbles in a barrel.

• • •

Perseveration

The term 'perseverate' derives from 'persevere', meaning 'to continue determinedly'. 'Perseverance' can be a very helpful trait in life, but when a person persists without any good reason, they are said to perseverate. In a more clinical context, 'perseveration' refers to insistent or redundant repetition that brings about extreme levels of distress if the person is not allowed to continue. Perseveration of thought indicates an inability to switch ideas or responses, for example returning relentlessly to a certain point during a conversation, way beyond rationality. People who perseverate may have physical challenges, such as a neurological condition, but it can also be a remarkably irritating trait of rigid thinkers, and sometimes it can be helpful for parents to introduce the teen to the concept of perseverating so that you can call it and help them to stop if needs be.

• • •

Post-traumatic stress disorder (PTSD)

Although certain kids emerge from traumatic experiences without major difficulty, nobody has yet figured out whether this is because of a genetic disposition or because of life experiences or the support they received during and after the event, or even a combination of these factors. Other people seem unable to 'bounce back' and struggle to cope with the memory of their experience, and PTSD can develop in this context. The teen with PTSD or traits of PTSD can feel unable to escape the impact of the trauma. Some might experience flashbacks of the event, and many engage in avoidance tactics. Parents can feel powerless in the face of their teen being held hostage to their mental pain, and this is why it is vitally important for the parent to access some professional help – for both the teen and the parents who are processing everything.

• • •

Selective mutism

Selective mutism is an anxiety disorder that typically manifests in children. They can't speak in certain places, with certain people or, most commonly, during certain social activities at preschool or school, but at home they can comfortably speak with their family and friends. Selective mutism is not a choice – they want to speak and try to speak, but their anxiety stops them. Anxious teenagers can develop selective mutism. Common symptoms include:

- freezing

- seeming restless

- paralysing tension

- trembling and blushing

- a racing heart, clammy hands or a sore stomach.

As with other manifestations of rigid thinking based on fear and tension, parents can help by gently guiding their child to overcome the necessary developmental milestones that face all teenagers, such as learning how to deal with emotional discomfort.

• • •

Perfectionism, fear of failure and performance anxiety

This generation's productivity is phenomenal, their performances are magnificent and their abilities are tremendous, but their anxiety is, perhaps as a direct result, off the scale. We can identify a fear of failure in an individual on match day or exam day as the person suffering from this fear is generally sick with worry, while the highly motivated, self-driven person feels buoyant and energised by the big day.

Perhaps as a response to the extraordinary pressure on young people to succeed and perform wherever they go, there has been an uptick in the number of young people speaking about their fear of failure in my clinical practice. Fear of failure is often related to being a perfectionist. Because perfectionists have such high expectations for themselves, they can often experience a nagging fear that they won't be able to live up to their often unrealistically high standards. A common response to this is to avoid the exam or the competition or to procrastinate so that you aren't at all prepared and can blame your failure on a lack of preparation rather than your ability.

It can often be difficult to identify a fear of failure and/or perfectionism in your teenager as it can be cloaked by many other manifestations of their fear. The following checklist may help:

- believing, despite evidence to the contrary, that they don't have the skills or knowledge to achieve a given task

- procrastinating to the point that it affects their performance or ability to finish on time

- self-sabotage, such as not turning up for the exam or missing a deadline

- elaborate avoidance tactics

- loss of control

- trying to convince everyone that they will probably fail
- dislike of expectation and continuous underestimation of their abilities
- worrying obsessively about their perceived imperfections or shortcomings
- worrying that they will disappoint others if they fail
- critical self-talk
- shame and feelings of worthlessness
- lack of motivation – intense fear creating a paralysing listlessness.

Fear of failure can produce a range of emotional and behavioural symptoms that might not seem connected but are completely rooted in anxiety. Some common emotional and cognitive signs of this fear include anxiety episodes, rage, emotional dysregulation and/or a series of unexplained maladies. Anxious kids often initially manifest their distress through their bodies, and parents often find that they have worn a path to the doctor seeking relief for various ailments.

ANNA, 15

Anna was an award-winning Irish dancer who became crippled by a fear of failure even as she grew more and more successful. Initially, when Anna first began dancing, it was all a joy for her. She had a natural talent and simply loved dancing. Then, as her medal collection grew, Anna became self-conscious because everybody began commenting on her great successes. Over the years, Anna would often find herself dancing for the gold medal against a girl called Laura. Sometimes Laura would win, and sometimes Anna would win. Anna began to dread the competitive aspect of dancing. Everybody seemed to care so much whether she won – her father's pride felt oppressive instead of a source of joy.

When Anna began to experience unexplained pain in her feet, she was brought to the doctor, who recommended rest and relaxation. This was surprising to Anna's family, who were focused on competition and uncomfortable with signs of weakness. Anna decided to give herself two weeks of R&R, as if she was an elite athlete – and to be fair, she kind of was. Anna generally won or got second place in the All-Irelands and was entered for the world championships.

When the pain in her feet subsided, she started to complain about headaches and then vertigo. Her doctor recommended cognitive behavioural therapy, and she landed in my office when she was 15 years old. She had stopped dancing by then – the vertigo had put paid to all that, and Laura was now the undisputed queen of dancing. Anna was disappointed about this, but not as disappointed as her parents, who had seen serious talent in their child and knew, with the wisdom of age, that not many of us have such a special talent.

Anna's inner life, meanwhile, was a mess of grief and competitiveness. She followed Laura's career obsessively. She saw Laura as the perfect version of herself, and she was very angry with herself for getting sick. We worked hard to widen Anna's landscape. Psychoeducation was a major feature of our counselling sessions as I explained to Anna how a fear of failure can ruin people's lives. Anna realised that her life was centred on silently competing with everyone. This wasn't working very well, and she procrastinated endlessly with her schoolwork and then generally missed the deadline or scrambled to submit a half-written assignment, unfinished and almost never reflective of her ability.

It took some time for Anna to learn about the simple joys in life. She was so used to assessing everything through a prism of competition. She only knew how to be happy whenever she won – she hadn't yet experienced the beautiful joy to be had in nature or in having a laugh that had no basis in competition or in simply just being, without trying or failing or winning. Anna learnt over time to make friends with herself and leave behind her terrifying fear of failure.

• • •

Academic intensity

Although parents are often justifiably proud when their teen becomes obsessive over their academic work, academic intensity can sometimes be an indication that the teen is tipping into a worryingly rigid mental thought pattern. As with eating habits, drinking habits and other behavioural habits, the response of the individual when they cannot perform their preferred task is a good indication that the parent should seek to help their teen loosen their grip.

When Sheila came to me in distress about her 17-year-old daughter, Juliet, she didn't quite know what to make of it. Juliet had been studying obsessively for some months. It was all very impressive. She had a very specific timetable that was never neglected. She woke up at 5.30 a.m. to get two hours' study in before school. She had no other interests and didn't socialise – all she seemed to do was study. One day, when their car broke down, Juliet became inconsolable as she 'needed' to get home to study. Her timetable was disrupted and Juliet couldn't handle it. It turned out that Juliet had tipped into an emotional prison, where she felt compelled to tap her fingers, eat certain foods, repeat certain phrases and study incessantly. Her mind was completely overwrought, and she needed to confront her excessive need for control.

• • •

Fear of success

Some young people develop a fear of failure because they suffer from 'imposter syndrome' – the debilitating fear that their achievements are undeserved, they are not as good as others and won't be able to live up to expectations. Often the individual feels that they simply aren't competent enough – they overestimate other people's abilities and underestimate their own. The young person might misinterpret their feelings of excitement as nervousness or anxiety and feel triggered by any sort of expectation or excitement about them. They might also be shy and dislike the inevitable attention that success will bring, so they might simply come to realise that a different life, perhaps a simpler, less competitive life, could bring more contentment. It is only self-awareness that will help the individual understand whether or not this is appropriate.

• • •

What parents can do

Although rigid thinking can be very impairing, there is treatment available that can significantly reduce symptoms and make them manageable. Sadly many young people cling to their obsessions and therefore are unwilling to recover. Mental rigidity can be treated by a range of treatments, such as medication, cognitive behavioural therapy, and/or exposure and response prevention (ERP). ERP involves slowly and gradually exposing the individual to the very thing that makes them anxious while providing them with healthy skills to cope with their anxiety and not allowing them to engage in the rituals that they would normally use in this context.

A successful form of treatment for obsessive thoughts and rigid thinking is a structured approach to exposure therapy, involving:

- learning coping skills

- increasing distress tolerance

- incremental exposure to the trigger.

The grand plan is that, over time, the person begins to experience less anxiety and is able to cope better. Also, the young person has learnt self-awareness and a more rational analysis of what is 'worth' worrying about versus what their brain has decided to fixate on.

Parents need to have boundaries of steel if their teen is prone to rigid thinking. Otherwise, the intensity of the teenager's emotion will lead to the parent folding every single time. It is more valuable if the parent learns to insist on a tiny bit of progress every single time the issue is raised and acknowledges the reality of any given situation, no matter how small, rather than colluding with the teen on their insistence that they 'must' do whatever maladaptive behaviour they tend to engage in.

· · ·

Takeaways

- Many of the great achievers in this world had rigid thoughts and achieved great success.

- Flexible thinking is healthier than rigid thinking.

- A professional evaluation can be helpful.

- Some people show traits without having the full disorder.

- Determination and intensity can slip into perseveration.

- Intensity can often be rooted in a need for control.

- Graded exposure can be valuable.

- Parents need to have boundaries of steel.

PART IV

THE RECKONING:
COMING TO TERMS
WITH OURSELVES AND
OUR BODIES

CHAPTER 10
BODY ISSUES: SELF-LOATHING AND DISORDERED EATING

'and i said to my body. softly. "i want to be your
friend."
it took a long breath and replied "i have been
waiting my whole life for this."'

— NAYYIRAH WAHEED

HAVING A POSITIVE RELATIONSHIP with your body is one of
the most difficult challenges for some adolescents (and indeed
adults). Yet being comfortable in our own skin brings a depth
to our sense of wellbeing that is hard to match, so this is a
challenge that is well worth tackling. If we can teach our kids

to appreciate their bodies and to think and speak about their bodies with kindness and affection, we are liberating them from unimaginable levels of inner pain and distress. Sadly, many teenagers utterly despise their bodies and are a very long way from being kind or affectionate towards them.

In my work, I have long noticed that teenage girls (and their mothers) are more likely to be critical of their bodies than males. In fact, until quite recently, it seemed that the vast majority of teenage boys were mostly unconscious of their looks, as long as they belonged in the wide band of people who could be described as reasonable looking. Of course, extensive ad campaigns that sought to fully capture the teenage market have driven a coach and horses through this liberating unconsciousness that boys had. Nowadays, boys are following the girls into obsessive vanity and mirror-checking. The problem is that although all this vanity might improve our looks – just compare school photos from 30 years ago and today: the teenagers today are much more polished and stylish – this improvement comes at a cost. Vanity might make us look better, but it doesn't improve our relationship with our bodies. In fact, vanity nurtures anxiety, seriously hinders self-acceptance and can lead to self-hatred.

Many teenagers, especially teenage girls, feel a sense of panic when they go through puberty. Their bodies are changing rapidly, and other people are suddenly noticing the changes and projecting upon them a sexualised nature that the teens may not yet be ready to accept. Boys and men may look at them in a sexualised manner and believe that these girls are fully sexualised, but for many girls, their bodies are developing faster than their minds, so it is a false projection. This can lead to a lack of control and even chaos. 'Maturity fear' can happen when a child has been propelled into an adult persona before they are ready for it. Girls need a bra, they get their period, and along with all this comes the male gaze and its intrusive assessment and evaluation of their bodies, which can feel very disturbing. The figure-hugging dress for the disco can induce panic, even though everyone else seems fine with it. The message from the world is that teenage girls need to look beautiful and sexy – but not too sexy, just sexy enough. This is complicated and overwhelming. Added to this, teenage girls often perceive a silent demand from the world that they should be small and cute. No longer do many people care whether they are brave or adventurous or good at scoring goals – now there is an intense focus on whether they are cute enough. It is little wonder that teenagers crumble under all this pressure.

Boys have their own pressures to deal with as they often wonder how they can possibly grow up to be a man. Many boys don't feel sufficiently masculine and worry that they will reveal their weakness to the world. Gender-nonconforming boys often have a very difficult time during adolescence as they might feel that they are failing at being male. Many more boys are becoming just like the girls: self-critical of themselves and their bodies.

Poor body image is horrible to live with, but it can also have dangerous consequences and lead to devastating conditions such as eating disorders or body dysmorphic disorder. The initial stages of these serious mental illnesses can begin in a very benign manner. If you think your teenager is falling into disordered eating patterns or perhaps body dysmorphic disorder, it is recommended that you seek professional help, as the most effective interventions occur in the early stages of the condition.

Parenting strategy: Lean in to your teen's online influences

Good self-esteem comes from doing what you love, not from looking at yourself in the mirror. Parents could do worse than limit the time their teenagers spend looking in the mirror. Parents should also limit teenagers' access to Instagram and other vanity-inducing sites. Subliminal messages sneak into our subconscious without anybody noticing. Social media bombards children from a very young age to be conscious of their 'brand'. Parents already limit the amount of junk food their kids consume, and it is also the parents' responsibility to consider how much online content their kids consume. Realistically, the only way parents can do this is by getting buy-in from the teenager and discussing what they like online. It can also help to find content that is interesting to your teen and makes the point for you – so TikTok clips that explain the corrosive nature of vanity or YouTube videos that explore the dangers of body-beautiful sites and the false reality of photoshopping could be helpful to your teen.

• • •

A sense of control

We all need to feel a certain sense of control in our lives. Teenagers who have sufficient choice, freedom and autonomy typically feel motivated and are active participants in life. It's important to note that it's the perception of control that influences motivation. When a teen feels they have no control, they can respond in a number of complicated ways.

Children often assert their need for autonomy by exercising control over what goes into their body (eating) and when it comes out (going to the toilet), as this is the last frontier of control. Consequently, issues with eating and constipation are often viewed as a bid for control by the child or the teen. If your teenager has issues in these areas, it could be valuable to ascertain if they feel a sense of autonomy and how they could feel more empowered in their life.

• • •

The critical inner voice

Many people who have body issues often have a critical inner voice that is vindictive and bullying. This inner voice is often unknowingly revealed by the way the teen speaks about other people – if your teen is very critical of other people, they are probably even more critical of themselves. If they are harsh and unforgiving, then you can take it as given that they are a lot more brutal and unforgiving in the privacy of their own mind. Taming the harsh inner critic can take some years, but it can be done. Many teens – but certainly not all – have learnt to be self-critical from their parents. We parents often see our children as extensions of ourselves, so when we see them fail, we can be as critical of them as we would be of ourselves. Yet our children are not extensions of ourselves, and regular criticism seldom achieves the desired effect. If parents can move away from the critical persona and instead demonstrate self-compassion, self-acceptance and a curiosity about their inner selves, it might help their teenagers more effectively than costly therapy.

> **Parenting strategy: Watch your self-talk**
>
> To soften our inner voice, we need to learn to watch our self-talk. We need to teach our kids to speak to themselves as they would speak to their best friend, or their dog, or their granny. Viewing negative self-talk as the beginning of self-harming behaviour can be valuable. More than anything, try to model gentle and forgiving self-talk.

• • •

Body dysmorphic disorder

Body dysmorphic disorder (BDD) is a disorder that causes an individual to have a distorted perspective on how they look and results in them spending an inordinate amount of time worrying about this perceived defect. BDD can be focused on any aspect of the face or body. It does not mean that the person is vain or self-obsessed. Rather, it suggests that the person is anxious, discontent, prone to self-loathing and has channelled all this distress into one thing.

Symptoms of BDD include:

- constantly comparing their looks to other people's
- spending a lot of time in front of the mirror
- avoiding mirrors altogether
- spending a lot of time concealing what they believe to be a defect

- becoming distressed by a particular area of the body (or the face)

- feeling anxious when around other people

- avoiding social situations

- feeling anxious that they will be seen to be vain or self-obsessed

- seeking medical treatment, such as cosmetic surgery, for the perceived defect

- dieting and/or exercising excessively.

In many ways, BDD is similar to ruminative OCD; for example, the repetition of compulsive behaviours is often evident in individuals suffering from either disorder. Individuals with BDD judge themselves primarily on their looks, which typically leads them to constantly worry about their appearance and develop distorted views about their perceived flaws.

BDD is a cruel and debilitating condition that requires a lot of effort to overcome. Perhaps your teenager is fixated on their nose, breasts or body hair? It can be exhausting and very irritating for parents to constantly hear the refrain 'I hate my nose.' It needs a wide range of responses from parents, including distraction, sympathy, humour, compassion and direct challenges.

• • •

Eating disorders

Eating disorders come in many guises and can be very difficult to detect. Many of us know about anorexia and bulimia, but less is known about orthorexia or, other specified feeding or eating disorder (OSFED; see below). There can be a deep sense of shame with eating disorders, and the corresponding secrecy makes it very difficult to unearth. Whether they binge and put on lots of weight or whether they are bulimic and binge and purge through vomiting or laxatives is immaterial; the drive to eat manically feels like a horribly impure, rotten part of their personality that must remain a secret. Although anorexics typically don't eat, and many sufferers report an intoxicating high that goes with this, they can often feel a shameful level of hatred for themselves and for any tiny desire to eat that emerges from their starved mind. There can also be an intoxicating high associated with fasting and purging, and many have reported that this can feel addictive.

· · ·

Anorexia nervosa

There can be a perceived hierarchy among sufferers, where anorexia is often considered the 'purest and best', while bulimia is considered a less impressive disorder. This hierarchy is shame-based, and those who don't have anorexia but have some less visible eating disorder such as bulimia or OSFED can feel utterly mortified about what they view as their dirty little secret. Secrecy is an integral part of eating disorders, as we'll see below – perhaps because the individual knows on an instinctive level that their thinking has gone seriously awry and that if anyone found out how consumed they were by food and body issues, they would be horrified. At the same time, even though those with anorexia are also secretive, they can also feel superior to others. Narcissism is often rooted in shame, so behind that show of omnipotence is usually an insecure and vulnerable person clinging on to their eating disorder as a coping mechanism to help them handle their more difficult feelings of inadequacy and shame.

Eating disorders come in slyly through the back door when nobody is watching. Perhaps your child had some puppy fat as they went through puberty and then went on a diet, felt fabulous when they lost weight – and then they were gripped? Or perhaps they were always conscious of their eating habits and liked being the thinnest girl? Maybe they were in a competitive friendship and what started as a game subtly turned into an obsession? Rigid thinking, perfectionism and the need for control often characterise anorexic thinking, and it can be more helpful for parents to focus on these issues than on the food itself.

The dieter can feel great about their ability to eat in a controlled manner and then, bang, they have fallen into the clutches of obsessive-compulsive behaviour and no longer feel any control over their mind or their behaviour. Parents suffer tremendously in this sphere and quite understandably feel that their teen has almost become possessed by a demon spirit.

The sooner we can intervene in an eating disorder, the more easily we can alleviate the condition. The teenager might have been quite loud and proud when they first announced that they were becoming vegetarian, and then they might have moved to veganism, and then less loudly decided to forgo all wheat-based food. Just as the mind registers that it is going insane with regard to eating, a flawed and disturbed instinct is awakened that teaches the compulsive dieter that they need to pretend that they are eating way more than they really are. They know that if anybody knew what was going on in their mind or their behaviour, they would be shocked and would interfere. For this reason, parents are often astonished when they find out that the fairly random diet that began way back when their daughter was 13 ended up being the beginning of a frightening eating disorder that only came to light when the child turned 16.

• • •

Orthorexia

The term 'orthorexia' was coined in 1998, and it means an obsession with healthy eating. Eating disorders often manifest in OCD-like symptoms, particularly with orthorexia. Although orthorexia is not a formal diagnosis, I have worked with so many teenagers who seem to show orthorexic symptoms that it feels important that parents learn about it so that they can recognise whether this is an issue for their teen.

Symptoms of orthorexia can include:

- compulsive checking of ingredients lists and nutritional labels on food

- cutting out an increasing number of food groups (e.g. all sugar, all carbs, all dairy, all meat, all animal products)

- an inability to eat anything but a narrow group of foods that are deemed 'healthy' or 'pure'

- an unusual interest in the 'healthiness' of what others are eating

- spending hours and hours every day thinking about food, exercising, practising yoga, Pilates, jogging and other 'purifying' pursuits

- experiencing deep distress when 'safe' or 'healthy' foods aren't available.

It can feel almost impossible to confront these individuals about their unhealthy obsession with food as they are often far more informed than anybody else. Orthorexics often obsessively follow 'healthy lifestyle' blogs on social media platforms. They can be sanctimonious, and many people feel slightly ashamed of their gluttony when in the company of the orthorexic.

The problem is that their perfection is completely joyless, their level of intensity is extreme, and they are experiencing considerable inner turmoil. It feels impossible to question the orthorexic's food habits or exercise habits. Doing so generally leads to futile arguments during which the orthorexic outsmarts the worried family member.

Lara, 16, was sent to me for counselling when her mother, Annie, discovered a file on Lara's laptop that diligently counted every single spoonful of food she ate – the spreadsheet of numbers seemed to go on for miles. This made Annie realise something serious was going on in Lara's mind. 'I knew she was always intense about food,' said Annie, 'and I worried about her weird behaviour around food, but it turned out to be a much bigger deal than I could have ever imagined.'

Body image concerns are often but not always present in the orthorexic – they are usually more driven by health or purity. They want to be perfect. Similar characters from previous generations might have become religious zealots – today's Matt Talbot lives on Instagram and is obsessed with pure food.

Parenting strategy: Focus on the need for joy and flexible thinking

Parents can focus on the value of flexible thinking and the need for happiness and joy in their bid to help this teenager. Speaking about food or body image is often a no-go area. The people who are prone to manifesting these symptoms are usually quite rigid in their thinking and have a sense of joylessness that can easily lead to despair and anxiety. If the parent can bring some gentle softness into the teen's life, especially in other distracting areas, it can really help loosen their tight grip on food.

• • •

OSFED

People who don't meet the full criteria for anorexia, bulimia or binge-eating disorder are often categorised under 'other specified feeding or eating disorder'. They typically have clinically significant symptoms and experience serious distress in their relationship with food. For example, they might have atypical anorexia nervosa, with all the behaviour of the anorexic but without the extreme weight loss, or they might swing wildly between anorexic symptoms, binge-eating symptoms and bulimic behaviour. Meanwhile, their weight might seem stable, and nobody in the household might even be aware that anything unusual is taking place. It can be unfathomably difficult for parents to figure out what's going on – the rigidity around food or exercise is probably the biggest red flag. If your teenager has an incomprehensible meltdown over food, it might be time to watch for other signs or to at least begin some conversations with them about their attitudes to food.

A version of OFSED is present among (mostly) boys who become very focused on developing their muscles and bulking up. They can begin to take supplements and compulsively exercise. Just like the orthorexic, it can be difficult to question their approach as they will often have memorised vast swathes of information about proteins and carbohydrates that can entirely derail the conversation. Speaking to a professional can often have more impact as it can be very difficult for the parent alone to scale the defensive wall the teenager has already erected.

SARAH, 18

Sarah's extraordinary rigidity around food was noted by her parents, but her seemingly normal weight suggested that all was well and that she was healthy enough, despite all the weirdness. None of this was true. Since the age of 12, Sarah had veered in and out of anorexia, bulimia, binge-eating and orthorexia. She was ravaged by her obsession with food. She ran obsessively for many miles every day, describing the experience as 'running ferociously fast, driven by the terror that [she] might put on weight'. Sarah was remarkably good in school, remarkable because she spent so many hours of the day thinking obsessively about food; what she should or shouldn't eat; what she had already eaten; how disgusting her body was; what was really in that cup of soup that she had been forced to eat three weeks ago; and when she could dispose of the plastic bags of vomit that had accumulated in the bottom of her wardrobe.

Sarah was outwardly very successful. She had friends, she made good academic progress and she looked well. The problem was that she had fits of rage especially if anybody tried to speak about her eating issues, she was also prone to anxiety attacks and had recurring episodes of self-harm.

When she first attended her local doctor for her anxiety, she initially felt gleeful that he didn't detect anything about her eating issues – even though her mother had called ahead and warned him about them – and then she felt a suffocating rage at herself for being so fat that the doctor didn't realise what was wrong.

Sarah engaged in a plethora of silent competitions with her equally food-obsessed and high-achieving friends in school. They had a habit of running their hands over each other's backs to check how bony their spines were as an evaluation of who was the skinniest of them all. They were all underweight and pretended to eat in front of each other and used various systems to purge the contents of their stomachs immediately afterwards.

Sarah viewed me as a fat fool – just as she viewed most people – and we took some time to establish any connection at all. She was ostensibly coming to me for her anxiety attacks, but we made little progress, perhaps because she hadn't yet divulged any of her body image issues or her disordered patterns of eating. Then one day, Sarah arrived in my office looking unusually distressed. I gently enquired about this, and the whole sad secret came tumbling out. She had binged all night and was feeling too sick to put up any defences. She had been trying to secretly get rid of the mice in her bedroom that had arrived as a result of her hoarding secret stashes of food, but the mice had returned, and she felt defeated by them. Sarah was simply worn out from years and years of overthinking and mental anguish.

The road to recovery was very long and very gentle. We took the emphasis off food and put it on rigid thinking, the pain of shame, the need for control and the root cause of her perfectionism and control. This worked for Sarah as she read up on the psychology behind these issues. Sarah was a good girl in every single sense of the word, and she did her therapeutic homework assiduously. She spent time building her self-awareness around perfectionism; she repeated her positive affirmations daily; she expanded her world beyond food counting; and she tried to re-engage with joy – this was the hardest task for her.

Finally, after a long time working together, Sarah was ready to tell her parents and her boyfriend all about the long and horrible mental illness she had been silently suffering from since she was 12 years old. None of them had suspected anything. However, for Sarah, the shame and perfectionism were reduced, and little green buds of self-acceptance had sprouted. Sarah even managed to crack a few jokes. We had come to a place of reasonable contentment, and we went our separate ways.

• • •

Bulimia nervosa

Bulimia nervosa is characterised by episodes of binge-eating followed by compensatory behaviour, such as vomiting or 'purging' or the abuse of diuretics or laxatives. Bulimic teenagers may feel a lack of control over their behaviour. Deep down, they know they have a problem yet are filled with fear as they cannot stop bingeing and then compulsively engaging in purging behaviour to avoid weight gain, so feelings of shame alternate with relief.

Bulimia can be an indescribably difficult condition for parents to detect as, unlike those with binge-eating disorder or anorexia, people with bulimia are often able to maintain a normal weight for their age (they may also be overweight or even obese). But they are often just as consumed with losing weight as the anorexic and equally filled with self-loathing about their body. The bingeing and purging cycle is compulsive, intensely secretive and filled with shame. As with other eating disorders, teenagers with bulimia often have coexisting psychological illnesses, such as depression or anxiety.

• • •

Binge-eating disorder

Binge-eating disorder is a very common eating disorder, but it is not often spoken about in relation to mental health and there is notably less sympathy for or understanding of this condition than there is for anorexia or bulimia. Binge-eating disorder involves repeated consumption of large amounts of food in a short amount of time. The binge typically involves eating more rapidly than normal, eating until uncomfortably full, eating large amounts of food when not hungry, and feeling disgusted or depressed afterwards. Just like the anorexic feels that they need to be secretive about their lack of eating, the binge-eater feels a compulsive need to hide their food intake. They may secretly remove the packaging from the house and put it in far-off bins.

Teenagers who compulsively overeat isolate themselves from public gatherings such as school because of their embarrassment and depression over their weight. Their compulsive secrecy about their habit sometimes means that nobody knows about their eating and the shame prevents them from seeking help.

Developmental milestone: Come to terms with the maturing body

Parents can help teenagers who are having difficulty coming to terms with their maturing bodies by being sensitive to the situation. They might offer online content, books or films that explore the idea of self-acceptance – the book *Wonder* by R.J. Palacio or the film *Little Miss Sunshine* might suit your teen.

Parents might also need to manage weight gain sensitively by bringing in effective household habits rather than making comments about sudden weight gain. For example, banning the consumption of food in bedrooms (as this is where secret eating generally takes place) and insisting that all food should only be eaten in the kitchen or dining room can be much more effective and less damaging.

As mentioned, some boys (and girls) can become fixated on developing muscle mass, and this can become a major challenge in the teen's life. Again, the rigidity of the individual's mindset is the clearest indicator of whether this is becoming an unhealthy obsession.

• • •

Seeking professional support

It is recommended that parents seek professional support
as soon as they believe that their teen is showing signs of
disordered eating because:

- Eating disorders are often noticed by loved ones quite late into
  the illness.

- This mental health condition can be very dangerous.

- Early intervention can save a person from years of mental pain.

Alongside therapeutic care, parents can help their teen by, first
of all, taking a step back and trying to figure out what was
going on for the child in the first place that led them to attack
their body in this manner. Was she lonely? Did he feel out of
control? Is she a perfectionist? If you, the parent, have some sort
of working theory of how and why the problem first began, you
can begin to help. If you have no idea why your child became
so filled with self-loathing, it can be more effective for you to
attend therapy as you could easily become as obsessed with their
illness as your teen is about their body or food.

If you also have an unhealthy relationship with food, now
is the time to address this with a therapist. Sometimes a
parent might guiltily wonder whether their low-level eating
disorder, which has been present for 30-odd years but generally
manageable (and yet unhealthy), is cause for concern. Frankly,
yes, it probably is. Anorexia and other eating disorders began
to emerge from the 1970s onwards, so we are one of the first

generations of parents where eating disorders were rampant while we were growing up, and many mothers have brought their continued unhealthy relationship with food into family life. A rigidity about food, an excessive fear of gaining weight or an over-the-top focus on food being the source of all good and evil can impact children's understanding of food. If this is the case, it is a significant gift for your child if you are willing to address these concerns.

• • •

What parents can do

Get therapeutic help

Teenagers and parents should access professional support. This is a very difficult condition that can have higher mortality and relapse rates than most. Your teenager may insist that they have everything under control and might be very resistant to therapy. It can be helpful if the therapy is framed in a manner that will help your teenager with their anxiety or rage rather than focusing on their eating disorder.

Lean in

This can be a very isolating illness. Try to get to know this frightening part of your teen's psyche, but be sensitive to the risk of enabling and collusion (see Chapter 16).

Role-modelling

Parents need to role model a forgiving approach to their bodies and lives in general. If you have spent decades harshly judging your own or other people's flaws, you will have a lot of work to do in convincing your child that you are either self-accepting or other-accepting. This can be a long and difficult row-back for many parents, but it is certainly worth the effort.

Monitor and limit social media content

Teenagers are swamped with images of heavily photoshopped bodies and faces these days. They inevitably compare themselves with these fake images, which feeds into further scrutiny, and none of it is healthy. Placing time limits on certain sites can be helpful for younger teenagers, while parents of older teenagers may send their kids content about how destructive Instagram, TikTok and other platforms can be to our sense of wellbeing.

Help your teenager reduce the time they spend looking at the mirror

Have a rational discussion with your teenager about the time they spend in front of the mirror and how it mostly exacerbates the problem. Begin with a challenge they can easily agree to, such as never spending more than three hours a day in front of the mirror. Then begin asking your teenager how much time they actually spend in front of the mirror. Suggest that they limit each looking-in-the-mirror session to 60 seconds. Ask them to check the time when they begin looking at the mirror and again when they stop. They will inevitably forget to do this as looking in the mirror is escapism into another world. But asking them about this brings about more self-awareness about the impact and the experience of looking in the mirror.

Help your teenager to begin cultivating their sense of style

Discuss their favourite style models. It can be fun to make an online or paper collage of their favourite styles or to help them put some creativity into their make-up. The approach is more important than the end result; perfection is the enemy and fun is the goal.

Learn about the dangers of perfectionism

Body issues and food issues can be rooted in anxious perfectionism, so parents need to help their child to learn to laugh at mistakes. There might be many slammed doors and rolled eyes, but you're sowing seeds. The message will one day get through.

Teach them about learning how to fail

Individuals with eating disorders and others with body issues and food issues are often consumed by a quest for flawlessness and, on a developmental level, they need to learn how to fail. They will utterly hate this task, but it might be the very issue that will lead to breakthroughs in their disordered eating.

Buy some treats that encourage your teenager to indulge their body

This might be a hair appointment or a trip to the nail salon – something different and indulgent that makes your teenager feel good about themselves can take the focus off the main issue.

Tackle their need to control by expanding their world

These teenagers often seek to live in a very controlled and orderly environment – indeed, they are often described as control freaks. It is valuable if parents help to loosen this rigid grip on life by expanding their world beyond this narrow path. This entails bringing complexity into the equation: they might need to accept that they will be nervous at a new club but they still have to attend; they might need to learn that it is essential that they leave their comfort zone if they are to expand their worldview. You, the parent, might need to allow them to attend parties and discos and other teenage gatherings to continue this expansion from a rigid life into real life.

Find some joy in life

The mindset of the teenager with food and/or body issues is often very joyless, and the only humour they engage in is spiteful wit and/or gallows humour. Bringing this teenager to a comedian or a funny film in the cinema can lead them to reconnect with spontaneous fun.

Help them appreciate what their body can do

It can sometimes be helpful for a young person who is in the grip of an eating disorder to begin to become proud of what their body can achieve rather than always focusing on what it looks like. This pride might be centred on learning a skill, such as sailing, horse riding or abseiling. The idea is for the young person to feel more connected with their body and to develop a sense of pride in their physical achievements.

• • •

Takeaways

- Disconnection with the body and alienation from the body can emerge during puberty – this can be helped with a focus on what the body can do rather than how it looks.

- Body issues can often arise out of the panic that happens when the individual goes through puberty and feels like their maturing body is out of control.

- Parents can help build awareness in their child about their need for control and how it feels when they lose control.

- Perfectionism can be a driver for many body image concerns.

- Role-modelling is a vital way to undo the feelings of self-loathing that can accompany the teenager who is obsessed with their body.

- A sense of joy is often missing in the lives of teenagers with eating disorders. Parents can help with this by increasing the sense of joy, fun and pleasure for its own sake in the household.

CHAPTER 11

SEX MATTERS

'Sexuality is one of the ways that we become
enlightened, actually, because it leads us to
self-knowledge.'

— ALICE WALKER

THE YEARS BETWEEN 10 and 20 are typically when the human
moves from being pre-sexual to being sexual, and society
hasn't really come to grips with this yet. It is natural for
teenagers to become more private as their sexual side begins
to develop, and this helps with the larger process of becoming
a mature adult who is independent from their parents. But it
means that speaking to our teenagers about sex is difficult. It's
important to note that the 'sex talk' should not be confined to
one talk; it should be a series of talks throughout childhood,

growing in complexity from childhood to adulthood. When the kids are younger, we can buy the books and show them the content, but as they grow older, eyes are rolled and the door is often very firmly shut. And yet it's our job to make sure that they understand sex and mutual enjoyment, intimacy and consent, and that, while other aspects of growing up might be practised at younger ages, sexual intimacy is an aspect of adult relationships that can go awry if we try it too soon. But how to properly communicate this to teens, who are filled with hormones, longing and romance, is a very hard nut to crack.

• • •

Sexual awakenings

Early adolescence is often reasonably innocent, but sometimes external influences can lead children into dark places. Many teenagers try to appear older than their years. This is all practice for future adulthood, but these practice sessions can often be deceptive for others as the teenager is often not as sophisticated as they appear to be. Leah self-referred herself to me when she was 19 years old. She felt disconnected from her body and worried that she might be 'frigid'. After we had established a therapeutic alliance, Leah told me all about her first boyfriend, Michael, whom she met when she was 14. Michael was 18 at the time, in Sixth Year, and he thought Leah was gorgeous. Leah also fancied Michael, and they became girlfriend and boyfriend. But Leah was way out of her depth. Michael drank and took drugs. He had a car. He expected sex. Leah had never even smoked a cigarette before she met Michael and enjoyed the sophistication of house parties where there were drink and drugs. She pretended to Michael that she had

had sex loads of times before. The first time they did it, in a friend's house at a party, was very painful for Leah. She bled on the sheets. Michael didn't notice as he was quite drunk at the time. Leah felt awful. She was ashamed of the blood and bundled the sheet into a cupboard. She thought the most important thing was to keep her prior virginity a secret. So began a false intimacy between Leah and Michael. Leah would pretend to have soaring orgasms even though she had never climaxed in her life. She watched porn to get tips on how to look best during sex. Michael thought that Leah was unusually mature – her body was certainly mature, so he assumed her mind was as mature as everything else. Leah stayed with Michael for two years. Her parents thought he seemed like a very nice solid boy, although they worried that he was a bit old for her. Meanwhile, Leah became completely disconnected from her body and her self – she exuded sophistication but never found the time or space to get to know her sexual self on her own terms and so lost the opportunity for a sexual awakening. It was some years before she reconnected with her body and herself.

Developmental milestone: Coming to terms with the sexual self

Although it's not the role of parents to interfere in their teen's sexual awakening, it is the role of parents to make sure that their teenager isn't out of their depth. Parents can take a healthy interest in what's going on, ask questions and make points about suitability. Parents can also relate stories from their own adolescence, identifying relevant issues and highlighting how easy it is to lose our way. This is a task of adolescence that can be difficult for parents to help with, but with some sensitivity and a well-placed comment here or there, you might be able to help your teen come to terms with their developing sexuality.

• • •

Consent, boundaries and saying 'No'

Both girls and boys need to be taught the concept of consent during their teenage years, even if it feels like the only person your teen can say 'No' to is yourself, the parent. Yet we must persist because teaching your teen how to have boundaries and say 'No' is one of the most important lessons we can impart.

Ideally, parents begin with a conversation about boundaries and consent in all sorts of contexts that aren't necessarily related to sex and can be applied everywhere. Some children might need to learn to practise on easy ground, such as saying 'No' to their parents. The wise parent will provide these more diffident children with the opportunity to say 'No' and will acquiesce when the 'No' is finally said. For example, you might explain to your kid that being able to say 'No' is very important and that you plan to give them opportunities to say 'No' so they can practise at home before bringing it to the world. Then you might let them – or even encourage them – to say 'No' to a chore they don't want to do. This doesn't mean they never have to do the chore again; encouraging them to develop their ability to say 'No' means that you respect that they might sometimes say 'No' to something you want them to do and they might need you to allow this to happen. This takes skill, and parents should be careful not to roll over any clumsy attempts by gentle teenagers who are learning to say 'No'.

For those who missed the memo, FRIES is an acronym that attempts to highlight the nuances related to sexual consent:

FRIES

F: Freely given
R: Reversible
I: Informed
E: Enthusiastic
S: Specific

This acronym is handy as a parent can have fun with each item — for example, wondering aloud exactly how enthusiastic we have to be to cross the line into consent.

A popular animated blog written by a blogger called Emmeline May explained sexual consent as similar to asking for a cup of tea.[34] This animation made clear that agreement is not unequivocal; you might say 'yes' to a cup of tea and then change your mind. It's also true that we can't make decisions when we're unconscious; nor does wanting a cup of tea (or sex) one day automatically equate to wanting it at any other time. But there are limits to the analogy. What if a drunk person insists they want a cup of tea but they don't actually have the capacity to make that decision? Then there is the issue of conditional consent, where a person might consent to sex with a condom but not without; and of course, we could extend the analogy to wanting tea with milk but not without. Content like this is great conversation fodder for parents and teens – not to agree but to discuss without feeling it's too close to the bone.

Sadly, despite all the talk about consent, despite all the policies around sex education, there still remains a steady trickle of distressed teenagers who report sexual assault and significant levels of unwanted sexual attention. In my work, I often hear about girls being subjected to porn on the school bus on the way to school. Although it's a generalisation, it is notable that it is the boys who share the porn freely and show each other different clips while the girls look away or show disgust or laugh along with the boys. Boys sending dick pics to girls in school has become a widely accepted practice. Girls often reciprocate with pictures of their own. Girls and boys who have never even had a first kiss are sending each other ever more explicit recordings of themselves in sexual poses. Some teens become hypersexualised by their consumption of porn and can feel a heavy weight of expectation to act like a porn star.

MADDY, 17

When Maddy was 13, the boys in her class added her to a WhatsApp group and described in detail what they would do to her, her sister and her mother. They regularly added pornographic pictures to the WhatsApp group chat. Maddy was the only girl in a group chat of 60 boys. She didn't know what to do. She didn't know who to tell. She thought it might make it worse if she left or commented or did anything. So she kept quiet, did nothing and compulsively checked the horrible group chat. This went on for months.

Some of the boys developed an unhealthy interest in Maddy. They sent her dick pics and made sure they were in her company when she received them so they could watch her reaction. They touched her body and laughed when she brushed their hands away.

One day, the school bus was delayed and Maddy found herself in the middle of a group of boys who began groping her. It was very frightening as she realised she was in the middle of a circle and nobody could see what was happening. The other buses had gone, and everybody else was looking away. The boys in the circle continued to grab her violently. They hurt her. She screamed. Maddy felt completely humiliated as one of the bigger boys pushed her to the ground and pulled at her clothes.

Eventually, the school bus arrived and the sexual assault stopped. Everyone acted as if nothing had happened, and Maddy, in a state of shock, got on the bus home. So did the boys, sniggering and commenting.

Years went by before Maddy told anybody about what had happened to her. The sexual assault had left its mark on her, and she had become depressed and turned to self-harming behaviour. It took a great deal of therapeutic work for Maddy to realise that her sexual objectification had not helped her sexual awakening – rather, it had stunted this process and taught her that sex was something that other people got pleasure from. Maddy learnt to please herself first by learning how to masturbate. Eventually, years after she experienced the sexual attack, Maddy learnt that sex could be reciprocal, intimate, vulnerable and beautiful.

Hygiene and the developing body

Parents often feel panicked if their teenager develops an aversion to hygiene. 'I feel like tearing my hair our when I see my gorgeous kid, smelly, hair falling around his face, living in squalor in his dirty bedroom. Why won't he shower?' asked Maria, mother of 14-year-old Jason, who came to me hoping I could give her the secret information that might make her son clean up his act. I didn't have the information to give, though. Teenagers' lack of hygiene and their smelly bedrooms can be a source of major arguments in a household. This can be difficult to handle, as teenagers can feel quite content living in filth and might not believe that they smell. Their newly developed body has started to sweat, and hair is trapping the sweat in a way it never did before. Perhaps these teens are becoming acquainted with their bodies in an animalistic manner? Their bodies are emanating a new smell as they start to sweat regularly. Maybe they like to live in this new smell so as to become habituated to their maturing body? Some teenagers go in the other direction and almost obsessively groom themselves. Some seem to feel overwhelmed by their maturing body and prefer to ignore all aspects of their developing body. They haven't yet learnt to clean their body properly as it all feels too grown-up. They often don't like confronting their new body, so they try to avoid showers and baths.

One way or another, the teen is coming to terms with their maturing body and, thankfully, most teenagers grow beyond their dirty, smelly stage and become perfectly clean and groomed young adults. Until this day arrives, parents often have to contend with the fact that their teenager lives in what could only be described as a chronically dirty lair – and that's the way they like it. Parents can help with this by making sure there are specific times and days for cleaning – for example, every Saturday they clean their bedrooms. They know it's coming, so it can't be avoided.

• • •

Masturbation and a joyful approach to sex

If possible, parents should include information about masturbation in their sex talks with their kids. Masturbation can be a wonderful way for teenagers to figure out their bodies and learn how to enjoy their sexual selves. These days, sex can often be spoken about in a foreboding tone and there is little sense of joy involved, but it is helpful for teens to develop a healthy and loving relationship with their bodies before they engage in sexual activity with others. This can be an embarrassing time for everyone. Parents generally hope their children will grow up to have sexually satisfying relationships, but our natural sense of privacy often prevents us from having useful conversations with our children about how to go about this.

An added complexity is that with the advent of high-speed Wi-Fi and smartphones, pornography has become a significant factor in the development of a teenager's sexual self. Few parents know what to do when they believe their teenager is engaging in excessive masturbation: 'How much is too much?' they worry as their teen dashes off to the toilet during the Sunday roast dinner. As always, conversation makes a difference

and the odd well-worded comment that has been prepared
beforehand and is then landed into the conversation at the right
time can make a huge difference. For example, a mother could
say in passing to her daughter, 'It is better to teach yourself to
orgasm so that you can show others how to do it for you.' This
doesn't take long to say, and once said, it generally lands – even
if the teen rolls her eyes and stamps out the door in disgust.

• • •

How porn has changed

Porn has always been with us – pictures found on a cave wall in
Germany were dated to 35,000 BC, and pornographic sculptures
in Babylonia were estimated to be from 1800 BC.[35] From the mid-
to late twentieth century, porn magazines and videos were an
accepted rite of passage for most teenage boys, but then, from
the 1990s onwards, as the internet became more widespread, a
revolution happened in the porn industry that made porn today
unrecognisable from that of previous generations.

The decision by the porn industry to capitalise on children's
sexual awakenings by offering cartoon porn and video game
porn to young boys is arguably a reflection of the predatory
nature of the porn industry. These kids are often quite innocent
when they first begin watching porn but can be quickly led into
a darker world of sexual violence and pain before they really
understand what they are consuming.

The musician Billie Eilish has described how she used 'a lot of
porn' since she was 11 years old. Eilish was an advocate for porn
use and said that she initially thought it was 'really cool' to talk

about using porn. Some years later, Eilish has changed her mind and described how she feels her porn habit impacted her sexual experiences: 'The first few times I had sex, I was not saying "no" to things that were not good. It's because I thought that is what I was supposed to be attracted to.' Just like many others, Eilish's porn use escalated into only watching BDSM (bondage and discipline, dominance and submission, sadism and masochism): 'It got to the point that I couldn't watch anything else [...] unless it was violent, I didn't think it was attractive.'[36]

The word *hentai* ('hen-tye') is derived from the Japanese word for 'perverted' and is the label given to a genre of Japanese manga and anime that is characterised by overtly sexualised characters and sexually explicit images and plots. Over the last decade, hentai has become one of the most popular forms of pornography in the world. It is known for showing the gross mistreatment of women through horrific acts of bestiality and images of children having sex. The characters are completely malleable, as artists can make the characters look exactly the way they want. Every fetish can be fulfilled, no matter how bizarre or violent. Consumers can use any kind of abuse and tell themselves, 'No one is really getting hurt.' Cartoons can depict sex scenes that are too vile or violent to act out in real life. Because the films are animated, this has a disarming effect on the viewer. The consumer doesn't need to practise any compassion for the characters because they aren't real. It's 'just' art.

• • •

The Coolidge effect

A key element of testosterone is that it thrives on the new. The Coolidge effect is a biological phenomenon whereby males (both animals and humans) exhibit renewed sexual interest whenever a new female is introduced, even after sex with other sexual partners who continue to be available to them. The term derives from an old joke about US President Calvin Coolidge and his wife. They were taking tours around an experimental farm. When Mrs Coolidge saw a rooster in the chicken yard mating very frequently, she asked the attendant how often it happened and was told 'Dozens of times a day.' Mrs Coolidge said, 'Tell that to the President when he comes by.' The President was duly informed, and in response, he asked, 'Same hen every time?' The reply was no, that it was a different hen each time. Without missing a beat, the President replied, 'Tell that to Mrs Coolidge.'

Porn industry moguls know all about the Coolidge effect, and this is why they continuously offer new content on their free sites. Every click offers new and wondrous sexual acts and makes the moguls more money. To stay new, porn has become ever more illicit and weird. Teenagers who would be perfectly happy being able to simply view bare breasts are offered all sorts of hardcore content that they don't seek out. Heavy users need new content, hence *hentai*, cartoon porn and other digitally produced content are becoming more popular – the more novel and unusual, the more likely they will engage the porn user. In addition, the combination of the childishly familiar alongside the illicit could be attractive for young teenagers; this is a new issue that has not been fully researched.

An unexpected consequence of freely available hardcore porn is that teenage boys are experiencing sexual dysfunction in higher numbers than ever before. The number of Google searches for 'porn addiction' and 'death-grip syndrome' reveal how excessive male masturbation can lead to sexual dissatisfaction and sexual dysfunction. A 2016 study of 205 Canadian adolescents revealed that nearly half had erectile dysfunction problems.[37] Websites such as NoFap (https://nofap.com) have been created to help people to overcome porn overuse and compulsive sexual behaviour.

CONOR, 12

Conor was 11 years old when his friend Kevin first showed him some hardcore pornography on his phone. Conor felt disgusted but also compelled to search for more. Kevin's older brother was something of a connoisseur of hardcore pornography and had been exposed to this adult content from a very young age. Kevin became hypersexualised and spoke about sex constantly to his friends in school. The boys didn't quite know how to handle it. Some of them were sexually immature but wanted to keep up with their pals; others had some sexual awakenings but felt way out of their depth in the face of Kevin's brother's porn habit.

Conor's mother, Michelle, noticed that Conor had become excessively secretive about his phone and decided to do a spot-check on it. She was appalled by what she found. Videos containing bestiality, necrophilia, rape and mutilation were among Conor's more innocent football clips and Pokémon games. Michelle felt like she had been hit by a bus: What the hell was going on?

She decided to contact Kevin's parents, but they were unperturbed by it all. Kevin's parents reckoned that boys would be boys and that it was only screen stuff – nothing serious was happening. Michelle then spoke to Conor, and it turned out that Conor was pretty distressed by the content – he was in over his head and didn't know what to do. Michelle made a tough decision and took his phone off him, shut down all the devices in the house and decided to reduce technology in general in the household. Conor was very angry, but Michelle reckoned it was one of the best parenting decisions she had ever made.

• • •

Sexual orientation

Many parents believe that a liberal approach towards sexual orientation automatically frees their children to come out as gay, lesbian, bisexual or whatever. But this doesn't seem to be panning out all that well. Despite the Pride marches and the constant waving of rainbow flags, many young adolescents feel very conflicted about their sexuality. It remains unclear why this is.

Many of us thought that all we had to do was rid ourselves of the shackles of the Catholic Church and we would bounce exuberantly into a new era of wonderful sexual freedom. But this is not the case. Parents might feel sexually liberated, but adolescents tend to experience an intense need for privacy around their burgeoning sexuality. Some lucky families seem to have cultivated a healthy and open approach to sex, but many more are furtive and secretive. As a result, many teenagers seem to have difficulties in having pleasant sexual encounters, and many gay, lesbian and bisexual teenagers feel ashamed of their sexual orientation.

Shame is a toxic emotion that can lead to a whole range of destructive behaviours. Although we can't turn a switch and suddenly remove our sense of privacy around sex, we can ensure that we make a strong attempt to remove shame from our child's experiences. This takes courage from parents who might not want to speak about sex with their teenagers, but it is worth it.

Introducing your child to role models is very important for children who are questioning their sexuality. This might mean that you need to involve yourself in diverse cultures, watch films, read books, and immerse yourself in what might help your child before you dive in and recommend anything. It may also be important to give your child the opportunity to experiment without feeling that they need to describe their sexual preferences, so they might have girlfriends and boyfriends for some time before they label their sexual orientation – or you ask them about their preferences.

MICHAEL, 16

Michael was a gentle, creative boy who always felt different from the other boys. He had good friends and a gentle, pleasant childhood. When puberty struck, it hit hard. Suddenly, Michael had intense, overwhelming feelings for different boys in his school. He felt assaulted by the strength of his emotions and didn't know what to do with them. Michael's mother, Sasha, had often suspected that her youngest son was gay, and she had tried to gently lead him into some sort of acknowledgement of the situation. But Michael was intransigent. 'I'm not gay,' he said, 'And you need to stop asking me about this.'

Michael turned in on himself and went from being a self-contained and self accepting type to a secretive, shame-filled boy who blushed intensely whenever anyone spoke to him. Michael often felt like he had lost the power of speech as his overwhelming feelings so often rendered him speechless. He retired into his room and refused to come out. He had no friends. He didn't want to interact with anyone.

When Michael came into my clinic, I saw a shy, intense boy who seemed lost. Although the first few sessions were deeply awkward, we got to know each other through a shared love of music. That created the opportunity I needed to connect with this lonely teenager.

It turned out that Michael didn't want to be gay; he suffered from both internalised and externalised homophobia. Internalised homophobia was evident in his view of gay people. 'I don't like nightclubs and screaming queens and drag acts,' Michael explained to me. 'I just want to get married here in my locality, have some kids and have a normal life.' It took some time for us to unpack this as I believed that Michael could have a conventional life and still be gay, while Michael believed this was impossible. I used different films, music and novels to make my point; Michael argued that these were far from his home town. A turning point was when Michael's mother introduced him to some gay people who lived nearby, and he realised that being gay didn't have to involve going to nightclubs every night.

The externalised homophobia didn't help, however. Many of Michael's schoolmates were homophobic in their comments and their actions. Gay slurs were everywhere, even though all his pals believed themselves to be perfect allies. An interest in politics helped Michael along the way. He started to follow a local politician who was gay and who wanted to eliminate bullying in schools. Michael could see that this politician had suffered as Michael had, and he realised that many other gay men had experienced as much shame as he had. Michael became more politicised in his outlook, and this gave him a sense of purpose and meaning. He had started the long road towards self-acceptance, and by the time he was ready to go to university, he was finally ready to come out as gay.

What parents can do

Talking about sex is often awkward for parents and teenagers. Nonetheless, talk we must. For example, many men have learnt to view female bodies through a sexual lens, so some fathers can feel a sense of panic around their teenage daughters' developing sexuality. The father's response to their daughter's sexual body can be pretty irrational. A certain level of self-awareness is necessary to help rather than hinder their teen's sexual development.

Too many teens I work with have no idea about the impact of hormones. Many girls are profoundly impacted by their hormonal fluctuations in terms of energy, mood and libido. The sooner they learn to understand their bodies, the better. Some boys become overwhelmed by their sexual urges and could do with some parental guidance. Generally, but of course not always, it can be helpful if mothers can pass on their knowledge about their bodies to their daughters, while fathers can speak with their teenage boys about the impact of testosterone.

Over the course of childhood, parents need to be prepared to have a series of conversations with their child that clearly makes certain points about, for example, sex, periods, masturbation, pleasure, joy, love, porn, intimacy, vulnerability, consent, hormones and boundaries. Each talk can be short, but it's important that parents think about it beforehand and figure out what they want to say. It's also important to ask your teen if they have any questions and follow up with a book, a YouTube clip or a TikTok that further makes the point.

· · ·

Takeaways

- Premature sexual experiences can impede a sexual awakening.

- Teenagers who have never experienced their first kiss can feel like sexual connoisseurs when they are consuming online porn in the privacy of their own bedroom. This can lead them to view sex as transactional, and they may develop an aversion to intimacy.

- Boys and girls are experiencing sexual dysfunction as a result of porn use in a manner that has never been seen before.

- Porn is leading to violence in teenage sexual experiences.

- More girls are consuming porn than ever before, and this is shaping their approach to sex.

- Sexual orientation can take some time to develop, and adolescents need space to find their way through this.

- Role models and normalisation can be pivotal in helping a teenager accept their sexual orientation.

CHAPTER 12

IDENTITY EXPLORATION

'I am not what happened to me. I am what I
choose to become.'

– CARL JUNG

AS ADOLESCENCE PROGRESSES, the teenager develops a sense
of their personal identity so that they can become a fully
functioning adult. The plaster is ever so slowly pulled off as
the child moves from complete dependence on the parents to,
hopefully, complete independence from the parents. In many
ways, it can feel like the adolescent is ever so slowly dumping
the parent, a metaphorical death by a thousand cuts, and believe
it or not, this is developmentally natural!

As with all stages of development, each individual is progressing
at a different pace, so some teenagers are incredibly focused
on their identity while others don't pay much heed to it. As
children grow, so does their circle of influence. Right up until
puberty, children tend to be influenced by their parents; they

are easily impressed by their parents' jobs, political opinions, views on sports and music and whatever else. Then, at the beginning of adolescence, kids begin to tune their parents out, as if they are an annoying radio station. They need to do this so that they can allow other influences into their orbit. If they leave the radio blaring at your frequency, they will never find the bandwidth to discover themselves, so it is developmentally appropriate for them to flick you off and turn to their peers and other role models. One day, usually by the time they've hit their twenties, they'll flick you back on again to see if you have anything interesting to say.

• • •

Stages of development

Erik Erikson (1902–1994) was a German-American developmental psychologist and psychoanalyst most famous for coining the phrase 'identity crisis'. Erikson's mother, Karla Abrahamsen, conceived Erik out of wedlock and the identity of Erik's birth father remained unclear. When Erik was born, he was given the name Erik Salomonsen, but in 1905 Erik's mother married Theodor Homburger and told Erik that Theodor was his real father. The truth was revealed to Erik in childhood, and he remained bitter about this deception all his life. It comes as no surprise to budding psychologists that the development of identity was Erikson's greatest concern throughout his life. Erikson noted that his identity confusion was at times on 'the borderline between neurosis and adolescent psychosis'.[38] Not knowing his own father, he rejected his stepfather's name in adulthood and declared himself to be his own son with the name 'Erikson'.

Erik dropped out of school as a teenager and roamed around Germany and Italy as a wandering artist. He eventually realised that he would never become a full-time artist and returned home to become an art teacher. He worked well with children, and when he was 25, he was invited to tutor art in Vienna for children whose wealthy parents were undergoing psychoanalysis by Sigmund Freud's daughter, Anna Freud. She noticed Erikson's sensitivity to children, and encouraged him to study psychoanalysis. Erikson specialised in child analysis and underwent analysis with Anna Freud while simultaneously studying the Montessori method of education. His diploma from the Vienna Psychoanalytic Institute and his Montessori diploma were Erikson's only earned academic credentials for his life's work – yet he is now considered a leading psychologist of the 20th century. A salutary tale for parents who are tearing their hair out because of their child's lack of focus and a reminder that there is more to life than exams.

Today many mental health professionals, especially those who work with children, use Erikson's stages of psychosocial development as a way of understanding children's concerns. The general idea is that each individual works through each stage, right through adulthood until death, and it is up to the individual to resolve the challenges associated with each stage. If the challenges remain unresolved, the issue continues to reappear as unresolved conflict during crises in our adult life. According to Erikson, adolescents are mostly preoccupied with identity and role confusion and their significant relationships are with their peers and role models. The main existential questions of the adolescent, according to Erikson, are 'Who am I?' and 'Who can I be?'

Between the ages of 12 and roughly 20, we parents are mostly sharing platforms with our teen's best friends, with their crushes, with YouTube sensations and with social media influencers. It's a crowded field, and many parents feel outraged that their children refuse to take any more notice of them than they do of their very new bestie, whom they met last week. It can be some consolation for parents to learn that these teenagers are behaving exactly as they should – it is developmentally appropriate for teenagers to demote their parents. Frustrating and insulting, perhaps, but also developmentally appropriate.

● ● ●

A developing identity

It's very understandable for teens to have little sense of themselves; they have literally just discovered the greater depths of themselves and the world. They aren't sure who they are, what they like or how they might appear to others. As they feel so insecure about their sense of self, they can be very influenced by other people's identities.

Sometimes when we feel most unsure of ourselves, we project an air of certainty. Akin to a person drowning in quicksand who will grab on for dear life to any firm structure, these kids will wholeheartedly grab on to any identity that provides them with feelings of certainty. This can be very difficult for parents to watch as they can see their child grab hold of any random identity and proclaim it as their own. The more parents view this as the teen trying on an identity to see if it fits, the easier parents will experience the various identity crises. We adults need to be careful that we don't roll our eyes when we think the teen is being fake. They aren't being fake; what they are doing is checking to see if this identity could be suitable for them one day and this is exactly what they should be doing at this developmental stage. Each identity change should not be dismissed as a 'phase' as each 'try-on' has to feel like the real thing if they are to fully explore this identity. Complicated to watch and equally complicated to experience. For example, your teen might suddenly declare themselves to be an emo. They might radically change their appearance by dying their hair and wearing dramatic make-up. This is an important period. They are working through whether they like to be noticed; whether they revel in attention from strangers; whether they want to join a particular club. It isn't helpful for the teen to be undermined in this attempt to get to know themselves better.

• • •

Who am I and what can I be?

In developmental terms, adolescents are mostly concerned with how they appear to everyone else. Role confusion is an integral stage of this stage of development, and teens will experiment with their friends, with their activities and with their roles in life.

During this stage of development, teenagers seek their identity in their pastimes, occupations, gender roles, sexual orientation, politics, religion and other areas of interest. Teenagers are often trying to attempt to form a reconciliation between the person who they think they are, who they might one day be and what society expects from them. Their sense of self emerges from resolving these inner conflicts by forging meaning from past experiences and beginning to anticipate future experiences.

This can make every decision feel like a crossroads or a turning point in their life as they continually choose between society's expectations, their inner self and their ideal self. It is for this reason that many teenagers come to believe that *everything* is incredibly important and also become fixated upon their 'true self' and other intangible and subjective concepts.

Adolescents feel exercised by the need to establish and re-establish identities for themselves in a world that is filled with other challenges. At the very same time, the wider world of school, their peers and society are asking these young people to commit to a particular identity role, right in the middle of their period of transition. This is a problem with society that is laid at the door of the teenager: if they are acting authentically, they simply cannot commit to one specific role – they are busy trying out a multitude of roles, and roles within roles, and nuances of these roles. Despite the laconic image they often present, these kids are mentally very busy but don't yet have the neural ability to ascertain which is the most appropriate road for them to follow. It couldn't really be less appropriate that at the very time teenagers are determinedly trying out different roles, they are expected to choose their future careers and courses to study at university. The timing couldn't be worse and perhaps explains the tenuous connection most middle-aged people's careers have with their third-level degree.

JOEY, 15

Joey found his tribe at age 13 when he became friendly with a rebellious crowd. Always an independent type, whatever slim control his parents had on him suddenly disintegrated. Joey left the house at the merest sniff of an argument. When he was in the house, his headphones were on and he was glued to his phone.

The crunch came when Joey was 15. He refused point-blank to go on the family holiday. His mother, Paula, realised that Joey had completely disengaged from family life. He didn't speak to them, he wouldn't eat with them, he hated school, his room was a pigsty and he viewed himself as an outcast who didn't fit the family mould. Ciarán, his older brother, was the one who was good in school. Joey preferred to be with his friends because they liked and appreciated him.

When Joey first came to me he was completely disaffected. He didn't know who he was. He wasn't mad about his friendship group, but this was the only place in life where he got respect, and so, like a moth to a flame, he always returned to his friends. Joey had developed a heavy habit of playing video games late into the night. This was a form of escapism; mindless distraction is very attractive when there is nothing interesting going on in your life. Joey's identity as the disaffected teen was becoming entrenched, and it was important that he became motivated to begin exploring other aspects of himself.

Joey was bored out of his mind, unmotivated, and he couldn't see a future. It was clear to me that he needed some sense of purpose or meaning. We connected well and he became willing to try different activities in a bid to find some sense of energy. I sought out adrenalin-inducing activities for Joey to try. He tried mountain-climbing – it was 'OK', but it didn't take. He tried horse-riding – it was 'grand', but again it didn't take. He also tried kayaking, but he hated it. All along, Joey had mentioned his interest in buying a broken-down cheap car and doing it up to sell it. I was averse to this as I remembered all too well the stories of joyriding from my own youth and knew about the statistics for the dangerous combination of fast cars and teenage boys. Eventually, as there seemed to be few other options and Joey was becoming increasingly nihilistic, I supported Joey in his bid to buy a car and do it up.

Paula was dead-set against this, but John, Joey's dad, who had been completely disengaged because he had always felt out of his depth with Joey, suddenly spoke up. He said that he had always harboured this ambition himself and was willing to go for it if Joey was. For me as a therapist, this was a gift from the gods. I encouraged the idea as an opportunity for some father–son bonding. I counselled Joey intensively during this stage. Joey had no interest in doing up a car with his father – he wanted to take it to his mate's garage and do it there.

This was when the therapeutic alliance came to our aid as it helped Joey see that there needed to be some give and take. Joey needed to put up with his dad if he was to get his car. We met for an hour every week, and he often spent most of the hour ranting about how his dad was a 'FOOL' and a 'GOBSHITE' and how he couldn't bear him. Over time, as the project began to take shape, Joey began to become more expansive about his life, he became more ambitious and talked about one day owning his own garage – this was a long way from the disaffected teenager I had met some months previously.

At one point, Joey dismissed a car part as unimportant, but John disagreed and went to the trouble of dismantling the entire engine to put the part back in. Joey railed against this for weeks. John eventually declared the part safely installed, and then, in a golden moment, when Joey put the key in the ignition, the car started. Tears of joy came to Joey's and John's eyes. The car was finally running.

Joey decided to become a mechanic. He realised that he needed to finish school – even though it was 'stupid' – because not doing the exams would cause more trouble than it was worth. Joey eventually became an apprentice to a local mechanic and settled down a little. He was still stormy and obstinate and often had fights with authority figures but was no longer disaffected, unmotivated and listless. We can't have it all.

• • •

Providing brain space

It is helpful for parents to provide their teenagers with brain space (what Erikson termed a 'psychosocial moratorium') when they are in the middle of sorting out their identity amidst their role confusion. This moratorium should make allowances for even the most fixed identity so that the teenager has room to manoeuvre beyond whatever identity they have fixated on. Generally, but not always, the intensity of the commitment to any given role is matched by the inner sense of confusion and insecurity of the teenager. This is not easy to figure out – neither for the parents nor for the teenagers. One of the many difficulties related to adolescence is the challenge for parents to handle the declared certainty from the teen that each preferred role is the 'real thing'. If teenagers are provided with the appropriate mental space, they will have enough space and time to freely experiment and explore. This experimentation and exploration will allow a firm sense of identity to emerge, along with a deeper emotional awareness of who they are.

The social environment can be an obstacle to this moratorium. For example, a school could demand that the child choose certain subjects to guide them towards a particular career. Although this can feel oppressive, the parents set the tone in a household, and these matters can be dealt with by encouraging a certain lightness around subject choices. Although everyone else might be excessively intense about their subject choices – or even about their college choices – the role of the engaged parent is to provide perspective. Few among us are working where we thought we'd be working when we were 16 or 18. It is often only the very zealous or those who are imprisoned within a rigid mindset who end up following through on their 17-year-old self's ambitions. The more the parents emphasise a flexible approach to their future career, the freer the teenager is to explore their psyche and land on choices that help them form their emerging identity.

. . .

Career choices

Future career choices can be an issue where parents often don't cover themselves in glory. But there is a good reason for this! We parents know our children very well. We've changed their nappies, watched them grow up, and seen them face various challenges. From the moment the baby is first placed in our arms, many parents wonder how the child will turn out. Most parents have silently evaluated and dismissed many more career options for their teen than the teen has, and it is perfectly understandable that parents might be filled with consternation when the teen declares out of the blue that they are going to study business even though you know they are a born teacher and you also know that their decision to study business is a direct result of some vague grandiose idea that they will become a high-flying businessman because they recently watched *Wall Street*. It can be almost impossible to keep your mouth shut. Being dismissive or going to war over this might feel like the only options, but be warned, this might backfire, and the teenager might become even more zealous. Far better for the parents to subtly bring more flexibility into this conversation.

Because of changes in child-labour laws, this generation of teenagers often don't have the opportunity to work in part-time jobs and this lack of responsibility seems to lead to a lack of meaning and purpose in their lives. In addition, previous generations of teens started to feel autonomous because of the money they earned during adolescence; however, today's teen seldom has the opportunity to earn money. If at all possible, parents should help their teenager find some sort of paid work to help them build a sense of pride in who they are.

DAVID, 22

When Joanne's son David stopped attending his lectures at college, Joanne contacted the college administration on his behalf. Joanne liaised with the staff, who continuously told her that David needed to attend. David, meanwhile, was avoiding everything. As a child growing up in a small rural town, he had been considered the clever kid, described as the 'brainbox' by his peers. Then, when he found it difficult to keep up with his electronic engineering course, he felt completely thrown off and ensconced himself in his childhood bedroom, playing video games and escaping from the reality of life.

Joanne was very frightened by this and made it her mission to make sure David wasn't kicked off his course. And yet, in doing so, she was avoiding the main problem: the engineering course didn't suit David, and he needed to confront this fact. What happened instead was that

David remained on the course. David successfully avoided facing his fear of failure and continued on a course that didn't suit him. His fear caused his still-maturing brain to revert back to a childish mode. He stopped trying to grow up. His college course became his mother's problem. He didn't care about the money that was being spent on his education.

A huge conflict arose between David and his parents. When David first arrived in my office, he said, 'There are two things you need to know about me – one, I have a degree in engineering and two, I definitely don't want to be an engineer.' He had hated his course for some years and had felt painted into a corner. He chose to respond by focusing on whether he was winning or losing at Fortnite. He isolated himself and lost all interest in having a social life. In many ways, David's failure became much more prolonged and destructive because it was delayed and avoided, enabled by a parent who simply wanted to help.

• • •

Coming of age

Great strides have been made in neuroscience in recent years, and, as described in Chapter 1, we now know that the brain isn't fully formed until we are around 25 years of age. This rings particularly true for me, as I can recall feeling pretty insane until I was 25. Then, slowly but surely, I began to settle. Erikson wrote a psychobiography of Martin Luther, *Young Man Luther: A Study in Psychoanalysis and History*, and determined that Luther's identity crisis ended when he was 25; Erikson also wrote a Pulitzer-Prize-winning psychobiography of Gandhi, *Gandhi's Truth: On the Origins of Militant Nonviolence*, in which he concluded that Gandhi's identity crisis ended at 30 years of age. Equally, it wasn't until Erikson himself was 25 and moved to Vienna that he began to settle within his own identity. Parents who are concerned about their adult children can take heart that, according to Erikson, an identity crisis for people of genius is frequently prolonged and also that identity formation tends to be longer in our industrial society because it can take us much longer these days to learn the skills needed for the tasks of adulthood – for example, it can take many years to become a qualified doctor. The upshot is that sometimes, typically when we are in our twenties, we begin to tune into the tasks of adulthood and respond accordingly, so long as our family and society have given us the freedom to find ourselves, and it is only then that we come of age.

• • •

Gender identity and gender roles

An individual's identity can be composed of many different aspects of the person, such as race, ethnicity, gender, sexual orientation, physical attributes, personality, political affiliations, religious beliefs and professional identities. At the moment, there is a heavy emphasis on gender identity and sexual orientation. Gender has become a politicised and controversial issue; but the fact remains that no matter the cause of distress, the situation is improved when parents lean in with love and boundaries.

Parents often find the terminology involved in gender issues confusing, and it can be helpful if they learn the various terms, such as cisgender, non-binary and gender-questioning, so that they can keep up with their teen. While the term 'sex' represents either of the two main categories (male and female) into which humans are divided based on our reproductive functions, the term 'gender' is broader as it describes the range of characteristics pertaining to femininity and masculinity and the differences between them. Meanwhile, 'gender identity' refers to an individual's personal sense of their gender. This is a concept that was initially developed in the 1950s and 1960s by two clinicians, John Money and Robert Stoller, who put forward the idea that every one of us has an unidentifiable, invisible element inside us that motivates us to behave in certain ways and that may contribute to certain gender norms and expectations. Others do not subscribe to this theory of gender identity; they consider that we are simply born in our bodies, and our experiences, our bodies and the hormones in our bodies shape our minds and our behaviour. Whatever we believe about gender identity, many people reject the gender roles that are often imposed upon us and feel very distressed by society's expectations that anybody should, for example, 'act like a boy' or 'look like a girl': some boys don't feel brave or adventurous, and many girls don't want to wear pretty dresses.

• • •

Gender dysphoria

Gender dysphoria is a clinically diagnosable condition that refers to the psychological distress that results when an individual feels a disconnect between their sex and their sense of gender identity. Though gender dysphoria typically begins in childhood, some people may not experience it until after puberty or much later.

Clinicians like myself who work to a developmental understanding of gender dysphoria believe it is valuable for the person to come to terms with their body and also to develop a degree of self-acceptance that will lead to them feeling better. Young people can also benefit from learning about gender roles and gender identities so that they can better understand where their distress is coming from. On the other hand, gender-affirmative clinicians believe that they should help individuals change their bodies with medical interventions if the individual believes it will help them feel more aligned with their personal sense of gender. Neither of these treatments always works, so it is recommended that parents use a thoughtful and compassionate approach that helps the teen to alleviate their symptoms with the tools that are already at their disposal.

Developmental milestone: Coming to terms with the body and the sexual self

Gender dysphoria can manifest as a coping mechanism for adolescents who are having difficulty with the developmental task of coming to terms with the maturing body and the sexual self. They might also have difficulties with reaching emotional maturity, coping with independence, developing coping skills, learning to maintain relationships and acquiring healthy methods of communication. It is the parent's role to try to make sure their child doesn't become narrow-minded or obsessive and instead remains open to further development of their identity. For example, the young person can further develop a sense of personal identity as a result of seeking meaningful moral standards, values and belief systems. They might also benefit from exploring other aspects of their identity, such as their ethnicity, nationality, personality, political affiliations and vocational interests – we contain multitudes and none of us is simply a walking gender identity. It is important that parents help their children to keep their options open as they move through various identities during adolescence. When teens enter the phase of emerging adulthood, they can then make their own adult decisions about their lives. Until then, it is recommended that parents don't allow their child to foreclose on future options as a result of the intensity of emotion within identity politics.

I recommend you proceed cautiously and carefully if your teenager has gender dysphoria and wants to medically transition. Childhood is short, and we are adults for much longer. It is arguably impossible for a child to imagine what it is like to be an adult. Medical transition causes infertility and impaired sexual functioning and lays a very heavy medical burden on the adult body.[39] It is perhaps more liberating for your child to explore their gender identity by changing their style and gender expression rather than turning to medication. Other people don't agree with my reasoning and think it's better to medicalise the teen's gender identity as soon as they want this. As there is no long-term research base that shows the benefit of childhood transition, nobody actually knows which is better. Essentially, the parent has three ways to help the teen who wants to transition:

- help them to change their body (with medication) so that it aligns with their mind

- help them to change their mind so it aligns with their body – perhaps by exploring their style and gender expression

- teach them a range of ways to help them build their distress tolerance and increase their coping skills.

This last option – improving their ability to handle stress – is arguably the safest approach, as learning how to best handle mental pain is a gift for life and always worth learning. It is important that parents help their children to keep their options open as they move through various identities during adolescence. When the teens grow into emerging adulthood, they can then make their own adult decisions about their lives, but until then, it is recommended that parents don't allow their child to close down future options as a result of the intensity of their emotion and their difficulties with distress tolerance.

• • •

External influencing factors

Parents need to be aware that external influencers such as YouTubers, social media influencers and certain online platforms can have a heavy influence on teenagers' identities – especially with regard to gender identity issues. Many parents have reported that their teens became more comfortable online than in real life and, as a result, left behind their real-life identities in favour of hanging out online. As much as possible, parents need to limit heavy influencing factors and instead help the young person live an expansive life way beyond the confines of the laptop in their bedroom. Often parents will need to take the decision to limit their teen's tech use if they are to ensure re-engagement in real life (see Chapter 7). Teenagers often seek meaning and purpose and are more likely than older, more jaded adults to engage with new conceptual frameworks that promise a better world, be this identity politics, queer theory or critical race theory. While young people benefit from exploring different concepts, a key aspect of health is flexible thinking. If the teen clings too rigidly to any given concept, parents need to seriously consider appropriate interventions.

• • •

What parents can do

As they move into adolescence, many teens try to cope alone as they intuitively perceive this as an adolescent challenge. They want to see if they can face the challenge, and it's important that parents don't trample all over this effort. It doesn't help the teenager if the parent becomes over-involved in the teen's identity. If the parent is obtrusively present, it impedes the teen's progress, and they may respond to this by becoming entrenched in their identity – often shutting off other options as a result.

Parents who try to over-involve themselves, perhaps by providing inspirational speeches in the manner of an American sports coach from a made-for-TV movie, may miss the fact that often a more subtle, compassionate and tender approach might be more valuable. Caitlin Moran spoke eloquently about how her teenage daughter didn't want solutions from her mother; she didn't want to hear how much more difficult Caitlin had it when she was her age. According to Moran, what her teen wanted was for her mother to present in the manner of a cow (yes, a cow), mooing sympathetically as the teen related her stories – no suggestions, no advice, no coaching – just sympathetic noises. This is wise but often difficult to carry out – especially when we can see plainly what both the problem and solution are. Just like when your child is learning to ride a bike or tie their laces, it is more valuable for the teen if they can learn this for themselves, so parents need to hang back with care and sensitivity.

Parents can be the safe harbour representing consistency and fortitude while the teen is out on the stormy seas. Parents can make their teen's favourite dinner; buy them something nice; watch a movie with them; moo sympathetically; and sometimes, when it's asked for, give their well-thought-out tuppence worth. Being a neutrally supportive presence when all you want to do communicate your brilliantly thought-out solutions is a challenging task, but if the teen is provided with enough space to try on their various identities, they will be more likely to eventually blossom into an integrated and authentic adult.

Parents can also support their teens by acting as a sounding board so the teen can bounce different ideas off them. This doesn't entail supportive speeches – it means thoughtful and mind-expanding conversations that provoke further thinking. Teenagers can benefit from learning about different theories, such as queer theory and gender identity theory. They can also expand their worldview by learning about the fa'afafine of Samoa or the muxe in Mexico. Misinformation is a serious challenge for teenagers today, especially in the online world, so it is imperative that parents first become experts on the subject before they begin to speak with their teens about it. It's not helpful if the teenager becomes the apparent expert in the house and parents don't keep up, as then the teen will lead the way and parents won't be able to give mature guidance on the subject. Teenagers are supposed to push at the boundaries of life – that's their job. The parent's job, meanwhile, is to maintain these boundaries.

• • •

Takeaways

- A key task of adolescents is to come to an understanding of themselves and an acceptance of their strengths and limitations.

- During adolescence, teens need to try out different identities.

- The more intense the adolescent is about any given identity, the more likely they are to feel insecure about their sense of identity.

- External influencing factors can have a heavy impact on teenagers' identities.

- Teenagers may need their parents to provide them with a psychosocial moratorium on irreversible decisions during this period.

- People tend to come of age some time in their twenties. This is a process that does not benefit from being hurried along.

PART V
FACING COMPLEX
CHALLENGES

CHAPTER 13

NEURODIVERSITY AND OTHER ISSUES

'Do I contradict myself?
Very well, then, I contradict myself;
(I am large. I contain multitudes)'

— WALT WHITMAN

WHEN A CHILD is diagnosed with a condition, their parents often feel a complex range of emotions during the psychological evaluation process. The diagnosis provides parents with a framework for understanding their child and also access to the necessary supports their child needs. However, parents often then worry that the much-needed diagnosis in childhood will follow their adult child around and hinder them in the future. For some children with chronic conditions, it's clear that they will continue to need a lot of support in adult life, but the focus of this chapter is on the more ambiguous scenarios: the countless children who could perhaps go on to live fully functioning lives, or lives with a minimum level of support. Ultimately, some of these kids might end up needing slightly more help than anticipated and others slightly less. The upshot of all this is that the teenage years of the neurodiverse child can feel very intense as the adult slowly begins to emerge.

The rise of diagnoses for this generation has had a profound impact on the psyches of young people. Young people have grown up learning about complex neurological conditions that few are able to understand, so they often have a simplistic understanding of a diagnosis. Some people believe that we need to centre a person's diagnosis in most conversations about the individual while others believe that there is too much emphasis on diagnosis and not enough on the individual themselves.

Parents are often wondering non-stop whether their child might one day move beyond the diagnosis or further into the diagnosis. This is exhausting for the parent, and the child can feel like they are under surveillance. Parents can become very sensitive and overreactive about how the teenager is managing their condition, perhaps because they believe that every event is an indication of how they will cope in the future. Other parents respond in the opposite way entirely and may even pretend to themselves that the diagnosis is no longer a problem. To further complexify the issue, although a teenager can give us glimpses into the future adult, they can also give us fake news – sometimes the teenager's personality is very similar to the adult they will become, but equally often, the teenager becomes a strikingly different adult. We contain multitudes.

It is recommended that parents seek out a full educational and psychological assessment to understand and address the teen's individual needs. Many neurodiverse people have overlapping conditions, so teens with dyslexia might also have dyscalculia, or a teen with dyspraxia might also have ADHD or ASD. Although different conditions are outlined in this chapter, parents might find relevant information in places they don't expect.

. . .

Assimilating the diagnosis

Many teenagers I see in my clinical practice seem to be shaped by their diagnoses. Some build their identity around the diagnosis; others reject their diagnosis and view it as a source of great shame, remaining secretive about their condition and fearful about whether they are in some way inadequate. Both responses need attention. Parents can help their teenagers learn how to give an appropriate level of understanding to how much their condition impacts them and how it is also simply an aspect of their rich and multi-faceted psyche.

The issue of over-diagnosis and 'diagnosis creep', in which expert panels get together and decide to expand the definition of any given disease, has heavily impacted this generation. According to InSight magazine, published by the Medical Journal of Australia, this happened with osteoporosis in 2008, when a new definition increased the number of elderly women with the condition from 21 per cent to 72 per cent.[40] It also seems to have happened in diabetes, with a sharp uptick in the number of people deemed to be 'pre-diabetic'.[41] And it has also arguably happened with many neurological conditions such as ASD, ADHD, generalised anxiety disorder, gender dysphoria and others.[42]

Diagnosis of neurological conditions is a fallible science that relies heavily on self-report and interpretation. Your teen might go to one doctor and receive a diagnosis of ASD and go to another and be diagnosed with ADHD. Previously, when a person received a diagnosis, it mostly remained constant, but the issue of diagnostic creep has arguably led to the sharp rise in teenagers arriving into my office telling me, 'I was originally diagnosed with ASD, but that was a misdiagnosis, and I was then diagnosed with ADHD, but then recently I attended a new clinic, and they concluded that I don't have ASD or ADHD but instead have anxiety disorder.' This can lead to deep insecurity – the teenager feels that there is some big answer out there if only the experts could figure it out. It can reduce the inherent existential angst of what it is to be human to a simplistic idea that there is a solution to be found in the correct diagnosis. But this is reductive as, sadly, a diagnosis doesn't actually provide any answers. Although a diagnosis can bring about a tremendous sense of relief, it seldom provides much more than a framework to understand how the person might operate.

• • •

Support for the neurodiverse teen

The level of support that the neurodiverse child receives in primary school can be quite extensive. But the support and scaffolding tend to drop off in secondary school, and some teenagers can spiral as a consequence. This can be a very frightening and tense time for everyone. The teenager naturally wants to prove to themselves that they can manage just fine – this is often their first major challenge in moving towards independence, and they can become determined to manage without the supports they feel increasingly embarrassed about. Consequently, the teen can make a significant effort to keep their loving parents at bay as they are all too aware that their parents are eager to jump in and help. At the same time, everything is changing as the move from primary school to secondary school typically involves a new school, new schoolmates and new teachers who don't understand the issues that impact your child. Calls to secondary schools often go unanswered, and it can take some time for the teenager to even realise that they aren't coping. This doesn't just apply to teenagers – many of us are prone to thinking that we're just fine, really, when in fact we are feeling close to collapse.

Parenting strategy: Create a plan

At the start of the school year, parents can help by creating a basic plan with their child about how they might manage the year ahead. The plan should reflect on the potential pitfalls and where the joy might be found. This will give the child grounding and a long-term perspective about their school experience that might help them when they experience troughs.

Many neurodiverse teenagers benefit from a visual reminder system or a clear visual schedule hanging on the wall that can be referred to regularly to keep them on track. These can be found online, but many prefer to make their own visual plans and often use wit and humour in creating them.

Socialising the neurodiverse teenager

Socialising is often quite challenging for the neurodiverse teen, and parents might need to teach their teenagers how to interpret certain social interactions. The teenager can be very resistant to their parents' input and can end up struggling with isolation and turning to the internet and online relationships to stave off loneliness. While the internet can be a great salve against loneliness, it can also be a poisoned chalice, and parents need to monitor their child's content.

A large-scale study of ASD teens revealed that more than 43 per cent never saw friends outside of school, and 54 per cent were never called by friends.[43] It's not just ASD teenagers who find socialising difficult – teens with ADHD, OCD, dyslexia, dyspraxia and other conditions can find socialising difficult for a range of reasons. Consequently, not having any friends is often the hardest part of adolescence for neurodiverse teenagers. It is developmentally natural for these kids to look beyond their family to their peers for kinship, but it is not always on offer. Parents can find it almost unbearable to watch their lovely, kind child, who merely wants to be accepted and make friends, suffer cruel rejection. My book *Bully-Proof Kids* explores how parents can respond most effectively if bullying arises.

Sometimes the 'special interests' common to neurodiverse teenagers can help them find friends. The teenager can become absorbed in a particular interest and can also build a network of like-minded peers. This might become tricky when the special interest is not conducive to wellbeing. For example, many teenagers these days are very into identity politics and critical race theory. For some, this can be a great addition to their social awareness, but for others, especially those prone to perseverating and/or polarised thinking, it can have a detrimental effect. If your teenager is spending their life warring online, you will need to be vigilant about the content they access. You should remain interested, ask them about their online interests, seek to expand their life and also support their attempts to maintain some sort of social network while making sure they don't lose the run of themselves. None of this is easy.

If your neurodiverse teen has trouble getting along with others, you can take steps to help improve their social skills and their ability to maintain relationships (see Chapter 6). The earlier your child's difficulties with peers are addressed, the more successful these steps can be. The following strategies can be helpful for parents:

- Before your child goes to a social event, talk to them about what they should expect there and what others might expect from them.

- Resist the temptation to go overboard – don't try to do too much at once.

- Remember that having one or two close friends can be more valuable than having lots of friends.

- Involve your teen in activities that they enjoy, as this will help them have the confidence to focus on engaging more with peers.

- In the early years of adolescence, set up social behaviour goals with your teen.

- If your teen is excessively shy or tends to disengage, encourage small social interactions in your day-to-day life, such as in a shop or café.

• • •

Autism spectrum disorder (ASD)

Autism spectrum disorder is a neurological and developmental disorder that affects how a person communicates, learns, behaves and interacts with others. An individual with ASD often has challenges with sensory processing and gravitates towards repetitive behaviour as a coping mechanism. The term 'spectrum' reflects the fact that symptoms vary in type and severity. The behaviour of a person with mild ASD (also known as 'high functioning') can be unrecognisably different from a person with severe ASD.

Often missed in girls, there are arguably different criteria for females with ASD compared to males. Even so, the primary characteristics of ASD are typically poorly developed social skills, difficulties with communication, restricted interests, repetitive behaviour, and sensory processing issues. People with ASD may appear indifferent and remote. They can have difficulty forming emotional bonds with others, and some parents find it difficult to bond with their autistic children. This can feel taboo to speak about and yet can be perfectly understandable.

A common complaint I hear from parents is that they believe their teen's autism is getting worse. But this may be a misunderstanding of what's happening. Often the teen is not becoming more non-compliant because their autism is getting worse – it's because they are a teenager. Like all teenagers, they are seeking more independence. Although it might frighten parents, independence should be encouraged, and parents can help by giving them more control over their schedule. Yes, of course it will be difficult for them, and there will be many failures, but ASD teens also have to confront certain developmental challenges if they are to progress.

· · ·

Puberty and sexual development for the ASD teen

Research shows that ASD teenagers are often gender-nonconforming and can be distressed by the division between boys and girls that can happen naturally in the social context when puberty arrives.[44] Perhaps due to the difficulties with puberty and gender nonconformity, gender-related distress often arises for the ASD teenager. Parents may need to be extra vigilant and monitor their child's online content to ensure what they consume is helpful.

A teen with ASD may not intuitively know what types of information about sex and bodily activities should be private and may unwittingly make a faux pas by, for example, speaking about menstruation at the lunch table. They often miss social cues and may not understand the importance of hygiene or grooming for social acceptance. If your teen is shunning the shower, you might need to set up a rota that is checked often to ensure they are sufficiently clean. Some ASD teenagers can use masturbation as a way of stimming (self-stimulatory behaviour) and as a method of self-soothing. They also might masturbate to fulfil a sensory need rather than a sexual one, and some young neurodiverse children use masturbation as a calming strategy, much like thumb-sucking. Older kids may use masturbation more as a form of sensory input or as a way to tune out other things that are overwhelming in the sensory environment. This might not be born out of the sexual drive but from other needs. This is difficult and awkward territory for parents and teenagers to navigate, and compassion and openness is probably the most helpful approach.

• • •

Executive functioning and the neurodiverse teen

Anxiety and executive functioning are often challenges for neurodiverse teenagers. They can feel a widening gap between themselves and their pals as they may mature at a slower pace and often have particular trouble with flexibility, organisation, initiating activities and working memory.[45]

If we imagine our brain as an orchestra, executive functioning is the conductor, making sure all the musicians are working together, in tune, at the right rhythm and speed. Executive skills are applied to make plans, change plans when necessary, keep track of time, ask for help, maintain self-control, remember past experiences and relate them to present actions, and work successfully within a group. Even something as basic as shopping for food requires executive functioning, as Dr Michael Rosenthal, a neuropsychologist from the Child Mind Institute, points out:

'First, you need "initiation" skills to get yourself off the couch. The next step is to "plan and organise" a list of the items you need to get. You need to think about how many meals you need to make and how much money you have in the bank. Let's imagine the first thing on your list is pears, but when you go to the produce section, the pears are all bruised. You have to have the "cognitive flexibility" to say, "Instead of pears, I will buy apples." You need "inhibition" to keep from going to the candy aisle, and your "working memory" will help you keep track of the items you've purchased.'[46]

A degree of flexibility is required for a person to successfully function in society, and flexible thinking can be challenging for the neurodiverse teenager. This is why it's valuable to break down plans into smaller steps and to warn the teen that things might not go exactly as planned.

Parenting strategy: Seek some support before you need it

Sometimes it can be positive if parents seek a 'big brother' or 'big sister' presence in their teen's life. Foróige, the leading youth organisation in Ireland, has a Big Brother Big Sister programme that 'matches a young person (10–18 years) in need of friendship and support to a caring adult volunteer mentor. They meet once a week for an hour or two and do something both enjoy, like kick a ball around, play Xbox, learn guitar, bake a cake, or listen to music – the possibilities are endless.'

If you can't access a 'big brother' or 'big sister', shrewd parents can find their own by looking to older cousins or some other trusted family friend and asking them to pitch in. The parents can be financially generous with the older cousin, which might encourage them to go on outings with the neurodiverse teenager. This is semi-babysitting but also mentoring. It is preferable if this plan begins early in the teenage years and is supported by the parent in a low-key manner, as otherwise the teen will probably be resistant. If the parent makes too big a deal about it, acting like the cousin is saving the teen's social life, your teen might become embarrassed or resistant.

• • •

Attention deficit hyperactivity disorder (ADHD)

ADHD is a condition that affects a person's behaviour. It has three primary characteristics:

- **Inattention:** Poor organisational skills, difficulty listening to others, easily distracted, forgetful.

- **Impulsivity:** Often interrupts others, difficulty waiting their turn, blurting out answers, high risk-taking.

- **Hyperactivity:** In constant motion, fidgeting, difficulty remaining in their seat or engaging in quiet activities, talking excessively.

Although ADHD and Tourette's syndrome are two separate conditions, they are often similar in presentation, and children can often be diagnosed with both conditions. Individuals with Tourette's syndrome demonstrate behavioural tics and/or vocal tics while a child with ADHD might experience a different flavour of compulsive behaviour and vocal output.

As the hormonal changes of adolescence are happening and the demands of school and social interaction become more challenging, ADHD symptoms may get worse. It is no surprise that the ADHD teen's grades might fall; they may forget assignments, lose textbooks, interrupt constantly, and become bored with their daily class work. Parents can become very impatient with their ADHD teenager, as they are often aware of the child's potential and find it very difficult to witness their failure to make a good representation of their abilities through their school work. And yet some of us – many of us, in fact – do not suit school. Sometimes it can be challenging for parents to face up to the fact that their child is not academically inclined.

· · ·

Impulsivity and risk-taking for the ADHD teen

As we saw in Chapter 1, teenagers are more likely to take risks as their ability to assess the consequences of their decisions is underdeveloped as the teenage brain focuses on recognising the rewards and disregarding the consequences. Being neurologically more likely to be an impulsive risk-taker who is thrill-seeking and immature in judgement and having ADHD is a heady combination: it's like being a turbo-charged teenager. These traits make accidents and serious injury more likely, and issues such as fast driving, drink-driving and substance abuse are more prevalent among ADHD teenagers.

Certain issues pose special risks for teens with ADHD because they can be:[47]

- two to four times more likely to have a car accident

- more likely to be heavy drinkers

- more likely to have problems as a result of drinking

- twice as likely to have abused alcohol within the past six months

- three times as likely to abuse drugs other than marijuana.

It can be difficult to strike the right balance of treatment for ADHD while acknowledging the challenges that many teenagers have. Clear and consistent rules might be more necessary than ever. It's the parent's responsibility to establish rules and expectations and the teenager's responsibility to try to meet them. It is important to review privileges and sanctions with your teen in relation to their overall ADHD treatment plan.

• • •

Dyslexia and dyscalculia

Dyslexia is a specific learning disorder that involves difficulty reading and affects areas of the brain that process language. Dyscalculia involves difficulty in acquiring arithmetical skills. Teenagers with these conditions may need their parents to advocate for them to receive the support and adjustments they are due in secondary school. Very bright children can often compensate for their dyslexia and/or dyscalculia in primary school but find the greater intellectual demands of secondary-level schooling overwhelming.

Another source of stress for teenagers with dyslexia and/or dyscalculia is that they feel different from their peers, which can lead to struggles with low self-esteem. One teenager I worked with evocatively described the 'fizzing frustration' communicated by everybody in relation to her difficulties with reading and writing. It was a heavy burden to bear. Attending school, where academic progress is the primary focus, Monday to Friday, 9 a.m. to 4 p.m., can lead the teen to believe that academic prowess is everything. Not being able to keep up with their peers can bring on feelings of panic, helplessness and inadequacy.

It is recommended that parents help these teens choose their school subjects with care and consideration, keeping the demands of the state exams at the forefront of their mind. These subjects should be chosen with reflection on how much coursework can be done before the exams, how much is focused on reading, writing and arithmetic and how much is practical. Foreign languages and subjects such as history, which have a heavy focus on reading and writing, should be limited. The focus could instead be on practical subjects such as metalwork, woodwork and art. Teens with dyscalculia need to anticipate where arithmetic can pop up in other subjects. It is important that parents of kids with these conditions keep their own ambitions in check. Yes, perhaps the teenager can achieve great grades – but at what cost to their wellbeing? There are many ways to succeed in life.

• • •

Dyspraxia

Dyspraxia (also known as developmental co-ordination disorder (DCD)) is a specific learning difficulty that affects the brain's ability to plan sequences of movement. It is often associated with problems of perception, language and thought. Disorganisation, difficulties with forward planning and short-term memory problems can become an issue as peers, parents and teachers can become exasperated by the teen's inability in these areas. Many people with dyspraxia find social communication difficult as they do not always pick up on social cues and might misinterpret body language, jokes, metaphors or sarcasm. Teens with dyspraxia may also have very different interests and hobbies from their peer group, and this can lead to isolation, especially in early adolescence. These kids need patience. Parents can help cultivate the teen's hobbies and make sure they have a soft place to land when they come home from the stressful school atmosphere, where everyone seems to be ahead of them.

• • •

Medication and neurodiversity

Some people swear medication saved their lives; others say it ruined them. This is a complex issue that deserves a book of its own. As a psychotherapist, I am not qualified to prescribe or recommend medication. This suits me as I always tend to focus on the individual's inner world and the psychological progress that can be made rather than the impact of medication. Having worked in the area of mental health for many years, it is perfectly clear to me that some people need medication – how much and for how long is a debatable question. I remember working with one parent who always took her ADHD teenager off medication during the school holidays as he could cope with school only when medicated. This eventually called other issues into question, as the mother began to wonder if it was healthy to make her son take medication in order to attend school. In the end, the child left school early, came off the medication and entered into a field he was interested in – horses – and has had a very successful working life ever since. There is more than one way to skin a cat, and when your teen is neurodiverse, you probably need to be open to the road less travelled.

• • •

Takeaways

- Focus on building self-esteem in your teen during these difficult years.

- Work with your teen to create workable plans.

- Some teens benefit from a reminder system or a visual schedule for their various tasks.

- Help your teen to set a daily schedule and review plans and schedules often.

- Make sure your teen knows their limits.

- Keep distractions to a minimum.

- Show clear, consistent expectations; give clear and easily understood directions.

- Be sensitive and caring about how school can be very difficult for a neurodiverse child.

- Grades can sometimes but not always indicate how the teenager is doing.

- Work with your teen's school – try to find an involved teacher who can help if you need it.

- Be vigilant about bullying, exclusion and alienation. Talk with your child about what they might do if they get teased or picked on. Make sure they know that bullying is universal and says more about the bully than it does about the target.

- Monitor their online content.

- Support activities in which your teen can easily succeed.

- Keep your boundaries: reward positive behaviour; set consequences for bad behaviour.

- Set a good example. Teenagers may not show it, but the adults in their lives are very influential and important to them.

CHAPTER 14

SELF-DESTRUCTION, SELF-HARM, SUICIDALITY

'The habit of despair is worse than despair itself.'

– ALBERT CAMUS

THE EARTHQUAKE that unfolds because a teenager can't find her favourite T-shirt can shake the foundations of the house – and then ten minutes later, it can be very disorienting when this same teenager can be found giggling happily on her phone. The extraordinary force of these teenage emotions is shocking. Teenagers' seismic shifts in mood lead many parents to secretly wonder whether their teenager might, in fact, be mentally ill. Being told by your teenager that they love you and then, four seconds later, that they hate you feels very insane. But it is also difficult for the teenager who is engaged in this push-pull dance as they are trying to move away from you when they also feel very attached to you.

Some parents report feeling afraid of their teenagers, intimidated by the force of emotion and the feeling that literally anything could happen when they're around. Other parents describe a lack of comprehension of their teenager's emotions – one minute they are in the depths of despair, the next they feel blithe and heedless. In fairness, the teenagers I meet in my clinic often feel equally discombobulated by their wild mood swings. They sometimes reflect back on the events of the week with the fascination an anthropologist might have on discovering the strange behaviour of an Amazonian tribe. Cara, a 14-year-old girl I worked with, put it succinctly: 'I don't quite know what comes over me. The red mist descends and anything can happen. Then it fades away and it's all sweetness and light again. It's mad!'

• • •

Self-harming behaviour

Self-harm describes any behaviour where a person causes harm to themselves, usually as a way to help cope with overwhelming, difficult or distressing thoughts and feelings. Niall Breslin (the musician and sports star also known as Bressie) intentionally broke his own arm when he was 16 years old. Later on, describing the incident, he said 'It was an outlet for what was going on in my head [...] and when I did it, there was a euphoric feeling.' Breslin's book *Me and My Mate Jeffrey* revealed the challenges to his mental health and the way his harsh inner voice, which he called 'Jeffrey', would lead him into even deeper anguish. Self-harming most frequently takes the form of cutting, burning or non-lethal overdoses, but it can be any behaviour that causes injury – no matter how minor or high-risk the behaviour.

Sadly, self-harming behaviour is common, with 12.1 per cent of adolescents reporting engaging in self-harming behaviour.[48] Given a significant influencing factor for self-harming in children is knowing another child who self-harms,[49] the number of people who turn towards this maladaptive coping mechanism will continue to grow in ever-increasing circles. Nancy Tucker, in her book *That Was When People Started to Worry*, recalls laughing her head off with her friends at the message from the Samaritans that needed to be checked before they gained entry to a self-harming website. Perhaps they were so in thrall to the illicit glamour, secrecy and ceremony often associated with self-harming behaviour that the po-faced warning from the boring Samaritans seemed hilariously disconnected from their experience?

Self-harming behaviour usually starts as a way to relieve the build-up of pressure from distressing thoughts and feelings. It typically gives temporary relief from the emotional pain the person is feeling, but the underlying reasons for distress remain. Feelings of guilt and shame follow an act of self-harm, which continues the cycle of harm. As we see in the image below, the problem with self-harming behaviour is that it is a damaging and dangerous coping mechanism that creates a vicious circle. The person believes that this is the only way to relieve the mental strain, but they're wrong.

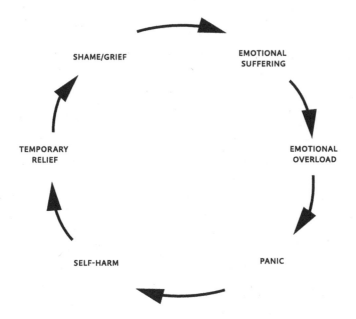

SHAME/GRIEF

EMOTIONAL
SUFFERING

TEMPORARY
RELIEF

EMOTIONAL
OVERLOAD

SELF-HARM

PANIC

Because it provides temporary relief, self-harm can become someone's automatic go-to for dealing with life's difficulties. Learning new coping strategies to deal with these challenges can make it easier to break the cycle of self-harm in the long term. Many young people believe it is impossible to live without self-harm as they become heavily dependent on this method to relieve the stress they feel inside their heads, yet with the right help and support, most people who self-harm can and do fully recover.

• • •

Why do people self-harm?

Animals who spend a lot of time on their own or enclosed within a small space often turn to self-harming behaviour. Similarly, in my work, I have noticed that a lot of teens who feel hemmed in and controlled often have a deep well of underlying rage within them that can turn into self-harming behaviour. Adolescents often harm themselves when things get too much; the more distressed they are, the more they self-harm. When a few issues come together, the teenager can quickly feel overwhelmed, which becomes too much to deal with. As one young person said, 'I self-harm to get out the hurt, anger and pain.' Self-harmers hurt themselves because they don't know what else to do to release the mental pressure and they don't feel that they have any other options that will work.

People who self-harm often speak about this behaviour as a means to communicate to themselves and other people the extent of their pain. When Liz was 15, she used to arrive at the dinner table with bloody arms. Her parents, who thought the world of her, were completely frozen in the face of this. Rather than asking her about her pain, they chose to get her professional help instead. This wasn't what Liz wanted. 'I wanted my parents to see my pain,' she said. 'This was the only way I could express how bad I was feeling. I wanted them to see me.'

Developmental milestone: Learn coping skills and acquire healthy means of communication

Teens who self-harm often need help with their difficulties in communication and coping skills and also need to find some self-compassion for themselves. They can feel over-controlled and may benefit from experiencing risk beyond the family home. Ultimately, the teen needs to be helped to find better ways to cope with emotional pain and to communicate their complex feelings.

When we don't express our emotions and don't feel able to talk about the things that make us distressed, angry or upset, the pressure can build up and become unbearable. Some people turn this in on themselves and use their bodies to represent the thoughts and feelings they can't say aloud. Some parents don't understand just how addictive self-harming can be as a coping mechanism for some teens. The social media post below reveals the nature of this destructive habit:

> Cw: self-harm
> This is something I try to never post about, but I just wanna post how proud of myself I am; this month marks 3 years of being self-harm free! That's 1,095 days! It's been so damn difficult at times but I'm so proud of myself for sticking it out!

Self-harming behaviour is complex. Some people self-harm because, when they feel numb, they want to feel something; others turn to self-harm as a way to express or distract themselves from unwanted emotions. It can also work as a way to symbolise and communicate their hurt and pain – even to themselves. It unleashes a punishment on the individual in a way that can feel suitably dramatic. Self-harm offers a solution to distressed teens; it offers a way to regain a sense of control when everything feels chaotic.

• • •

Harm-minimisation strategies

Harm-minimisation techniques should only be used as short-term solutions. These tactics might help when the person isn't quite ready to stop self-harming but needs to explore safer coping strategies. Coping strategies might help reduce the impulse to self-harm, but they generally don't resolve the underlying causes of emotional turmoil – so the desire to self-harm will resurface again and again until the individual finds a different way to process their emotions.

Harm-minimisation strategies include holding ice, running your hands under warm or cold water, squeezing a stress ball, punching a pillow or cushion and/or screaming into a pillow. Such tactics can also include safer self-harm practices such as sterilising self-harm tools, treating injuries immediately and reducing self-harm intensity (a person might scratch themselves instead of cutting, for example). Some people can be very ceremonial and feel good while setting up the self-harming equipment in an orderly fashion as they prepare to hurt themselves; others are much more chaotic in their behaviour. Afterwards, an alluring sense of calm and relief can set in – often followed by more complicated feelings of shame and loneliness. It is essential that parents don't allow harm-minimisation tactics to further entrench this maladaptive behaviour.

Here are some healthy alternatives to self-harm:

- Being slowly exposed to risk, challenge and adventure and other engaging activities.

- Talking to someone they trust can help a teen better cope with difficult feelings and overwhelming emotional pain.

- Learning about their style of communication and how it can work for them and work against them (see Chapter 2).

- Distraction can work very well for some.

- Changing the environment can give the teenager enough time away from self-harm tools so that the urge might pass.

- Spending time in nature can have a calming effect.

- Physical activity can also offer relief.

- Background noise and the commotion of other people can provide a sense of community and safety, offer a distraction and help some people feel less alone.

- Music, films, books and art can provide a temporary escape – but bear in mind that the type of music or art should be carefully selected.

- Creative work can offer a sense of control, since the person gets to choose what to express and how. Art, music and writing allow a person to express distress in their own way.

- A visual approach to relaxation can help create a mental 'happy place'. Guided meditations can help and adding vivid, specific sensory details to the mental image can help release stress and promote feelings of peace and calm.

• • •

Suicidality

Suicide is perhaps the most frightening issue that any parent can be confronted with. As it's so overwhelming, many parents can underplay the threat – they simply can't face it. But once it becomes an issue, parents need to be willing to confront it. Suicidality must be taken seriously, and the correct protocol should be followed. If your teenager has expressed suicidal thoughts, it is imperative that you bring your child to the doctor. I recommend that you also enlist in a short suicide training course (such as ASIST: Applied Suicide Intervention Skills Training) so that you can feel more equipped in the face of this terrifying event.

Suicidal ideation (or suicidal thoughts) means having thoughts, ideas, or ruminations about the possibility of ending one's own life. Most people who have suicidal thoughts do not go on to make suicide attempts, but suicidal thoughts are considered a risk factor for suicide. On suicide risk scales, the intensity of suicidal ideation ranges from fleeting thoughts to detailed planning. Passive suicidal ideation is thinking about not wanting to live or imagining being dead. Active suicidal ideation is thinking about different ways to die or forming a plan to die. Teens need to be taught that suicide is a massive deal and should never be spoken about lightly. Although it seems great that there is no longer a taboo in society when speaking about suicide, it is notable in my work that thoughts about suicide have inadvertently become normalised as young people have become so accustomed to hearing about it. Consequently, I strongly believe that we need to change our approach to suicide in society as soon as possible.

In 2020, an estimated:

- 12.2 million American adults seriously thought about suicide
- 3.2 million planned a suicide attempt
- 1.2 million attempted suicide.

In 2020, a total of 45,979 deaths in the US were attributable to suicide.[50]

· · ·

A search for meaning and purpose

Although this might be news to some parents, keeping things light and breezy will not necessarily lift the teen's spirits and can actually make them feel more isolated and hopeless than ever. There can often be a sense of meaning or purpose missing from the suicidal person's life. Sometimes parents are afraid to go deep when their teen expresses suicidal thoughts. Although it requires skill and sensitivity, philosophical conversations about the nature of life and death can be helpful to the individual who is having an existential crisis. Being truly understood is one of the deepest, most effective ways to help a person feel better.

Self-compassion, compassion for others, depth, authenticity and tenderness are needed when your teen is feeling a sense of despair. This can be really difficult as the parent is often simply terrified. We remember back when it was relatively easy to help our teens when they were young children – we took the time to figure out what was wrong and then we moved in and rectified it. But when the child grows up, our power and consequent ability to understand and then fix the situation is significantly reduced, and it can feel almost unbearable to witness our teens' pain. If we can turn and truly face the demons that are driving our teens, we are more likely to provide valuable help.

• • •

What parents can do

As the parent is embarking on a recovery process with their child, they may need some ground rules to carry them through; the rule of thumb is plenty of rules and plenty of warmth. This is difficult to carry out. We can become brittle when we are frightened, and some of us begin laying down the law in a bid to feel some sense of control over the chaos. We can even become hard-faced, trying to be stern so that the teenager realises that we are serious about the recovery. Others can become complete pushovers, without any sense of authority. This is when it's important to remember the need for love and boundaries. You might insist on the new rules about screens staying out of the bedroom because you are aware of their proclivity to look at self-harming videos but then, despite the teenager's shouts of protest, you could still cook their favourite dinners, treat them to a night out at the cinema or buy them something they have wanted for ages – anything that shows your tenderness and affection towards them.

It is valuable if parents try to be (but forgive yourself as you probably can't always be!):

- empathetic

- compassionate

- authentic

- patient and prepared for the long game

- willing to go deep; prepared to address the monster under the bed

- sensitive to the need for attention

- aware of the relapse cycle

- sensitive to the risk of collusion

- willing to seek out behaviour management techniques that might help.

When I was about 16, I was pretty furious with my parents. Our relationship had broken down and family life was pretty dysfunctional. One evening when I was in my room, pacing up and down, seething about one thing or another, my mother opened my bedroom door and, as if she was throwing a slab of meat to a lion in the wild, chucked a bar of chocolate at my bed and closed the door. It was a lovely gesture; there was no room for words between us – neither of us had the words to try to make our way back to each other again. Still, that chocolate bar showed me that she could somehow see my pain and wished to ease it. She couldn't ease it, of course – but the fact that she wanted to softened my heart, and I've never forgotten the gesture.

• • •

Takeaways

- The wild emotionality of teenagers can seem psychotic, and the subsequent emotional upheaval can cause parents to feel intimidated, deeply distressed and sometimes silenced.

- Self-harming behaviour is a maladaptive coping mechanism, and the person needs to help the teen to find healthier ways to cope with distress.

- Suicide is no longer taboo, and teens may speak about it more lightly than parents are accustomed to.

- Suicidality might be helped if the parents are willing to engage with the teen in seeking deeper meaning and purpose.

- Parents might need to be willing to explore the more frightening issues with their children if they suffer from existential despair – discussing different philosophies about what life is all about can be much more consoling than many think – and sweeping these questions under the carpet can make the teen feel more isolated.

- Boundaries and warmth are often essential to bring about serious change in the household.

CHAPTER 15

ALCOHOL AND DRUGS: SEEKING OBLIVION

'You're on earth. There's no cure for that.'

– SAMUEL BECKETT, *ENDGAME*

SOME TEENAGERS hit the ground running. At a certain age
– some very young, some older – they discover the illicit
delights of pushing boundaries and charge off, full steam
ahead, smoking, drinking, taking drugs and whatever you're
having yourself. There are many reasons why teenagers tend
to engage in this behaviour. Many teenagers with a natural
proclivity for risk taking and impulsivity tend to seek out the
adult thrills that alcohol provides. Some kids seek out drink
and drugs because it makes them feel stronger, confident, and

even invincible. Certain substances quell our natural feelings of vulnerability and can more easily take hold of vulnerable teenagers. In this chapter, I refer to drugs and alcohol interchangeably as it is generally a matter of the person's drug of choice. Their motivation for seeking oblivion is much more important than the actual method they use to get there – some find oblivion in alcohol, others find it more easily with cannabis.

Many alcoholics recall their first experience of an alcoholic drink as a remarkable experience that allowed them to feel a sense of peace for the first time. Drug addicts recall similar experiences with their initial experience of their drug of choice. Comments such as, 'It was like being wrapped in an emotional duvet,' or 'It felt like I was floating on a cloud and all my troubles felt suddenly manageable,' are often used to describe addicts' first experiences of drugs and alcohol. Psychoactive substances such as drink and drugs can command our emotional brain and create temporary feelings of euphoria. This sensation might feel natural and leave the user with a glimpse into a false world where everything is easier, softer and better in every way, but it is chemically manufactured. In this way, drink and drugs can offer a panacea to teenagers who feel awkward and insecure, and this can lead them to eventually become addicted.

• • •

Alcohol and drugs as a solution

Most addicts initially view alcohol or drugs as a solution to the challenges posed by life. Alcohol or drugs can be very alluring when they work as a tranquilliser, physically relaxing the individual and making them feel less inhibited and more confident. The release of the internal opiates called endorphins that are released by alcohol promotes feelings of satisfaction – characterised by the 'aaaahh' feeling when we take a nice long, satisfying swallow. What's not to like? Sadly, for anyone prone to addictive behaviour, this combination can create cravings and a destructive cycle where the person turns to alcohol or drugs every time they feel emotional pain. From my extensive experience and research on this subject, it is notable that some people seem to have a psychological disposition to become addicted, often described as a 'hole in the soul', and also seem to have a genetic predisposition to become addicted. (Alcoholism has a strong genetic component.) A small number of people can feel driven to get drunk and stay drunk from the very first time they drink alcohol.

A client of mine, Margery, described how her son Richard 'completely changed' after he took his first drink. According to Margery, 'He went out drinking with his mates that summer he turned 16, and it was like he had a personality transplant. From that day forth, he was hellbent on socialising. He went from being a quiet, gentle and nervous boy to becoming the life and soul of the party in a matter of weeks. In hindsight, it was all fuelled by alcohol. He seemed to become addicted that very first night he had a few pints of cider. I wouldn't have believed it if I hadn't seen it unfold.'

An added challenge facing parents is the remarkable drinking culture that still exists in Ireland today. Every celebration, from christenings to wakes, is drenched in alcohol. Boys often come to believe that drinking is manly while girls may believe it is sophisticated. People who choose not to drink are still regarded with suspicion, and alcohol is often considered the central focus of every gathering. The importance that is given to alcohol creates a huge level of allure around it. Parents can help to reduce this by drilling some holes in this culture with stories in the media that highlight the normalisation of drinking excessively in Ireland and how different cultures approach alcohol more calmly.

If you are concerned about your teenager's drinking, you might first take some time to figure out what the motivation is behind your child's desire to become intoxicated. Why do they want to get out of their mind? Why are they driven to tranquillise their emotions and lose their inhibitions? This is a task that should not be hurried but instead scrutinised with a cool head. If you examine the list below and decide that the reason why they might seek to drink or take drugs is likely to be a combination of two or three different factors, these are the factors that you need to focus on. Few lists are exhaustive, though, and you know your teen better than anyone else, so don't be afraid to come to your own conclusions about what is driving their behaviour.

Among the multitude of reasons why teenagers turn excessively to drink, drugs or self-destructive behaviour are:

- escapism

- rebellion

- peer pressure

- boredom

- thrill-seeking

- instant gratification

- lack of confidence
- a bid to seem grown-up
- lack of purpose.

• • •

Coping mechanisms: Why does your child seek oblivion?

Is your child seeking to escape?

Alcohol offers an escape hatch for some people. The liquid rolls down the throat and everything feels easier. Parents who have figured out that their child is driven to seek escape through drugs or alcohol need to seek out other escape routes for their child – other ways to relax and reduce their inhibitions and that provide this feeling of confidence. This might mean finding an activity that engrosses them or regularly bringing them on exciting trips to pique their interest. If they like sports, you might drive them to a soccer match; if they like music, you might buy them tickets to a concert. It might be hiking in nature or working with computers. What it is doesn't really matter. What matters is that this individual finds a healthier way to escape, because seeking escape through alcohol is an emotionally immature and dysfunctional coping mechanism.

Is it a need to rebel?

If your child is drinking due to a desire to rebel, it can be helpful for the parents to build a 'golden bridge' that enables the child to come to you. This particular child might benefit from being allowed to have a watered-down glass of wine or beer at home.

This needs to be done with open and frank discussion – why do they need to rebel? Do they feel over-controlled? Do you, the parent, need to loosen your grip a little? Can you negotiate safety behaviours alongside the adolescent's natural desire to break free?

Is it peer pressure?

A teenager who drinks to feel part of their peer group is often driven by an insecure attachment. These kids are ready to do anything to feel part of things – and if their friend told them to jump off a cliff, they would probably do it! The way to approach underage drinking with an insecure teenager is to attempt to strengthen your bond with them. This will take some time. In the meantime, you may need to lay down strict rules while simultaneously committing to projecting warmth towards the teenager and establishing stronger connections.

Is it boredom?

The child who is driven to drink or use drugs because they are bored and looking for thrills shouldn't be underestimated. Boredom has been a dangerously destructive force for so many people that it really should be given appropriate respect. Boredom is corrosive and can lead to reckless behaviour. It can create tension and existential angst and can be a driving force into self-destruction. People often dismiss their children's boredom as they believe the children are too busy to be bored, but this is misunderstanding boredom as having 'nothing to do'. A bored person doesn't just have nothing to do; they generally wish to be stimulated but are unable, for whatever reason, to connect with their environment. The psychologist John Eastwood, of York University in Toronto, describes the bored mind as the 'unengaged mind'. According to Eastwood, boredom is essentially 'the unfulfilled desire for satisfying activity', so a child can be very busy and also bored senseless at the same time.[51] A little boredom is good for most people, especially overscheduled children. It can lead to creativity and artistic pursuits – but relentless, long-term boredom leads to stagnation, especially when too much screen time is involved. This is bad for the psyche and needs just as much attention as other problems.

Is it thrill-seeking?

If your teen is drinking or using drugs because they are seeking thills, this might be resolved with some commitment from the parents. Some exciting adventures such as abseiling, water sports, circuit racing, go-karting or other adrenalin-inducing activities could bring some life into the disaffected teenager. This will need to be regular and challenging without being childish. The teenager might be reluctant to go; nevertheless, the parent needs to be committed to engaging their teen's interest. It is stressful and downright irritating to be in the company of a bored youth who refuses to engage and the parents could need further support to maintain morale as they attempt to find some thrills for their reckless, recalcitrant teenager.

Is it searching for instant gratification?

Instant gratification is the desire to experience pleasure or satisfaction without any delay. Basically, it's having it when you want it, right here and right now. For generations, we have been teaching children to practise delayed gratification, but as we now live in an age of high-speed Wi-Fi, instant gratification has become the norm, not the exception. No longer do we have to wait for next week's episode – we just download the entire series. Neither do we have to wait to make contact with people: instant messaging creates an expectation of immediacy that leaves us unsettled if we don't get a response.

If a parent suspects that their teenager is driven towards substance misuse in a search for instant gratification, they will probably see it in many other aspects of the teen's life. They probably have irrational demands about many things, so teaching teens the value of waiting and the pleasure of delayed gratification is a long-term exercise that should be combined with some additional bonding activities so the child might begin to feel more securely attached and less compulsive.

Is it a lack of confidence?

If your child is drinking or using drugs because they lack confidence, a course of counselling might be a good option. Building a teenager's confidence will take some time. In the meantime, their access to alcohol should be strictly curtailed in case they become habitual users before the long-term resolutions have time to take root. Plenty of love, consideration, tenderness and positive regard is essential for this child. They might be difficult and cranky, so bear in mind that it can be hard to maintain your equilibrium.

Is it a bid to seem grown-up?

It's developmentally natural for teenagers to wish to appear grown-up. It is the headache of the parents to figure out how to hold the tension between what is an appropriate bid for adulthood and what is inappropriate. With some thought and creativity, you could help them feel more sophisticated. Maybe attending certain more sophisticated events might satisfy this desire? Parents could do worse than introduce them to an older role model – maybe a cousin or family friend could be persuaded to bring them out every so often?

Are they missing a sense of purpose?

Many kids who act out are trying to escape an emptiness they feel inside them and could really do with finding a sense of purpose. The Roman Stoic philosopher Seneca tells us, 'If a man knows not to which port he sails, no wind is favourable.' Teenagers often feel bent out of shape by their lack of purpose – their parents and teachers tell them that school is everything, but many feel disaffected. They need something to encourage them to look beyond quick thrills. Indeed all animals need a sense of purpose – I know a little dog called Mindi who recently decided that her life's purpose is to protect me. Before she found her purpose, she was nervous and irritable (she's had a hard life), but now she knows what she needs to do, she is thrilled with herself. For a teenager, their sense of purpose might be fancying someone, getting likes and shares on social media or spreading the word about some new interest. Sometimes it doesn't really matter what our purpose is – simply the sense of having something that propels us out of bed in the mornings is enough.

• • •

Weed, hash, marijuana, pot, grass, skunk

A wide range of substances are available these days that were not available to previous generations, and, sadly, capitalism has arguably impacted this market in a pretty substantial manner, so there is little relation to the cannabis that parents might have smoked when they were teenagers and the cheap cannabis that teenagers today are smoking.

Hash, skunk and cannabis can all be described as 'weed', but the differences between them are significant. There are three main types of cannabis: hash (hashish or resin), herbal cannabis (weed, grass or marijuana) and skunk. Research shows that while regular unadulterated weed doesn't seem to cause an increased risk of psychosis, people who regularly smoke skunk are considerably more likely to experience psychotic episodes.[52] Having had considerable experience with young clients being adversely impacted by skunk in this manner, I believe it is vitally important that parents teach their teens about this issue. The link with psychosis is the reason why, while hash is considered a relatively harmless relaxant (which you might have smoked in your student days), skunk, a modified form of the cannabis plant, is known to be quite harmful.

The problem is that skunk has become more prevalent because it is often the cheapest way to get high; for example, 94 per cent of police seizures of cannabis in the UK in 2016 were skunk.[53] Based on my own clinical work, the situation in Ireland seems to be similar. Consequently, many new cases of psychosis are linked with skunk. It seems to be the modern equivalent of poitín. Prohibition arguably causes more problems than it resolves as it means that there is no quality control and consumers' reviews aren't easily available.

Nonetheless, even hash and weed are not harmless. Many young men are especially prone to becoming psychologically addicted to smoking weed. They can waste years playing video games, watching films and smoking weed. It can be a vacuous, superficial lifestyle that might have many passing pleasures but very little depth or satisfaction. If your child has become a habitual cannabis smoker, you must first ascertain whether they are smoking skunk or regular weed. If they are smoking skunk, I recommend an immediate and comprehensive response that tackles this issue head-on. If it is weed, you might need to consider your child's lifestyle. Think about the motivations listed above. Are they bored? Do they need some stimulating activities? Is it escapism? Whatever is driving them should be attended to, as it is all too easy to be waved away by the easy-going teenager who is very happy to live this low-key but self-destructive life.

• • •

Addictive behaviour

Some parents believe that the continental Europeans have a more sophisticated view of alcohol and often recount stories about how Europeans invite their children to have a watered-down glass of wine with their evening meal or a beer with their father when they watch a football match. Some say this works very well. Others say that it creates an unhealthy attitude and sends the message that adults need alcohol to oil the wheels of every social interaction. To figure out whether any behaviour is seriously worrisome, parents can ask themselves what the underlying need behind this behaviour is. They can also ask if the behaviour is having a negative impact on the person's life. Is the teen able to stop it when they want to? Another way to contemplate the issue is to assess the level of intensity the person has towards the activity – if it feels like there is too much intensity around it, it could be cause for concern. Do they grip the glass tightly? Do they slug the alcohol back as if their life depended on it? How do they handle it when their expectations to drink or take drugs are thwarted? The answers to these questions perhaps give you more insight into the problem than focusing on quantity.

· · ·

Hard drugs

If your child is taking heavily addictive drugs such as heroin or crack cocaine, they will need a correspondingly heavy response. A residential treatment centre might be an appropriate route, or teenager-oriented Narcotics Anonymous might be sufficient. Your teenager will need a good doctor, a good therapist and a good support group at the very minimum. Nonetheless, the motivations described above still apply. Parents need to prepare for a long, hard road to recovery, where relapse can break a person's heart and sobriety can create unbearable tension.

If your teenager is heavily involved in hard drugs and has little interest in stopping their drug use, you will need to batten down the hatches and prepare for the long slog. You will need to maintain your mental health for this, as it will take its toll on you. Having a child who is an addict is a long, dreadful and difficult marathon. Support groups such as Nar-Anon and Al-Anon are recommended as you will probably need to meet other parents who are on a similar path. You will also need to become an expert on boundaries and have a deep level of knowledge about the differences between enabling behaviour, colluding behaviour and supportive behaviour (see Chapter 16). Books such as *Tweak: Growing Up on Methamphetamines* by Nik

Sheff and *Beautiful Boy: A Father's Journey Through His Son's Addiction* by Nik's father, David Sheff, give good insight into the baffling, cunning and cruel nature of addiction and how it can destroy a family.

• • •

Heavy on boundaries, heavy on warmth

Seeing your child drunk or high is often a very disturbing experience. However, sometimes it is more important that parents put aside their visceral reactions and instead focus on analysing why their teen is seeking chemical oblivion. Most former addicts decry their lost years spent in the wilderness of addiction. Oftentimes people try to help them, but the addict can be an expert at masking what is wrong and the helpers may end up following their loved one down the rabbit hole. Becoming aware that your teen is in deep mental anguish and seeking to escape through alcohol or drugs can feel overwhelming, but this might be what you need to face. If this is a case of addiction, it is the teen's mountain to climb, not yours. If parents could suffer the addiction for their children, most of us would, but sadly this is not an option. The most useful response to addictive behaviour is providing boundaries and love. If it's not an addiction but simply inappropriate behaviour, the same response is required: you need to be clear that you will not tolerate drunkenness in the house, and you need to be ready to use tough love and to follow through if the rules are broken. This can lead to some very difficult choices, but the sooner the young person confronts the unmanageability of their lives, the more likely they will be to seek recovery.

· · ·

Takeaways

- Teens who seek oblivion often haven't yet developed their coping skills to be able to handle the more difficult challenges that life throws at us. They might need to learn emotional regulation and behaviour management.

- It is helpful to clarify the teenager's motivation to drink or use drugs.

- An emotional void can lead children to addiction.

- People who turn to drink or drugs as a means of escape tend to be emotionally immature.

- A long-term commitment might be needed to help their child to move beyond addiction.

- The parent needs to be heavy on boundaries and equally heavy on warmth when trying to help their child move towards more positive behaviour.

PART VI
ESTABLISHING POSITIVE
FAMILY DYNAMICS

CHAPTER 16

SUPPORTING YOUR DISTRESSED TEEN

'If there must be trouble, let it be in my day, that my child may have peace.'

– THOMAS PAINE

THE PANIC a parent feels when they see that their child is unhappy can be utterly overwhelming. We parents will typically do anything for our kids, and when they are very young, we can generally find a way to heal most wounds. But then, as they grow older, our powerlessness in the face of our adolescents' challenges becomes mercilessly obvious, and the teen begins to realise, often with a sense of panic and shock, that we are all essentially alone. Although parents can make a difference, ultimately it is essential that the teenager faces many of these challenges themselves as they are necessary developmental tasks that need to be overcome if the teen is to become a fully functioning adult.

· · ·

Take care of yourself

Some teenagers' emotional distress seems to tip into more serious clinical impairment, and it can be very difficult for parents to navigate these serious issues. It can be helpful to enlist the help of a therapist if you are seriously worried about your child, but don't discount the role a therapist might play in your own life. In my work, I often see the teenager, but I sometimes see the parent instead. I believe it is often more effective for the parent to undergo therapy as change can happen fast when the parents work on issues such as setting boundaries, holding authority, role-modelling, emotional regulation or whatever it is that would best help their distressed adolescent. Going straight for the target – the teenager – might seem like the best approach, yet sometimes coming at a problem in a more roundabout manner can yield infinitely better results.

Teenage distress can manifest in a number of ways – crying spells, bursts of anger, violence, substance abuse, disengagement, physical distress such as headaches or stomach pains, loss of interest and motivation, constant fatigue, or something else entirely. When your teenager is in the depths of distress, you might find that you become equally anguished: our barometer often rises and falls depending on our children's equilibrium. Yet it's important that you don't follow your teen down the rabbit hole of mental distress as it is all too easy to fall into the same level of distress as your kid. Bill Wilson, or 'Bill W' as he was known, set up Alcoholics Anonymous in 1935 as a fellowship so that people who were alcoholics could meet and find solace among each other. Sixteen years later, Bill W's wife, Lois W, and Anne B, the wife of another alcoholic, set up Al-Anon. They had come to realise that loved ones of alcoholics tend to match their partners' suffering. Likewise, we parents often follow our children into deep unhappiness. It's often said that we can only be as happy as our unhappiest child, but this does not need to be true and can be an unhealthy attitude. However, Herculean effort might be required to pull ourselves back from the brink so that we are sufficiently healthy to help our child.

• • •

Become an emotional detective

It can be valuable if you can figure out what is going on for your teen. Once you have a rough working idea about what's happening and you are open to amending this theory when faced with new evidence, then you can begin to devise a rough long-term plan of support.

Some parents find it helpful to role-play becoming a clear-headed detective and figuring out what is actually going on for their child. Why are they unhappy? Can you ascertain what their peers and/or teachers think of your teen? If parents can understand what is going on in the teenager's life, they are more likely to be able to help. Many parents tend to become secretive about their teen's distress, maybe to give their kid privacy or perhaps out of a sense of shame, but it can be very helpful to ask for input from siblings, from your friends and from the wider family as their view on the teenager is often more rational and sometimes more astute than the emotional, exhausted and harried perspective of the parent who is deep in the trenches.

Parenting strategy: Evaluate whether your child needs a psychological evaluation

Mental illness often emerges during adolescence, and as you worry about your teenager, you might often wonder whether these are the first shoots of serious mental illness. Sadly there is no real way for us to know this. What we can do, though, is offer compassion and tenderness and boundaries. This works whether the teen is facing a serious clinical disorder or is simply another crazy mixed-up teenager.

If a child's behaviour suddenly disintegrates when they were previously well-behaved, it is worth trying to view things with emotional depth and from a wider perspective – what do you think is going on? Is there mental illness in the family? Is it simply a manifestation of stress?

Serious mental health conditions, for example, bipolar disorder, schizoid disorder, borderline personality disorder and narcissistic disorder can first emerge during the adolescent years. Although these conditions are incredibly challenging, there is a lot of support available to families – the sooner you access this support, the sooner you can be helpful to your child, your family and yourself.

···

Evaluate the impact of family roles

Try as we might to avoid it, most families end up ascribing roles to each family member in a bid to more easily categorise and understand their behaviour. We know our kids, so monikers like 'the deep thinker' and 'the funny one' feel accurate. Sometimes, however, these tags can become a heavy burden. It is important that parents become aware of each child's family role, whether it is the golden child, the clown, the black sheep, or the rebel, and make sure that the teen has sufficient room within the family dynamic to move beyond their ascribed role.

Parents should keep an eye out for 'the lost child', who stays quiet and often goes unnoticed, or the scapegoat, who everybody blames and often ends up living up to their role as the troublemaker. We fall into using these categories because they make sense but if, for example, your teen has fallen into the role of 'the identified patient', you might find yourself trawling through therapists searching for the one who will 'fix' them, while it could be that this teen is manifesting all the emotional distress of the family through their 'dis-ease'. Another common family role is 'the truth-teller', who is often unpopular within the household because they reveal the family's unacknowledged dysfunctions. It can be very helpful if parents take a step back and consider each family member's role in the family and how it might be impacting their wellbeing.

MARY, 14, THE FAMILY SCAPEGOAT AND THE TRUTH-TELLER

When Mary first came into my office, it was immediately clear that this was a girl who didn't like herself very much. With a quick wit and a ready smile, she could be good company, but there was a storm of anger within her that was always threatening to bubble to the surface. She had a long fringe that kept falling over her face, and I thought about the message this was sending to the world. Mary also had a tendency to be prickly, no matter how banal the utterance.

When I asked Mary what the main problem at home was, she answered without hesitating. 'I hate my dad. He's a prick and a bully. I hate the way my mother panders to him.' As we got to know one another, it soon emerged that Mary's analysis was pretty accurate; Mary's dad, Tim, did indeed often behave like a bit of a prick. He was a self-absorbed problem drinker who was very loud when drunk and inclined to fight with anybody in the vicinity. Sue, Mary's mother, wanted to keep the peace, so the children were told to accept Tim's bad behaviour. But Mary didn't see why she should. In her view, her father was the one who was behaving badly, so he was the one who should be called out about it.

I often engage the parents in the therapeutic process, as long as it's appropriate and the teenager is happy with it. Mary and I decided that it might be helpful for Sue to join a couple of sessions. Sue was a kind and gentle woman who was intimidated by her daughter and overwhelmed by her husband. Sue sought peace at any price, and she hoped that I would teach Mary to learn to put up and shut up about Tim's bad behaviour.

But I didn't agree.

This family had become utterly dysfunctional. Tim was a malevolent presence when he was drunk and madly positive when he was sober. Sue revelled in Tim's positive sober persona, but Mary hated it. 'He's a fake,' she stormed, 'and I don't see why I should forget his horrible behaviour just because he's choosing to be nice one moment and horrible the next.'

Mary was the third daughter in the family. Robyn was born first, and the parents adored her. Robyn was a high achiever and proof enough for Sue that the family was fine, really. Then came Sinéad, the family clown, who was funny and easy-going and always able to make everyone laugh. By the time Mary had arrived, Tim's alcoholism was making its presence felt. Tim sank ever deeper into alcoholism, and Sue felt a sense of panic as her family was threatened. Mary's evident unhappiness made Sue feel resentful as it suggested that Sue should do something to change the household dynamic, and confronting the issue frightened Sue more than anything.

Sue didn't want to change anything. She knew that Tim's behaviour was dysfunctional, but she also knew that she needed him. He had a good job, and Sue didn't feel able to live alone. Also, Sue loved Tim and couldn't bear to live without him, despite his worsening alcoholism.

Mary, on the other hand, hated living with Tim. She hated living in a household that was fake and hated the way everyone endured Tim's aggressive mood swings as if they were a necessary evil. Mary wanted out, but she was only 14, so she was stuck. In situations like this one, I often think of the story of the comedian Bill Hicks who, when he was a teenager, was taken by his parents to a psychoanalyst hoping to ascertain the root causes of his rebellious nature. The analyst privately told Hicks, 'It's them, it's not you.' This gave Bill the fortitude that he needed to stay sane in a pretty insane situation. In the very same manner, I saw my role with Mary was to help her endure a dysfunctional lifestyle, in which she might be woken any given night by singing or fighting. I encouraged her to envisage her future adult life and plan for it accordingly.

Mary and I engaged in creating a holding space where she could let off steam in our sessions. Her growing self-awareness and insight could be used to help her become more content in herself. Some years later, I met Mary bouncing merrily along the street with her hair swept back from her face in a ponytail. She was with her boyfriend and seemed very happy. She had left home and had a full-time job. The furious, brittle and bolshy kid had grown up to become an interesting, engaging and cheerful adult.

• • •

Don't sweat the small stuff

Over the years in my work I have noticed that certain parents can worry themselves sick about issues that might not necessitate such agony. Perhaps your teen's bedroom is shockingly messy? Maybe family holidays have become disastrous? Or your teenager's friends are a troublesome crowd? This is when parents need to remember that the pattern of behaviour is much more important than any one-off behaviour. If your teenager's bedroom is the worst of the challenges you face, you're pretty lucky. If, however, their bedroom is reflective of a marked disintegration in their way of being, you need to have a serious conversation with them and access professional help.

Sometimes a new response from your teenager is simply a sign that they are growing up and away from you, as they must do. If your teenager previously enjoyed family holidays but has suddenly lost interest in family events and wants to be with their friends instead, perhaps you might consider bringing a friend along as it will make everyone's holiday more pleasant? Or you might allow them to stay with friends instead of coming on the holiday? Parents can feel dreadfully disappointed that their kids don't want to spend their leisure time with them, but if the teen is coping reasonably well with life, this might be a challenge for the parents rather than the teen.

• • •

Is it trauma catching up?

Past traumas that may have happened to the child can emerge either behaviourally or cognitively during adolescence. Until puberty or so, most children assimilate any trauma that they have experienced without properly processing what has happened. They have neither the emotional ability nor the verbal competence to articulate what has happened, so the trauma is most often manifested behaviourally. This behaviour can come out in a wide range of ways – for example, some children need constant reassurance, others are given to rage while others might display Tourette's syndrome in the form of tics or other anxious symptoms.

When adolescence is up and running, and the reality of life has well and truly hit, many teenagers feel entirely at sea as they begin to cognitively process what has happened to them since they were born. This is why many parents might believe that the child coped perfectly well with a problem in early or middle childhood – not recognising that some other behaviour was actually a manifestation of the distress – and then, when the child becomes a teenager they can suddenly demonstrate very clearly that they are very distressed and might need to improve their coping skills. We parents always hope that our children have emerged through each specific trauma unscathed – this is a natural hope but it can lead us to kid ourselves. And it can make us feel incredibly emotional when our teenager tells us that actually they aren't coping and a certain traumatic event has left a lasting mark on them.

Mental distress can manifest and channel in any given direction, depending on the context. A perfectly happy kid can suddenly become ravaged by anorexia while another kid might become addicted to alcohol or drugs. The specific way an adolescent manifests their distress might be of supreme importance to you, the parent, and yet, as you have read this book and considered the different challenges that face adolescents, you may have recognised your child in contexts you didn't expect. The specific way an individual behaves in order to try to get their emotional needs met is not so important – what is actually important is the need that is driving the pattern of behaviour.

Parenting strategy: Take regular breaks!

Parenting is a marathon, not a sprint. It is easy for our patience to become sorely tried and it can be helpful to take a break from the worry from time to time. If you do take a break from it – maybe by going away for a weekend or catching up with old friends – you might find that you come back with fresh eyes and a more considered insight into what is actually going on for your child.

• • •

Facing potential mental illness

When we consider that roughly three-quarters of mental health problems are established by the age of 24,[54] and that roughly 25 to 33 per cent of the general population will have mental health problems in their lifetime,[55] it becomes easier to understand why some teenagers behave so irrationally. A certain number of these very destructive and distressed teenagers will eventually suffer from mental ill-health. We don't yet know why some teenagers recover and why some become more distressed; indeed, we don't yet know why some adults recover and why others become stuck. Some of us experience dreadful life events and manage to avoid terrible mental illness; others experience relatively less difficult hardship and end up devastated by mental health troubles. Thankfully, some of our distressed teenagers will move beyond their pain and their adolescence will end up being the lowest point of their life.

In my own clinical experience, commitment to the process of recovery and the availability of appropriate support from family or friends seems to be the difference between those who recover and those who don't. The problem is that nobody seems to know why some people are able to commit to the recovery process while others at first seem equally committed but then, somewhere deep inside, they don't seem to have the tools to be able to overcome their demons. It is also difficult to ascertain what is appropriate support and what is not. Studies of identical twins who have been raised in different households suggest that 50 per cent of our happiness is genetic, 25 per cent is dependent on our circumstances and 25 per cent is dependent on our habits.[56] So, although some of us find it more difficult to be happy, our circumstances and our habits can have a radical effect on our happiness.

When to escalate, when to maintain and when to seek professional help

If the individual is in a constant state of stress and they overreact all the time, therapy is recommended, especially if any of the following are notable:

- always feeling on edge or tense; a pervasive inability to relax

- persistent worry, nervousness, fear

- depression

- despair

- a feeling of foreboding

- emotions/behaviours that interfere with daily activities

- fear or avoidance of non-threatening situations

- rage and other overreactive responses.

Professional help should assist the individual to balance their stress response and to determine the underlying cause of their feelings so that they can find better ways to cope with difficult but not life-threatening situations.

Certain people seem to have been born with a thinner skin than others. These kids will often have behavioural difficulties when they are younger – stomach pains, headaches, bedwetting, fussy eating, insomnia or other nervous habits – and then when they grow older, they might find it difficult to make friends or to maintain friendships. They may engage in self-destructive behaviour such as getting drunk or self-harming or develop a spiteful and harsh inner voice that never stops criticising. Why do some of us behave in that manner and others skip along easily? That is the million-dollar question that may never be truly answered. But we do know what works best to support these kids, and all kids: love and boundaries.

JACK, 27

Growing up, Jack was an intense, academic boy. He was the second youngest of four and prone to bedwetting and emotional outbursts, Jack's mother, Clodagh, worried about him more than her other three children put together. 'It's like Jack is just too soft for this world. He doesn't have a second skin,' she often said. Jack didn't make friends easily and he preferred to play alone rather than engage in more complex interactions with his peers. Jack loved Lego and in many ways this saved his childhood. He happily stayed in his room playing with Lego as long as he was allowed to. Unlike his two brothers, Jack didn't like sports and although his mother enrolled him in soccer, hurling and swimming, none of it stuck and he went back to playing alone. Clodagh had him psychologically evaluated and although it was interesting, it didn't make much difference.

When Jack reached puberty, he became even more solitary. He spent all his time in his room, only coming out when he was forced to. When he was 16, he discovered weed and took to it like a duck to water. Previously an A-grade student, Jack's grades dropped along with his interest in school. Prior to his weed habit, Jack had been expected to do very well in his state exams and perhaps study medicine or law at college. Six months later, there was doubt whether he would even take the state exams.

Tom and Clodagh were out of their minds with worry when they first came to see me. Although they made the appointment for Jack, he refused to go, so they decided to attend instead. Ultimately, Clodagh became my client as, week on week, Jack refused to attend. I never even clapped eyes on Jack although the stories about him became ever more frantic.

Jack's weed habit became out of control. He smoked in his bedroom all day and all night and refused to go to school. He robbed from his mother and father. He accessed their online banking details and transferred large amounts of money from their account to his and then he frittered it all away on random useless stuff. He dropped out of school and the great dreams of a doctor in the family faded away.

Jack's behaviour became even more erratic. He reported hearing voices in his head that were forcing him to behave in a certain way. One summer's day, Jack had a serious psychotic break, took off all his clothes and wandered through the neighbourhood singing to himself. The ambulance was called and Jack ended up in psychiatric care, diagnosed with cannabis-induced psychosis. He was 19 years old.

Jack has remained living between his parents' house and psychiatric care ever since then. Sometimes he seems to recover and begins to rehabilitate into society, getting a part-time job and making plans for the future. Other times, he is utterly reliant on his parents. Clodagh continued to attend therapy, as caring for Jack became very difficult.

As we worked together, it took some time before Clodagh was ready to acknowledge that she needed to renegotiate her own life so that she could take some pleasure out of it. She had become so obsessed with Jack's welfare that she found it difficult to allow herself even a small level of pleasure, such as singing along happily to a favourite song. She believed she wasn't allowed to be happy because her son was pretty much always unhappy.

Clodagh and I continued to meet and discuss Jack's life, the missed opportunities, the difficulties he had had as a child, her marriage, her other kids and then, finally, Clodagh. Clodagh's life, Clodagh's childhood, Clodagh's hopes and dreams. It turned out that Clodagh was a beautiful singer who had stopped singing as she focused on trying to make Jack feel better. She and her husband, Tom, used to take part in musicals before Jack's problems became unmanageable. Slowly but surely, Clodagh started to allow some joy back in her life.

The difference between supporting and enabling

The rule of thumb is that supportive behaviour supports the individual to behave in a manner that is healthy; enabling helps the individual to behave in a self-destructive manner, and colluding plots with the individual in order to deceive, for example, when a parent covers up for their teen. Although it can feel very satisfying to have lots of control over our younger kids, over-controlled kids don't tend to mature in a healthy manner and over-controlling parents can tend towards enabling and sometimes colluding with their teen.

If teens feel over-controlled, those with a rebellious nature learn to push against all authority, biting off their nose to spite their face. Meanwhile, those who are more obedient can end up being compulsively compliant and bounce from controlling parents to chronically controlling relationships and friendships in both their personal and professional lives. Over-controlled kids often seek enabling and collusion from their parents. This can lead to deep resentment and a limited ability to make decisions to help themselves.

Enablers are often problem-solvers who have kind hearts. Solving problems makes them feel useful but the truth is they are impeding the individual in learning how to function in a responsible manner. Parents' intentions are to help; sadly, acting as an enabler does just the opposite. Enabling involves acting in a way that prevents your teenager from dealing with the negative consequences of their actions. Not dealing with these consequences gives them the impression that their behaviour is acceptable. No matter what the behaviour, allowing your teenager to continue to choose damaging behaviour by being passive, or assisting them, only deepens the potential damage in the long term.

Supportive behaviour involves supporting or assisting with things that the teen is incapable of doing for themselves or doing things that facilitate them to improve their life in some way. If we are to be a supportive presence in our children's lives we need to make sure we don't enable or collude with self-destructive behaviour. When our teen is unravelling, we need to help them gain control of their behaviour and their life without overstepping into enabling inappropriate behaviour.

Consider these questions to ascertain whether you are an enabler or supporter:

- Do you find yourself repeatedly making excuses for your teen? 'Oh, she was just tired today,' 'She meant to text, but she was just too busy,' 'He was just blowing off steam, he wouldn't normally behave like that.'

- Do you continuously put your own needs (or the needs of your other children) second because your teenager needs your attention? This can be normal with a young child, but less healthy if your child is an adolescent and there is no give and take.

- Do you have a feeling (or maybe you know full well) that the behaviour you are witnessing is unhealthy, irresponsible or inappropriate but you're afraid to act as you know you probably should?

- Do you routinely lie for your child?

If you believe you might be tipping into enabling rather than supporting it can be helpful to learn to take some time before you respond to any request from your teen. If you answer automatically you will probably agree to 'help' every time, but if you pause, say you'll get back to them and remove yourself from the room to have a think, you might find that the most helpful response is to say 'no'. In doing this, you are role-modelling healthy boundaries for the teen and teaching them that 'no' can be a full sentence. We teach people how to treat us and it's important that we teach our children to treat us with respect.

• • •

The process of individuation

Individuation is the process of the formation of a stable personality. As a person individuates, they gain a sense of themselves that is separate from their parents, friends and family. This process of individuation generally begins in adolescence and pretty much continues throughout a person's life. The good news is that parents and children have never been so connected and open with each other. Children confide in parents much more than previous generations and they depend on parental love and guidance to a much larger degree than ever before. This is all to the good and long may it continue. But one downside of our deeper connection with our children is that many teenagers and young adults are finding it more difficult to individuate and this is preventing personal maturity. If the parent becomes over-involved in their teen's life, for example, by involving themselves in their teen's friendship battles, a toxic dynamic can develop where the child loses their ability to individuate because they are too enmeshed with the parent.

Signs that a teenager is seeking to individuate from their parents are:

- seeking privacy
- focusing on themselves more than others
- rebelling against family or cultural norms
- personalising their appearance.

We parents are used to doing things for our children. When they're very young, we feed them, bathe them, dress them and do pretty much everything for them. Then, as they mature, we slowly wean them off their dependency on us. This generally happens over the course of roughly the first 20–25 years of a person's life. As the teenager becomes more mature, they need to renegotiate their relationship with their parents and begin to understand that their parents are humans too, with needs and desires, and not just a being who is either supporting or foiling their life. This means that it is important that you begin to teach your teen that you are a human, not just a parent; that you bleed and hurt and laugh and cry just like everybody else. Initially, the teen is often horrified to learn this. Then, over time, as they mature, they begin to appreciate you as a human as well as a parent.

• • •

A supportive presence with a loose rein and a strong core

Just as we would when riding a horse, parents need to learn to hold on loosely while simultaneously maintaining a sense of control of the situation. With a loose rein but a strong core, the horse-rider makes it clear to the horse what direction they should travel in and which jump they wish to clear. Indeed, equine therapy is a rapidly expanding industry, perhaps because horses can provide good lessons about a mentally healthy approach to life. When a parent is filled with fear, they can react by keeping a very tight grip. This seldom works, though, and the parent needs to look for more productive solutions.

Parenting strategy: Have a small number of crystal-clear expectations

Parents need to have a small number of crystal-clear expectations for their children. This might mean an expectation of respectful communication: of leaving the phone downstairs before 10.30 p.m. and of getting up on time for school – and that's it. If you overload the teenager with expectations, this will quickly turn into too much control. Parents need to be wise about choosing when to be hard-line and when to let it go. It's never easy, by the way, and mistakes will be made. But that's OK. The grand plan is to have a couple of reliable, consistent expectations that are both fair and flexible. Specific, well-known consequences need to be sometimes enacted to remind the teenager that you are the authority figure in the house. (But it's important that you don't overdo this either!)

• • •

What parents can do

To a certain extent, you only really have control over your own life. You can read books, go to therapy and build self-awareness about what needs to happen for your child to feel better, but ultimately, by making yourself the healthiest, most in-tune and self-compassionate, self-accepting person you can be, you will automatically improve your child's chances of living a healthy and functioning life. You will also be happier. You can look at what's in your power and not what's in your child's power. Although you may not have had any part in causing your child's distress, you can change the part of yourself that's adding to the cycle of unhealthy behaviour in the household. Your child will benefit most if you can parent from your values rather than from your anxious place. If you walk around filled with grief and anxiety, your child will feel burdened by your distress. If you can access a wiser, more reflective place, your child will only have their own distress to contend with and will have you as a role model. It is hard, but it is valuable.

Parents can certainly help their distressed teenagers by acknowledging that a fundamental step in the process is understanding the limits of the parent's ability to help. There is only so much you can do – after that, you need to give a certain space for the teen to find their way. You can't do it for them. If you try to, you will impede their progress. Nonetheless, you *can* do any or all of the following:

• You can role-model a healthy, happy life; you can take care of yourself emotionally and physically and make sure that you take some joy out of life.

- You can attend to your friendships and other adult relationships.

- You can seek to resolve your own issues in a healthy manner so that your unresolved distress doesn't impact your kids.

- You can learn to communicate effectively and learn to say what's on your mind in an appropriate manner.

- You can learn to observe yourself and your family's patterns and family roles and seek to improve the less healthy patterns of behaviour.

- You can learn to examine the whole family drama and see how your and your family's emotional pressures might contribute to your child's distress.

- You can set limits and give enforceable consequences.

- You can take charge, not control; you can hold your parental authority.

- You can be parental and learn not to always parent with an 'anxious focus' on your child.

- You can do all this and life in your household will be better; your teenager might not get better, but *you* will feel better and *they* will have a better chance of getting better than if you followed them into the various rabbit holes of adolescent confusion.

• • •

Takeaways

- Past trauma might not manifest until the teenage years.

- The first stirrings of mental illness often emerge during adolescence and it can be difficult to distinguish mental health concerns from difficult teenage behaviour.

- Controlling parents can feel very satisfied in their child's early and middle childhood but can later feel frustrated by their teenager's tendency to be controlled by their peers.

- It is easy for parents to lose themselves within their child's distress and it can take a lot of effort to pull back from it.

- Supportive behaviour supports the teenager to behave in a healthy manner.

- Enabling behaviour helps the teenager to behave in a self-destructive manner.

- Teenagers seem to be thankful for the enabler's intervention but in the long term this typically turns into a seething resentment.

- The process of individuation leads the teen to move away from their parents.

- Our job as parents is to hold on with a loose rein as the teenager moves through the teenage developmental milestones.

- It is helpful if parents live functioning and healthy lives so as to be a role model for their children.

CHAPTER 17

THE MAGIC IS IN THE REPAIR

'Out beyond ideas of wrongdoing and right-doing there is a field. I'll meet you there.'

— RUMI

MANY PARENTS FEEL incredibly disappointed and distressed that their connection with their teen is not how they want it to be. As we come to the end of this book, it is vitally important that you realise that no matter how ruptured you feel your relationship with your teenager is, parenting is a very long game, and you are unlikely to be even halfway through it at this stage. Secondly, relationships are hard. We humans are both very fallible and very complex. We can misunderstand each other for years. And we can also reconnect. Pretty much every long-term relationship carries some disappointment with it, but that's perhaps what makes this world so wonderfully complex – we love our loved ones despite their and our many, many faults.

When the poet Maya Angelou was three years old, her mother, Vivian Baxter Johnson, abandoned her by sending Maya to live with her paternal grandmother. Maya experienced some very difficult challenges, and when they reunited some years later, Maya found it hard to forgive her 'glamorous if feckless' mother.[57] Maya left her mother's home when she gave birth to a baby boy at 17. Yet Vivian helped Maya tremendously as she entered early adulthood. Some years later, as Vivian lay in a coma on her deathbed, Maya said to her: 'You were a terrible mother of small children, but there has never been anyone greater than you as a mother of a young adult.' In reply, Vivian squeezed Maya's hand twice. Maya kissed her fingers. Vivian died the following morning.

The magic of a relationship happens in the repair. Relationships deepen by recognising moments of distress and meeting this distress with honesty and care. You do not need to ensure that you never get into a fight. Rather, the everyday moments of disconnection, the long hard wars filled with coldness and the crazed, turbulent fights highlight how important any given relationship is to us. It is only because we care so much about a person that we are willing to have a passion-filled, long-drawn-out war. If you can acknowledge the distress and take the time and effort to authentically try to repair the rupture, you and your teen could one day have a better relationship than you can possibly imagine.

Regaining your sense of authority

In many ways, we're still using the equivalent of leeches when it comes to psychology. This is a new science, not much more than 150 years old, and there are *a lot* of unknown unknowns. Additionally, psychology hasn't exactly covered itself in glory in those years – there have been many disgraceful episodes such as the lobotomy scandal, the multiple personality craze and the terrible scandal of false memory syndrome, where many innocent people were falsely accused and imprisoned for child sexual abuse. Mind-altering medication has had a chequered history, with many people angry and regretful about being prescribed certain medications, while others report feeling very relieved to have been prescribed what they believe to be life-saving drugs. For this reason, it is not safe to distrust your own instinct in favour of the latest expert advice. Parents need to instead tap into their own mind and find their authority in this fast-moving landscape where what was recommended to parents merely one generation ago is frowned upon today. In such an unreliable landscape, the most important approach parents can take is to ensure that they parent with all their love and according to their own values and beliefs; not according to this book, that book, or anyone else's beliefs.

• • •

Parents are the world experts on their children

As the Jungian analyst Lisa Marchiano has noted, parents are the world experts on their children, and they need to be careful not to give their power away to other so-called experts. Experts aren't all-knowing gods – they are as fallible as everybody else. A lot of power has been removed from parents in recent years and bestowed on mental health professionals, social workers and the authorities. This change came about mostly as a result of harrowing cases of extreme parental neglect, but the tendency has seeped into more ordinary families. Parents often feel disempowered, and those in authority often disagree with each other. Even though a lot of power has been moved from the parents to the professionals, at the same time, and quite paradoxically, a lot more responsibility has landed on the parents' shoulders. Parents feel increasingly disempowered with regard to the freedom to raise their kids according to their own values. Yet they are increasingly being held responsible for issues such as school refusal, teen criminality and delinquent behaviour.

For these reasons, if parents believe their relationship with their teenager is veering out of control, they must retain a sense of authority within the household – and if they have given this authority away, they must retrieve it. You, the parent, can be good enough. Your teen will benefit more from you leaning in with love and boundaries than from what any professional can offer. Professionals who are involved in your teen's life are unlikely to have a fraction of the love and commitment that you have to offer, so your teen will benefit more if you lean in to the situation and make sure you are holding your authority. You can read this book and other books, you can watch the YouTube videos and listen to the podcasts, but then one day, you will need to close the books and trust yourself. The time is now.

Remaining curious

Curiosity derives from the Latin word for 'care' and curiosity is an important element that leads us from the darkness into the light. If we can remain openly curious about our teen's pain, we will be more likely to be able to reach into the inner depths that will explain what's going on for them. Suppose your teenager has lost it, yet again, and now, having screamed at everyone in the family, is in her room crying and thinking furious thoughts. In that case, when the storm has passed and the time is right, it can be valuable to make some space for curiosity as this will quiet the self-blame. So the parent might say, 'I can see you feel wretched about what just happened. I wonder what would you think if we were watching a movie and that was a scene from the movie?' The idea is that you metaphorically take your kid by the hand and lead them to take a bird's eye view of the situation. What was she feeling before she yelled? What has been on her mind today? What is hard about life these days? This enables the teen to become more self-aware and even self-analytical. She might become more motivated to begin problem-solving as she considers other options.

• • •

Don't be afraid to choose the nuclear option

Perhaps teenagers fared better when their journey to adulthood was marked with a ceremonial rite of passage and, other than that, mostly left to figure out life for themselves? Certainly, now that we have lost the official religious ceremonies that helped previous generations contemplate their movement from childhood to adulthood, this post-religious age seems to have left many teenagers rudderless. Perhaps visiting another culture might bring about some much-needed depth for your teen – or perhaps they might benefit from experiencing a rite of passage? Sometimes, though, we can see that our teen is flailing and needs a more significant change if they are to improve. This might be as big as moving continent, lock, stock and barrel, or it might be that one of the parents takes a sabbatical and travels beyond the cultural context to provide some perspective for their distressed teen – perhaps a house swap for a year, an extended trip abroad or a series of visits to some friends and relations. Other changes might involve moving schools or simply quitting a hobby that no longer brings joy. Sometimes we need to be brave.

• • •

Pebbles in a barrel

We don't have to go for the nuclear option – it doesn't suit everyone. Hollywood has a lot to answer for – so many of us assume that, when trouble arrives, there will be some sort of Hollywood-style denouement. In truth, this is pretty unlikely to happen. Sometimes we need to go large, but at other times we need to be aware that resolution will come slowly. It is much more likely that all the random remarks have been like pebbles in a barrel. It is achingly slow, but the little comments, the throwaway lines, the heartfelt gestures and the tender moments add up until, eventually, the barrel is full and your teen feels capable and ready to set forth into the adult world. Only when you have bestowed your wisdom on them for 20-odd years will you see the emotional maturity taking root. Until then, don't put too much pressure on yourself. Not every utterance needs to be filled with wisdom: peppering their lives with regular, supportive and loving comments will be enough to see your child grow up secure in the knowledge that they are loved.

• • •

Strengthening the parental bond

If a parent realises their bond with their teenager is not as strong as it could be, it can be valuable to commit to a long-term project that will strengthen the bond. This project will need to be planned, it will take commitment, and it might take some years. Teens might be heavily resistant to this, so the parent might need extra support to help them stay the pace. It's very easy to lose heart when half of the group of two is completely uninterested. The project will also need to be well chosen – if bonding isn't occurring, it is often up to the parent to call the shots and change tack. This can feel almost impossible as you will have to also give time for the teenager to be resistant, recalcitrant and unenthused. Again, extra emotional support for the parent is often necessary so that they can untangle whether any particular project is helping or causing even more problems. Nothing about this is easy, but it might end up being a project of a lifetime and could feel incredibly worthwhile once the parent gets some response from the child.

One parent I met described setting out to climb the peaks of Ireland with his teenage son. At the beginning of the project, his son had little interest. After a few months, the teenager began to feel a sense of achievement, noted the height of each peak, and became more ambitious. The emotional gap between father and son was reduced, and they stopped feeling so awkward in each other's company. A mother I spoke to went on a road trip all around Australia for a summer with her teenage daughter. They camped at night and toured the sights. The teenager came back from this trip a changed girl: more confident, more easy-going and with a new-found gentle tenderness towards her mother.

• • •

Rekindling the joy

It is not easy when we're in the trenches, trying to connect with a teenager who is resistant in every way. Holding the line and maintaining boundaries can be utterly exhausting. But this is the very reason why we need to make sure that we have some joy in our lives. When you have rekindled some joy in your own life you can then begin to establish some positive family dynamics in the household. If you try to establish the positive family dynamics when you aren't feeling better yourself it can quickly turn into a brittle affair – movie night can descend into a brawl about the choice of movie and the treat at the restaurant can become an evening of sniping. Perhaps if things are very difficult with your teen you might begin by finding your joy elsewhere? You could choose to refresh old friendships, join a choir or a drama group or find some other way to relieve your troubled soul? My mother had a very hard life when I was growing up, but every single Wednesday and Friday she played badminton and always came back in better form. Through this she showed me that no matter how hard a person's life is they can still find some joy within it. We need to nourish ourselves when we are going through hardship – otherwise we will fall into despair. This might take some time, so make sure to be kind and gentle with yourself in the meantime.

• • •

And finally ...

Forgive yourself and forgive your teen. Finding forgiveness and acceptance when you feel at your worst is no small feat, but it is essential for the wellbeing of the family. Parenting teens offers you many opportunities to hate everybody as you discover just how difficult it is to keep your head when everything is going crazy. However, if you can cultivate an attitude of self-compassion and self-acceptance, you will find yourself in a place of wisdom and transformation. You are the parent you are – not the one you hoped you would be. Equally, your kid is the kid they are, and no other. Neither of you was ever going to be perfect.

Even though we live in a culture that expects parents to soothe, discipline, inspire, teach, entertain, motivate, encourage and mend our children, we can't actually do all that. It's too much. And it leaves parents feeling permanently inadequate and hopelessly flawed, simultaneously forgetting that this is what it is to be human. You might be skilled at listening to your teen but hopeless at disciplining them; your partner might be brilliant at motivating them but useless at soothing them. We all bring different things to the party. You bring yourself. Your family is just that: your family, to shape and nurture with tenderness and playfulness or whatever else you choose.

Accepting your parental shortcomings is a radical act that will open up the entire family to a more expansive and forgiving way of living.

Your teen is trying to convey a multitude of emotions to you. They are not fully formed, so everything is chaotic. They can be funny and crazy, cheerful and angsty – all in the same minute. As parents, all we can do is try to buckle in, try to keep perspective and know that it will probably be OK in the long run. As the poet Philip Larkin told us, 'What will survive of us is love.'

NOTES

1   Damour, L. (2017) *Untangled: Guiding Teenage Girls Through the Seven Transitions into Adulthood*. Atlantic Books.

2   Pickhardt, C. (2010) 'The disenchantment of adolescence', *Psychology Today*, 23 February <https://www.psychologytoday.com/ca/blog/surviving-your-childs-adolescence/201002/the-disenchantment-adolescence>.

3   Thompson, D. (2018) 'A brief history of teenagers', *Saturday Evening Post*, 13 February <https://www.saturdayeveningpost.com/2018/02/brief-history-teenagers>.

4   Steinberg, L. (2008) 'A Social Neuroscience Perspective on Adolescent Risk-Taking', *Developmental Review*. 28(1):78-106. doi: 10.1016/j.dr.2007.08.002. PMID: 18509515; PMCID: PMC2396566.

5   Hendriksen, E. (2019) 'Failure to launch syndrome', *Scientific American*, 18 May <https://www.scientificamerican.com/article/failure-to-launch-syndrome>.

6   Brown, B. (2011) 'The Power of Vulnerability'. TED Talk <https://www.youtube.com/watch?v=iCvmsMzlF7o>.

7   West, C. (2020) *The Karpman Drama Triangle Explained: A Guide for Coaches, Managers, Trainers, Therapists – and Everybody Else*. Buntingford: CWTK Publications.

8   Hall, G.S. (1904) *Adolescence: Its Psychology and its Relations to Physiology, Anthropology, Sociology, Sex, Crime, Religion and Education*, Vol. 1. D. Appleton & Co. <https.//doi.org/10.1037/10616-000>.

9   Brennan, D. (2021) 'What is Emotional Immaturity?' *Web*

MD, 25 October <https://www.webmd.com/mental-health/what-is-a-emotional-immaturity>.

10   Gu, Y., Gu, S., Lei, Y. and Li, H. (2020) 'From uncertainty to anxiety: How uncertainty fuels anxiety in a process mediated by intolerance of uncertainty', *Neural Plasticity* 22 November 8866386. doi: 10.1155/2020/8866386. PMID: 33299402; PMCID: PMC7704173.

11   Heubeck, E. (2019) 'Teens seem to be taking longer to grow up. One reason? A closer bond with their parents', *Washington Post*, 4 September <https://www.washingtonpost.com/lifestyle/2019/09/04/teens-seem-be-taking-longer-grow-up-one-reason-closer-bond-with-their-parents>.

12   Ibid.

13   Burkeman, O. (2015) 'Misery, failure, death and a slap in the face. Great advice for life from James Hollis', *Guardian*, 10 August <https://www.theguardian.com/commentisfree/2015/aug/10/not-self-help-great-advice-life-james-hollis-what-matters-most-jung>.

14   Bowlby, J. (1969) *Attachment and Loss*, Vol. 1: *Attachment*. New York: Basic Books, p.194.

15   Neufeld, G. and Maté, G. (2004) *Hold on to Your Kids: Why Parents Need to Matter More than Peers*. Ballantine Books.

16   Carvallo, M. and Gabriel, S. (2006) 'No man is an island: The need to belong and dismissing avoidant attachment style', *Personality and Social Psychology Bulletin* 32(5):697–709, doi:10.1177/0146167205285451

17   Robinson, K. (2006) 'Do Schools Kill Creativity?', TED Conference <https://www.ted.com/talks/sir_ken_robinson_do_schools_kill_creativity?language=en>.

18   Miller, A. (1998) *Thou Shalt Not be Aware: Society's Betrayal of the Child*. New York: Farrar, Straus and Giroux.

19   Silverman, E. (2017). 'Facebook's first president, on Face-

book: "God only knows what it's doing to our children's brains"'. The Washington Post, November 9. <https://www.washingtonpost.com/news/the-switch/wp/2017/11/09/facebooks-first-president-on-facebook-god-only-knows-what-its-doing-to-our-childrens-brains/>

20   Wacks, Y. and Weinstein, A. (2021) 'Excessive smartphone use is associated with health problems in adolescents and young adults. *Frontiers in Psychiatry* 28 May, 12:669042, doi: 10.3389/fpsyt.2021.669042 <https://www.frontiersin.org/articles/10.3389/fpsyt.2021.669042/full>.

21   Everri, M. and Park, K. (2018) Children's online behaviours in Irish primary and secondary schools. Research report. Zeeko, NovaUCD, University College Dublin.

22   Ibid.

23   Edwards, R. (2020) 'More young people addicted to online gambling', 11 October, *The Sunday Independent.* <https://www.independent.ie/irish-news/news/more-young-people-addicted-to-online-gambling-39608919.html>

24   Pope, C. (2021) 'Most children aged 8–12 have smart phone and social media profile', *Irish Times*, 9 February <https://www.irishtimes.com/news/ireland/irish-news/most-children-aged-8-12-have-smart-phone-and-social-media-profile-1.4479406>.

25   O'Connell, J. (2018) 'How's your 'digital wellbeing'? Facebook's anti-addiction drive', *Irish Times*, 8 September <https://www.irishtimes.com/culture/tv-radio-web/how-s-your-digital-wellbeing-facebook-s-anti-addiction-drive-1.3620629>.

26   Caden, S. (2018) 'The reality is there is no one in charge', *Sunday Independent*, 28 January <https://www.independent.ie/irish-news/news/the-reality-is-there-is-no-one-in-charge-36538074.html>.

27 Clear, J. (2012) *Atomic Habits: An Easy and Proven Way to Build Good Habits and Break Bad Ones*. Penguin.

28 Vonnegut, M. (1975) *The Eden Express: A Memoir of Insanity*. Praeger Publishers.

29 Walton, A. (2016) 'Why uncertainty is more stressful than certainty of bad things to come', *Forbes*, 29 March <https://www.forbes.com/sites/alicegwalton/2016/03/29/uncertainty-about-the-future-is-more-stressful-than-knowing-that-the-future-is-going-to-suck/?sh=45b4731d646a>.

30 Taleb, N.N. (2012) *Antifragile: Things that Gain from Disorder*. New York: Random House.

31 Mason, G. (1991) 'Stereotypies: A critical review', *Animal Behavior* 41:1015–37.

32 Bodfish, J.W. (2007) 'Stereotypy, Self-injury, and Related Abnormal Repetitive Behaviors', in J.W. Jacobson, J.A. Mulick and J. Rojahn (eds), *Handbook of Intellectual and Developmental Disabilities* (pp. 481–505). New York, NY: Springer.

33 McCullough, M. and Emmons, R. (2003) 'Counting blessings versus burdens: An experimental investigation of gratitude and subjective well-being in daily life', *Journal of Personality and Social Psychology* 84(2):377–89 <https://greatergood.berkeley.edu/pdfs/GratitudePDFs/6Emmons-BlessingsBurdens.pdf>.

34 White, D. (2015) 'St Albans woman writes blog which inspires viral "cup of tea" sexual consent video', *Herts Advertiser*, 12 November <https://www.hertsad.co.uk/news/st-albans-woman-writes-blog-which-inspires-viral-cup-of-5037542>.

35 Driver, K. (2005) 'Archaeologist finds "oldest porn statue"', *The Guardian*, 4 April.

36 Stern, H. (2021) 'Billie Eilish opens up about surviving covid and hosting "SNL"', 13 December <https://www.howard-stern.com/news/2021/12/13/billie-eilish-performs-2-songs-

live-in-studio-and-opens-up-about-surviving-covid-and-hosting-snl>.

37   O'Sullivan, L., Byers, E., Brotto, L., Majerovich, J. and Fletcher, J. (2016) 'A longitudinal study of problems in sexual functioning and related sexual distress among middle to late adolescents', *Journal of Adolescent Health* 59(3):318–24 <https://www.jahonline.org/article/S1054-139X(16)30056-8/fulltext>.

38   Erikson, E.H. (1970) 'Autobiographic notes on the identity crisis', *Daedalus* 99(4):730–59. <http://www.jstor.org/stable/20023973>.

39   Cheng, P.J., Pastuszak, A.W., Myers, J.B., Goodwin, I.A. and Hotaling, J.M. (2019) 'Fertility concerns of the transgender patient', *Translational Andrology and Urology* 8(3):209–18; Wierckx, K., Mueller, S., Weyers, S., Van Caenegem, E., Roef, G., Heylens, G. and T'Sjoen, G. (2012) 'Long-term evaluation of cross-sex hormone treatment in transsexual persons', *Journal of Sexual Medicine* 9(10):2641–51.

40   Wilken, H. (2017) 'Diagnosis creep: The new problem in medicine', *InSight*, Issue 20, 9 May <https://insightplus.mja.com.au/2017/20/diagnosis-creep-the-new-problem-in-medicine>.

41   Ibid.

42   Haslam, N., Tse, J.S.Y. and De Deyne, S. (2021) 'Concept creep and psychiatrization', *Frontiers in Sociology* 12, 16 December, doi: 10.3389/fsoc.2021.806147.

43   Shattuck, P.T., Orsmond, G.I., Wagner, M. and Cooper, B.P. (2011) 'Participation in social activities among adolescents with an autism spectrum disorder', *PLOS One* 6(11):e27176.

44   Churcher Clarke, A. and Spiliadis, A. (2019) '"Taking the lid off the box": The value of extended clinical assessment for adolescents presenting with gender identity difficulties',

Clinical Child Psychology and Psychiatry 24(2):338–52.

45 Rosenthal, M., Wallace, G.L., Lawson, R., Wills, M.C., Dixon, E., Yerys, B.E. and Kenworthy, L. (2013) 'Impairments in real-world executive function increase from childhood to adolescence in autism spectrum disorders', *Neuropsychology*, January 27(1):13–18.

46 Sarris, M. (2013) 'Autism in the teen years: what to expect, how to help', *Interactive Autism Network*, Kennedy Krieger Institute. <https://iancommunity.org/cs/simons_simplex_community/autism_in_teens#:~:text=Rosenthal%20said.,you%20have%20in%20the%20bank>.

47 Bhandari, S. (2021) 'ADHD in Teens', WebMD, 14 June <https://www.webmd.com/add-adhd/childhood-adhd/adhd-teens>.

48 Doyle, L., Treacy, M.P. and Sheridan, A. (2015) 'Self-harm in young people: Prevalence, associated factors, and help-seeking in school-going adolescents', *International Journal of Mental Health Nursing* 24(6):485–95.

49 Fox, C. and Hawton, K. (2004) *Deliberate Self-harm in Adolescence*. London: Jessica Kingsley.

50 Ibid.

51 Eastwood, J., Frishchen, A., Fenske, M. and Smilek, D. (2012) 'The unengaged mind: Defining boredom in terms of attention', *Perspectives on Psychological Science* 7(5).

52 Kelland, K. (2009) 'Smoking skunk raises risk of psychosis, study finds', *Reuters*, 1 December <https://www.reuters.com/article/us-psychosis-skunk/smoking-skunk-raises-risk-of-psychosis-study-finds-idINTRE5B000G20091201>.

53 Roberts, M. (2018) 'Most UK cannabis "super strength skunk"', *BBC News online*, 28 February <https://www.bbc.com/news/health-43196566>.

54 Kessler, R.C., Berglund, P., Demler, O., Jin, R., Merikangas,

K.R. and Walters, E.E. (2005) 'Lifetime prevalence and age-onset distributions of DSM-IV disorders in the national comorbidity survey replication', *Archives of General Psychiatry* 62(6):593–602.

55 Steel, Z., Marnane, C., Iranpour, C., Chey, T., Jackson, J.W., Patel, V. and Silove, D. (2014) 'The global prevalence of common mental disorders: a systematic review and meta-analysis 1980–2013', *International Journal of Epidemiology* 43(2):476–93 <https://doi.org/10.1093/ije/dyu038>.

56 Brooks, A. (2022) *From Strength to Strength: Finding Success, Happiness, and Deep Purpose in the Second Half of Life.* Portfolio.

57 Als, H. (2002) 'Songbird: Maya Angelou takes another look at herself', *New Yorker*, 5 August.

ACKNOWLEDGEMENTS

Thank you, my darling Henry, for being so good to me this past year. Of course you've been good to me over the past twenty years too – great to me, in fact! But thank you especially for this year – I could never have written this book without you.

Thank you to my lovely, kind Róisín and my sweet-natured Muiris for being so patient as I became increasingly distracted and cranky about my work as the year unfolded.

Thank you to Alasdair for the chats. If the best of life is conversation, and I believe it is, then we're having the best of life.

Heartfelt thanks to Claire and Lorraine, who keep me sane.

Thank you to Sarah Liddy for your light but magic touch and to Aoibheann Molumby for your brilliant work and commitment to producing the very best work possible. It has made such a difference to this process. Warm thanks to everyone on the Gill team and to Swift Press for understanding the need for this book and for supporting my work.

Thanks to my family, friends and colleagues, scattered all over the world. Thank you to Jo, Joseph, Lisa, Michelle, Saoirse, Sasha and all my friends and colleagues at Genspect, GETA, SEGM, CAN SG and Thoughtful Therapists. Our work together means the world to me.

Finally, a special thanks to the parents and teenagers who I've worked with over the years. I have cherished the time we've spent together, analysing things, figuring things out and collaborating together in our bid to find better pathways for the road ahead.